Hazing Aging

How Capillary Endothelia Control Inflammation and Aging

Robert Buckingham, MD, FACP

PAPERBACK: 978-1-948779-10-4
EBOOK: 978-1-948779-11-1

Ordering Information:

For orders and inquiries, please contact:
1-888-375-9818
www.toplinkpublishing.com
bookorder@toplinkpublishing.com

Printed in the United States of America

Acknowledgments

I want to give thanks to the many people involved in the writing of this book.

First, to my parents and grandparents who nurtured my curiosity and encouraged me to verbalize questions.

To Jackie Colvin, for being my guardian angel for so many years.

To all of my patients throughout thirty-six years of medical practice, both in and out of the hospital.

To the hundreds of nurses and ancillary professional staff who have put up with me over the years and yet understand my nature.

To the dozens of fellow doctors I have shared cases with over the years and who have given me insight into patterns of illness.

To Scott Bennett, for his time and effort in designing the book cover.

To Sherrie McClellan, for giving me the technical assistance I needed with my graph designs.

To my adult children, Tyler and Lily, who, together, have been a source of inspiration and delight as I have watched them find their own unique gifts.

Finally, to Kate, who has made it clear that I have the right stuff to write about the insights that I have regarding the origins of aging. She, along with God, has given me both hope and encouragement on a daily basis, and for this I am grateful.

Contents

Illustrations

Introduction

Most of us live with our health concerns on autopilot. We become passive about our health, and so we fail to integrate into our behavior the discipline and proactive principles required to limit premature adverse outcomes. Our wake-up calls are usually serious life-changing problems like heart attacks, strokes, or cancer. We then wonder why these problems have occurred. Inevitably, we blame it all on too much stress, bad relationships, our boss at work, our kids, our parents, or our financial concerns. We often avoid or postpone taking a hard look at ourselves and our habits, neglecting to address the hard question of what we could have done to make things different. Can we become intentional about our health in order to effect change that could make a difference in how we feel?

Certain assumptions that we make about aging are wrong. Our joints don't have to make us cripples, our hearts do not have to fail, and our brains certainly don't have to atrophy, resulting in our becoming a shell of who and what we once were. In other words, if we intentionally preempt our health management, living to an advanced age does not have to hurt; it can be joyful and full throttle. We now have enough information about the consequences of lifestyles choices to make pronouncements that, when changed, can result in major improvements to our health.

In the first decades of life, we pay little attention to good health maintenance by getting comfortable with bad habits and addictions. This is when we learn to use sugar as a snack food and passively submit to television and mobile devices for entertainment. As with anything addictive, these early imprinted behaviors can lead to an avalanche of more serious addictions with deadly consequences as time passes. As this occurs, the vascular inflammatory changes are often initially felt as vague symptoms that don't get our attention. We get used to feeling that we are in what I will call "a light shade of gray," as vascular inflammatory changes establish a foothold throughout our bodies. At the same time, as we look for comfort from the world we live in, incipient breeding of well-known addictions to overeating, alcohol, drugs, cigarettes, shopping, pornography, and gambling consumes us and feeds the inflammation. Much of this behavior begets a sedentary lifestyle, poor sleep hygiene, increased stress, and other risky lifestyle choices. When these behaviors stack, intertwining with one another, tremendous effort is required to unravel and remove them.

As a practicing physician of thirty-eight years, I have had the privilege of watching the processes of aging in my practice—and seeing its consequences. There is the inevitable sense of "if only I had done things differently" from every afflicted patient. I myself experienced my own health crisis, with a near-fatal outcome, requiring a stent in a coronary artery at age fifty-four. Was all this just random processes of natural aging? The answer is a categorical *no!*

Throughout this book, I will unravel this mystery, using a piece of my own medical experience as a patient. My heart problem caught me by complete surprise, but it should not have. I will expose the wrong assumptions that I made about myself and also share how I acknowledged these mistakes, which then allowed me to begin the real process of healing.

The healing process led me to understand *hazing aging,* the relationship of aging and vascular inflammation as related to the decline of capillary-cell function. Clinical experience clarified that certain behaviors correlated dramatically with inflammation to the arterial tree, disturbed capillary-cell function, and then marginalized end organs, such as the heart and brain. These changes caused disease and accelerated aging that compromised life and led to premature death.

Moreover, the pace of this decline often mirrored lifestyle choices and habits. In other words, chronic illness and aging consequences were not random. Making the arterial tree and capillary endothelial cell a focal point of cause and effect created a clear path to unlocking the door to understanding preventative health care.

Rather than getting lost in biochemical minutiae, this book will translate cellular physiology and chemistry into understandable processes. Blood, and what it contains, provides the lifeline for all end organs to function effectively. How and what the end organ receives from the blood is determined by the capillary cells that support the end organ. These tiny cells at the farthest end of the arterial tree orchestrate seamless exchanges of all the resources offered from blood to end-organ cells. Capillary cells are part of a large vascular network of cells that line the arterial and venous systems; these cells are known as the *vascular endothelium,* or *endothelial cells.* All of these cells have direct exposure to blood and its constituents, but it is the capillary endothelial cell that has adapted to facilitate effective exchange between blood constituents and end-organ cells. When capillary cells become disturbed, end-organ function suffers.

By providing a cohesive theory of aging through the arterial-tree endothelium and the capillary cell, we will establish a sound foundation for understanding the vulnerability of disease and aging to cause and effect from evolving inflammation of the vascular system. This inflammation is largely the result of lifestyle choices. When behaviors change as part of a comprehensive package, the result is a substantial health payoff.

The thousands of hours spent in writing and editing this book have been a labor of love. The process has involved putting together myriad complex and sometimes disjointed information, in order to achieve a resultant simple understanding of how capillary cells, inflammation, and subsequent disease cascades respond to lifestyle changes. The combination of a sedentary lifestyle, highly processed food, and addictive behaviors has birthed a perfect storm of vascular inflammation. Out of this inflammatory morass and what it causes, comes a sense of urgency to increase our awareness of this process and make the necessary changes before we are consumed by irreversible progression, much like trying to escape from quicksand. Vascular-tree and capillary-cell health specifically, with its far-reaching effects on all body organs, provides the key to understanding the process that unlocks these improvements to end-organ function, which are associated with comprehensive lifestyle overhaul.

For those in basic science, pursuing an understanding of the feedback loops in capillary cells that optimize immune function could yield breathtaking advancement in limiting infections, autoimmune disease, and cancer, through improved immune surveillance. In addition, developing strategies to develop optimal fatty-acid and pyruvate (glucose) metabolism for energy production is important. Understanding the role of antioxidants and how they target toxic ROS (reactive oxygen species, or free radicals) is critical, yet this important work is still in its infancy.

For those in clinical research, my hope is for well-controlled studies that isolate specific vascular inflammatory factors and their cause-and-effect relationships on the capillary endothelial cell. This could lead to improved understanding of treatment venues and subsequent disease prevention. A secondary benefit would be in the development of simple tools to accurately measure endothelial-cell function in clinical practice. The outcome would be to preempt adverse clinical outcomes and add credence to early vascular anti-inflammatory behavioral change. All of these effects would produce preemptive treatment of vascular inflammation before symptoms of disease emerge, rather than waiting until their progression produces serious health compromise. These simple tests would become the foundation for preventative health care. If both health-care providers and patients can become motivated to become intentional rather than reactive to vascular inflammatory behavior and subsequent illness, this book has served its purpose.

To primary health-care providers, a return to holistic medicine for preventative health care, using the vascular inflammatory model, is both prudent and refreshing. A unified discourse on disease prevention, versus the current model of treating chronic health problems that appear complex and disjointed, gives patients and providers relief in establishing goals and setting an understandable path to better health. Educating patients about powerful prevention tools can become the central theme in primary care. For the first time in decades, momentum can build to shift priority from treating disease as it emerges to preventing disease before it occurs, through education. This will restore a quality provider-patient relationship. An outcome to this approach is empowerment of the patient to make changes to improve health based on an understanding of choice, rather than becoming dependent and addicted to a stockpile of prescription drugs that treat disjointed diseases.

There will always be a place for health-care providers to intervene, diagnose, and treat disease. However, engaging patients with a priority to prevent disease helps create a better relationship. Taking the time to provide preventative education is not lucrative, but it intuitively makes for better caring and perhaps a better chance for modifying behavior. This is in sharp contrast to how we currently practice medicine, which is to see patients in five- to ten-minute blocks and quickly diagnose and treat signs and symptoms of disease. Is there any question as to why health-care providers are burning out in record numbers and patients are equally dissatisfied? The health-care provider-patient relationship is on resuscitation and needs an urgent reset for improvement.

Inherent in this new model of primary prevention involves early interventions and education of young adults, who, for the most part, are largely ignored in our current system of health-care delivery. These early interventions will go a long way to weed out vascular inflammatory tendencies, as well as to establish adaptive behaviors early in life that would prevent expensive midlife encumbrances to health.

An inherent aspect of preventative health care is understanding that it is never about instant gratification, and it always involves behaviors that provide long-term benefits. That said, this book will offer a plan that can help break the string of addictive comfort behaviors. This process never comes easily, and failure is common and expected. Each failure can be used to build techniques to counter adverse behavioral influences. Positive change is a process with hills and valleys, with the end result becoming a game changer to well-being. Living fully becomes more of a reality than dying slowly.

It is never too late to take the necessary steps to begin the process of restoring arterial-tree and capillary-cell health. Starting with exercise, momentum builds toward modifying other behaviors, and then the process toward vascular inflammatory mitigation has begun in earnest. This journey can be both exciting and life changing, leading to a breakthrough of improved health that could not have been imagined. Goals of life are reset, new possibilities emerge, and living becomes more of a priority than dying. You too can wake up from the fog. The choice is yours. Have the courage to take that first step. Your life depends on it.

[AUTHOR'S NOTE: *Please refer to the glossary in the back of this book for a list of the clinical terminology used throughout the text.*]

1

Are You Kidding? A Lesson in Denial

"Having a hard time getting through there?" I muttered as I lay partially naked on the cardiac catheterization table.

Doctors and technicians were bunched near my right groin, all of them wearing surgical gowns, their faces covered by masks. My question ignored, there was absolute silence in the room except for the regular chirping of my heartbeat on the monitor above my head. Everyone appeared to be frozen and speechless, as all eyes were fixed on the x-ray monitor that was well visualized by the group huddled around my groin, where the catheter to my heart arteries had been inserted. My own eyes were fixed on the monitor as well. In fact, I was surprised at how easy it was for me to view the x-ray images from my vantage point. The image of the blocked artery, after dye was injected into it, was not pretty, but the drugs I was being given suspended my angst.

The catheter tip was abutted up against an obstruction in one of my coronary arteries. Every time the doctor tried to burrow through it, I felt a gnawing dull ache in my chest. At that very moment, I felt impending doom; and yet I also felt very detached, as if at a movie theater watching someone else's possibly fatal experience, not my own. In retrospect, the doom was from my heart rhythm being disturbed from blocked blood flow through the affected coronary artery caused by the catheter burrowing into an already severely narrowed blood vessel. The changes in heart rhythm caused my blood pressure to transiently fall, leading to the pressure/pain in my chest and the feeling of impending doom. The cause of the artery narrowing was critical plaque buildup that caused a near-complete blockage of my coronary artery from processes of long-standing vascular inflammation.

In spite of this drama, the drugs made me not care much about what happened to the catheter. I was more or less an inquisitive bystander. My thoughts turned to a synopsis of my life as I knew it. In snapshot moments, it passed before me: my childhood, medical school, my family, my patients. It was as if I was suspended in animation, as my mind wandered aimlessly to the best thoughts of times past. And then, suddenly, the room went dark, and my consciousness abandoned me. I sank into a dark space, a black hole, as if in a deep sleep. I was out. Was this death knocking?

I woke up in a large well-lit room filled with noisy chirping monitors and surrounded by pulled curtains. I had an IV in my left arm, a blood pressure cuff on the right arm, an oxygen cannula in my nose, electrodes all over my chest, and a dull, pervasive ache in the right groin. I felt as if I were strapped onto the bed, as I could not move because of all the paraphernalia. Bewildered, my first thought was, *Where am I?*

Relief followed, as I realized that this room could not be the afterlife, which I was not prepared for. With some additional passage of time, I began to be aware of gnawing pressure and pain that centered on the right groin: a large heavy bag of some kind rested there.

I yelled, "Can someone get this bag off my groin?"

A nurse, businesslike but friendly in her demeanor, came to my assistance, quickly checked the groin bag, and with a smile explained, "The bag is there to keep the hematoma from getting bigger. Things went well; you are in the recovery room." With that, she left as quickly as she had come, closing the curtains as if I required isolation.

Mission not accomplished. The bag stayed, and the pain increased. Recovery was not all that it was cracked up to be.

All voices outside the curtains were drowned out by the incessant chirping of the monitors around me.

The next time the nurse poked her face around the curtain, I blurted, "I'm hungry. Got anything to eat around here?"

Amused, as if I was some type of drunken sailor rather than a doctor, she gave me a Mona Lisa smile. After once again checking my groin, she politely said, "Once you get to your room, you will get some lunch. Not too much to eat here."

I had completely lost track of the clogged artery and the intervention that had just transpired. Eventually, with postanesthesia amnesia fading and having been transferred to another floor and room, I came to understand that a stent had been placed where the critically narrowed coronary artery would soon completely occlude—and which would have likely caused my death. I was spared the details of what actually happened to get it open. The plaque that I had in the left anterior descending coronary artery of the heart is known as the "widow maker." Translated, this means that if completely occluded, absent blood flow through this artery would cause the heart to stop beating and result in sudden death.

That said, changing rooms did not improve my bed-bound dependency or capacity to move, as I was still hooked up to monitors, IV drips, oxygen, blood pressure cuffs, and the large uncomfortable bag in my groin. That night, still with groin pain, I had a glass of wine and a sleeping pill. My next conscious moment was to say hello to my cardiologist in the morning.

"How do you feel?" he said briskly, appearing rushed as he quickly perused my chart. Clearly, he did not expect me to answer with anything short of "fine." "I will let you go home today," he continued. "But you have to take it easy and let the hematoma in your groin heal. Continue the Crestor as well as the aspirin. You will need to take Plavix to keep your stent open. See you in a week." Without giving me a chance to respond, he scurried out of the room almost as quickly as he had come. Although the exchange was curt, what he *didn't* say caused relief. The "to do" list that he rattled off was short, and I was going home. The medications I was to take included Crestor, a statin drug used to lower low-density (LDL) cholesterol, as well as Plavix and aspirin, which are blood thinners, to prevent the stent that was placed in my coronary artery from clotting.

Case closed. Or so I hoped. Could my life as I knew it continue? Was this just a bad dream?

As the cardiologist left, a parade of nurses and aides followed, checking my groin, unhooking the IV, and leaving me a lukewarm breakfast consisting of eggs and soggy toast.

Unbeknownst to anyone, with the door to my room closed, I decided to test my newfound freedom. Staggering out of bed with my swollen groin, somewhat dizzy and light-headed, I got to the shower, fumbled with the water controls, and eventually let the hot water pour over my fatigued body. I felt totally hungover.

After several minutes, the hot water relaxed me but did nothing for my fatigue. In slow motion, I stumbled out of the shower and managed to towel-dry myself. It was then I noticed the softball-sized bruise in my right groin. Unfazed, and knowing that I had been on powerful blood thinners overnight, I then proceeded to shave with a razor blade. I looked terrible in the mirror. The entire process had left me gaunt, pale, and old looking. After shaving, I shuffled back to the bed where I could sit and get dressed. With no reason to stay but with judgment impaired from the mix of drugs still affecting me, I then picked up the plastic bag holding my belongings, preparing to leave. Dizziness and groin pain made this difficult. I could barely bend to tie my shoes.

With a bag of clothes in one hand and a plant, courtesy of the hospital CEO, in the other, I slowly limped out, waving good-bye to the nurses at their glass-covered station as I passed it. They appeared oblivious to what I was doing and where I was going, and actually waved back in perfunctory fashion. I took the elevator down to the first floor, where I met my then wife in a waiting car. To this day, I can't remember how this had been arranged, but it was effective in getting me home seamlessly. As I found my way outside to freedom, I heard over the hospital intercom, "Dr. Buckingham, please return to your room."

It was then that some brain fog lifted, and I realized that I had miscalculated one small detail before leaving: my nurse was required to discharge me from her care and go over all the discharge instructions and follow-up. Not feeling any need to know about more details of treatment, and still lacking judgment from being under the influence of drugs, I mustered all the speed that my swollen groin would allow and limped briskly to the waiting car. As I got there, I felt myself swoon from the deep ache in my groin. I struggled to sit and get comfortable on the front passenger seat, placing my plant and clothes behind me in the backseat. At this point in our marriage, my then wife expected these kinds of shenanigans and drove me home without any meaningful verbal exchange. She seemed indifferent, almost detached. In retrospect, even in a failed marriage, she did care and was coping with fear from my stubborn behavior and from what could happen to me. Relieved to be going home, I was in a total fog as to what had just happened. I had no plan or purpose for dealing with a condition that could easily have taken my life.

What had happened? Or more to the point, how could this have happened to me? Just the week prior, I was grinding out twelve-hour days with my busy medical practice. Except for some arthritis, allergies, and asthma, which had gotten a lot worse recently, I had no known health problems. My cholesterol numbers were on the high side, but I thought not alarmingly so. I was not too terribly overweight, and I exercised up to several times a week. My diet on the surface appeared well balanced, but I had my share of cookies, ice cream, and pizza. Sure, I was under some stress, but at age fifty-four, with two teenage kids in high school, and with expanding professional responsibilities, I expected this. After all, who wasn't stressed? I did have some fatigue and heartburn, but I chalked that up to the stress of twelve-hour workdays, the extra cup of coffee in the morning, and not getting enough sleep from hospital night calls.

It would be an understatement to say that I was in total denial of my poor health and the fact that I was on the verge of sudden death. And, even though I had seen this pattern hundreds of times in my own patients, I did not recognize it in myself. My denial had rationalized insomnia, arthritis, difficulty breathing, grumpiness, short-term memory loss, and fatigue. These were all part of just getting older.

As fate would have it, I was very lucky. A few weeks prior to my stent intervention, on a typical morning of answering messages, making calls, and signing off on patient prescription renewals, I got a call from the hospital's surgery suite. "We need you here stat. Your patient is coding!"

I hustled from my office, about one hundred paces to the hospital, thinking about my patient. At age eighty-eight, this man was getting a permanent pacemaker. What could have gone wrong to cause sudden death in the operating room? After unsuccessful resuscitation efforts, he was pronounced dead, with signs pointing toward a pulmonary embolus (blood clot in the lung). I was emotionally drained and terribly upset by the outcome. And then, as I sat there in the operating room, mentally agonizing over the just then concluded resuscitation, I felt pressure in my chest.

Within minutes of our pronouncing my patient dead, someone called, "Code blue!" Another patient in the ICU (intensive care unit) had gone into shock and required resuscitation. As I opened the ICU door, there were people bustling around with crash carts, chirping monitors, and alarms. The usual chaos that accompanies a resuscitation ensued. After about an hour, the patient was stabilized: intubated with a breathing tube, placed on a ventilator machine, and hooked up to IV central lines and pressor drips.

I was exhausted like I had never been before at that time of day. The pressure in my chest became more like a constant ache. I dismissed it as chest-muscle or -wall pain.

I walked slowly back to the office, breathing deeply, now two hours behind schedule. I slipped through the private back door and quietly lay down on an exam table.

My plucky office manager found me with my eyes closed. "What are you doing?" she asked. "You never come in like this to lie down. I am getting an EKG."

Before I could get up, she had me strapped onto an EKG monitor, as she swiftly placed twelve adhesive patches on my chest and abdomen to run an EKG.

"Just as I thought," I said under my breath. "Nothing to worry about. It looks fine. Just give me a few minutes to catch my breath from this crazy morning, and I will be okay."

But she feared the worst. Before I could get off the exam table and get dressed, several more people came into the crowded exam room. I was surrounded by nurses and an echocardiogram technician; I could not leave. Too weak to resist, an echocardiogram was performed, nitroglycerin spray was shot into my mouth, and some oxygen by a nasal cannula was even lodged into my nose. All of this was occurring as a nurse friend of mine was summoned and then walked the eighty or so paces from the hospital to my office to begin checking my vital signs.

The echocardiogram (ultrasound of the heart) and EKG (electrocardiogram) looked normal, and after all the drama, I simply had enough. Thanking everyone for their concerns, I was ready to start my morning office hours, almost three hours late. I was sure there were at least a half dozen patients waiting to be seen and probably not too happy about my being late.

My frustration mounted as my persistent office manager proceeded to tell me that my morning patients had been canceled. Instead, she had me scheduled for a CT angiogram of the heart (this test is a special type of computerized tomography scan). In spite of my objections, she would not take no for an answer, and so I was stuck.

At this point, although frustrated and even angry, I had no recourse. My office manager, who had relayed all of the morning's drama to my then wife, did not trust the assessment I had given myself. That is, I felt the prevailing circumstances of the day were sufficient reason for fatigue, and that my heart and chest symptoms were from stress-related chest-wall pain. I was not very convincing.

I realized that to appease both my office manager and then wife, I would have to submit to the test. There was no wiggle room for negotiation. I would follow through and have the imaging heart scan that they had scheduled. After all, it was scheduled over the noon hour and would not interfere with what was really important: seeing my patients.

Even when scheduled and arriving on time, getting the test took longer than planned. Paperwork, explanations, consents, and inability to get an IV started all created delays and further added to the stress of a clock-driven individual like me. Finally completed and taking forty-five minutes longer than expected, my thoughts were not about the result, which I was sure would be normal, but about how I was going to manage my afternoon of patients an hour behind schedule.

I quickly got dressed, and on my way out the door, a staff member in a calm but firm voice blurted, "The doctor wants to see you in the consultation room. It is to your right at the end of the hallway."

The radiologist and I were acquaintances, and my first thought was he wanted to know about my kids and college plans, as one was graduating from high school. When I arrived in the consultation room, the atmosphere changed; it was as if air had been removed from the room. The handshake, coupled with an intense concerned look and furrowed brow, made it clear this was not about the kids. He paused, fumbled for his glasses, and then sitting and leaning forward, with measured words, he told me to look at the screen behind him.

Images of my heart scan appeared, and with a pointer, he beamed a light to one of my heart arteries. In a monotone, he hesitated and then grimly asserted, "You have a 90 percent narrowing of the left anterior descending coronary artery." Even in denial, the picture did not lie. I could see the dye in the artery and the subsequent abrupt cutoff. There was no way I could rationalize this away. He continued, "This has to be confirmed, but you need to see a cardiologist to have a coronary angiogram and stent placement sooner rather than later." With a look of concern and without much emotion, he shook my hand, led me to the door, and wished me well.

I slowly walked out of the office to the front door, head down, slumped over, speechless, and shocked. Driving the thirty minutes back to my office, I became oblivious to everything around me. I could not focus on any one thought. It was almost as if I were suspended in a vacuum. Thoughts wandered from retirement to planning my funeral. Should I be buried here in Ojai or back in Iowa, near my mother? *At least I won't die with the indecency of being a confused, incontinent, and belligerent old man,* I thought.

As I lumbered into the office, my office manager already knew the verdict. Paradoxically, she appeared relieved that her suspicions were confirmed. As I collapsed and slumped into my chair, her five-foot frame stood before me as her eyes made contact with mine. Before my deflated spirit could muster an effort to ask about my afternoon, she calmly said, "You have a coronary angiogram scheduled in three days, at 7:30 a.m. You need to shave your groin and not eat breakfast that morning. You are required to be there no later than 7:00 a.m. to register. Make sure to take your insurance card. I have canceled patients for the next week."

I said nothing. Eventually, I staggered home. Depressed and anxious, I found respite with the coming of the weekend. Distracted by our golden retriever and watching some basketball on television, I postponed thinking about the dark reality of the previous week. The coronary angiogram was scheduled for Monday. I resigned myself to hunker down. My home for me became a cocoon: isolated, cozy, and comforting. Over that weekend, almost like some form of post-traumatic stress, images of the artery and the cutoff would flash before me, triggering painful and dark thoughts about retirement and diminished professional relevance. The vision that emerged haunted me, as I could not escape from the recurrent theme of an incapacitated, disabled, slowly dying man. My subconscious whispered that I had become my father, who, as luck and genetics would have it, almost died of a massive heart attack at about the same age, also from coronary disease involving the same artery.

What became even more sobering were the conclusions that I had to draw about my health. I had duped myself into thinking that I was okay, and, consequently, was completely wrong. My lack of judgment about my own health both haunted and disturbed me. There was no denying that the fatigue and chest ache were not just from stress, lack of sleep, or chest-wall muscles, but, instead, came from an impending life-ending heart attack. I had repeatedly misread my own symptoms, and that was not at all comforting. As a doctor who treated so much heart disease and was experienced in diagnosing all levels of preexisting heart disease, I should have known better.

I had the angiogram and stent intervention as scheduled (described at the beginning of this chapter). But knowing that I had additional plaque in the same artery, which could eventually cause more symptoms, I began the sobering process of personal assessment. Part of this process required me to admit that I needed to change and be more responsive to the warning signals my body was giving me. It was only after getting to this place of objective personal assessment that I could start from scratch and begin evaluating all aspects of my life in order to make meaningful changes. This would not be just a Band-Aid or knee-jerk bits-and- pieces change. Every aspect of my life would need an overhaul.

2

My Changes

To change fundamentally required deep and sometimes painful introspection. All of my behaviors had to be reviewed, put on the table, and then maintained, enhanced, or removed. This premise was the foundation of my initial literature search. To my surprise, and which was a major part of my denial, making behavioral changes could produce a major shift in vascular inflammatory risk. In my practice, I had given behavioral change lip service. My emphasis was always on medications to diagnose and treat disease. There was little room in the office visit to discuss details of diet, exercise, and other nurturing behaviors to improve vascular health.

I wanted to know which behaviors favored vascular plaque stability or regression, and which ones did not. As a result, I began to evaluate my behaviors and what I thought I knew.

A major breakthrough came when I became honest with myself. A major assumption that I had made prior to the coronary stent was that I had lived a decent and balanced life and this would protect me from adverse health outcomes. I did not smoke; I ate what I thought were quality meals, with only occasional desserts; I exercised several times a week. Although I had gained about thirty-five pounds since age twenty-five, I did not see myself as overweight.

I made a bet with myself that this lifestyle of moderation, although not perfect, would more than make up for my twelve-hour work grinds, sleep deprivation, and the accumulated stress of being a doctor. It should also trump my father's genetics, which I assumed I would inherit. After all, he smoked (and I didn't) and was mostly sedentary. As the years went by, it was easy to rationalize the subtle increases that I noticed in my untreated high blood pressure and elevated LDL cholesterol. The changes were minor and not enough to worry about. In looking the other way, I ignored standard-of-care guidelines as they applied to my own health.

All these assumptions were wrong—every one of them. But I had used them to make myself feel comfortable with the status quo. One by one, I began the process of making difficult behavioral adjustments, now post-stent, as if my life depended on it. The emerging renaissance had begun in earnest.

At age fifty-four, now with a heart-artery stent, I realized I had become a liar to myself. I could not admit that I was experiencing changes that were all tied to each other. The list included the following effects:

- I was thirty-five pounds overweight, did not exercise regularly, ate poorly, and slept unevenly.
- Short-term memory, and the capacity and speed of learning new information, had also decreased, as I became grumpy and less tolerant of others.
- In addition to cholesterol problems, blood pressure was inching higher, breathing had progressively worsened from asthma and cough, and GERD (esophageal reflux of acid) symptoms had also increased.
- In addition, knee, hip, and back arthritis had worsened.
- Balance, vision, and hearing had decreased.
- Colon polyps had emerged.
- Skin cancer had been identified.
- I had swelling in my feet (peripheral edema).

No organ system was spared in the relentless progression of symptoms that impaired quality of life. And I was ignoring all of them. Like it or not, I was aging, becoming an older man, staggering, as if predestined, to the finish line of retirement and subsequent disability. As is typical of most people, I saw myself as a victim. I had become reactive, blamed everything on life circumstances and stress, and had no plan to mitigate any of it. Life, as I knew it, was circling the drain, and even as a doctor, I still was clueless as to how to intervene. Does this sound familiar?

As I came to grips with the harsh reality confronting me about my heart, something became very clear. What if all the emerging health problems that I now had somehow had a common thread? Although I had been unwilling to admit this, all the medical evidence kept pointing to its being an undeniable fact.

I refreshed my understanding of coronary artery plaques, their origin, and the cells that are most adversely affected from this pathology, known as *endothelial cells*. Endothelial cells line the *lumens* (the spaces within the blood vessel tube) of the entire vascular tree. As such, they interphase directly with the blood, acting as conduits that pass nutrients from the blood to all the end organs of the body. The entire vascular tree of the body is made up of endothelial cells that line the lumen of all blood vessels. Depending on the size of the blood vessel and the end organ they support, their structure and function can change dynamically. At the capillary level, their membranes interact with blood constituents to facilitate transport of nutrient to end-organ cells. (Capillaries have the smallest diameter of all the blood vessels.)

These capillary endothelial cells have adapted different membrane properties and different functions, depending on what end organ they serve. What surprised me in this research was how intricate and complex the endothelial-cell functioning was at the capillary level. There was far more going on than just passive transfer of oxygen, carbon dioxide, and nutrients to the end-organ cells. Within each end organ there were stark contrasts in how capillary cells function.

With complex and integrative signaling arrangements to and from the blood and end-organ cells, capillary endothelial cells adjust membrane morphology, manage immune function, blood clotting, and lumen diameter, and also provide nutrient/oxygen support while removing carbon dioxide to and from the blood and end organ.

In my case, the larger, 90 percent blocked heart artery was affecting tens of thousands of capillary endothelial cells; their function upstream was diminished by the blockage. With their capacity to deliver oxygen and nutrients to the heart-muscle cells compromised by decreased volume of blood as a result of plaque obstruction, those heart-muscle cells became affected and could not contract well to move blood out of the heart chambers. Fatigue and pain from lack of oxygen and nutrients were the by-products of this breach, and these symptoms were caused by compromised capillary endothelial cells. Reading article after article, it became clear that these tiny capillary cells at the very end of the circulatory chain were central to optimal healthy heart muscle, specifically, and to all other end-organ function as well.

Research revealed that healthy capillary-endothelial-cell management was precise, and required integration of signals from multiple informants in a given moment. These informant signals could come from the end-organ cells, blood constituents, adjacent endothelial cells, inflammatory cells, distant endothelial cells, or distant end-organ cells. It became clear that even small hiccups in capillary endothelial cells' capacity to perform could have significant consequences for the management and integration of all of these signals. The responsibility of these cells to the efficient coordinated functioning of blood constituents to end-organ capacity was nothing short of spectacular.

Armed with this understanding of endothelial-cell function, I soon came to understand that the vascular inflammatory process that was narrowing my coronary artery and about to kill my heart muscle—and me—was a diffuse process that involved the entire vascular tree. Furthermore, it was likely compromising endothelial-cell function everywhere, and hence was affecting all of the body's organs in similar fashion. Differences in which organs and how they were affected would depend on environmental exposures, the physics of blood flow, and genetics. With this incriminating evidence, I declared a personal war on vascular inflammation of the endothelium.

What I didn't know, when I declared this war, was how much change I needed to do, how comprehensive these changes would be to inflammation and the capillary endothelial cells, and how well I would actually feel from making these changes. I soon came to understand that much of the inflammatory process could be contained, and even reversed, and this directly correlated with how well I felt.

A week after the heart-artery stent was placed, and now committed to taking Crestor, aspirin, and Plavix regularly, I began to walk to the office at a moderate pace: about fifteen minutes to and from my home. Walking, particularly first thing in the morning, helped me reflect on my health situation and center my commitment to genuinely effect change. I became aware of birds chirping, squirrels and rabbits scurrying, and the fresh cool morning air. With this routine, I started to internalize the walking process. I became more aware of my pace, breathing patterns, and scope of movement. Walking felt good, and, gratefully, I had no chest pain or unusual shortness of breath with this level of exertion. Baby step number 2 of the rehab process had begun in earnest. Walking every day had become a part of my routine.

After about six months of taking full-dose Crestor and niacin, my blood lipids—including LDL cholesterol and lipoprotein (a), also known as lipo(a)—were at goal. Mission accomplished. I was now on maintenance therapy and free of side effects. Intuitively, I felt I had mitigated my inherited genetic deficiencies in abnormal LDL cholesterol and lipo(a) lipid levels which made me prone to premature heart attack and stroke.

In conjunction with medication and regular exercise, I started the process of adjusting my diet. This is where the biggest surprise came, and to this day, it is still a work in progress. Looking back, most of what I was eating, which I thought was good food from reliable food companies that I had trusted since childhood, was really highly processed, contained high quantities of sugar, salt, and saturated fats, and contributed to inflammatory changes to my arteries. This food was poisoning my body, and I didn't even know it. Initial efforts included eliminating cookies, candy, ice cream, red meat, cold cereal, and snack food. Later, most bread and pastas were also eliminated. The common thread among these foods was the excessive amount of sugar they contained. I began reading labels and was surprised to find so much sugar in products thought to be healthy, such as yogurt, most dairy products, dry cereal, and fruit juices. The combination of hidden sugars and saturated and trans fats were increasing vascular inflammatory risk by producing higher levels of blood sugar, LDL (so-called bad) cholesterol, and triglycerides.

Modifying my diet was not easy. Sugar is addictive, and I loved certain kinds of cookies and ice cream. The process of withdrawal produced a psychological war of gratification followed by guilt. Eventually, after several failed attempts, I was able to overcome my weakness, but I can't keep ice cream or oatmeal cookies in the house, as they are just too tempting.

With the gradual changes in diet, moving away from processed, sugary foods, combined with the addition of regular exercise and taking the prescribed medications, other benefits were realized:

- My weight dropped from 214 to 194 pounds. This surprised me, as I was not trying to cut calories or intentionally lose weight.
- Over a period of six months, the daily walks had turned to longer walks, which then became jogs of about one and a half miles every morning. My knee, hip, and back joints did not betray me with pain as they had in the past. Previously, over several years, any regular exercise was always associated with

some type of weight-bearing joint pain the next day, limiting momentum to any regular exercise.

- My breathing became deeper, with less coughing; at the same time, there was less need to take asthma medication. (I still took it, but not as much.)
- I no longer had any GERD symptoms, and I began to sleep seven consecutive hours each night, without waking up coughing or having to urinate.
- The swelling in my feet, most noticeable at night, had noticeably decreased.
- Moles and skin cancers stopped forming, and fungus in my toenails improved.
- Most important, my thinking became crisp and focused, with more precision and less resistance to learning new information.
- I started to care again about my appearance. I found myself smiling more and feeling less irritated about unexpected problems. Patience and empathy had returned, and because of that, I became less grumpy.

All of this produced momentum for even more change. Diet and exercise continued to be refined, and I began looking into supplements to further improve my health. As my resting pulse, blood pressure, and weight fell to levels I had not seen in thirty years, blood tests confirmed a 25 to 30 percent reduction in serum creatinine, which reflected improved kidney function.

I had planted an herb and vegetable garden and was learning to cook whole food that tasted good. All the juices and colas were replaced for the most part with water. These changes were part of a five-year process that has culminated in a near-complete reversal of symptoms that had plagued me previously. I began to think and feel like I did decades ago. Being my own guinea pig, I had come to understand a mystery, a deep truth. By supporting the capillary endothelial cells of the entire vascular tree with anti-inflammatory living, optimal health and even age reversal was possible and involved every organ system in the body.

The personal revelations of mitigating vascular inflammation became even more relevant to me as a doctor, insofar as how I could help patients improve their lives to prevent and clarify the origins of illness. Since the capillary endothelia permeate all parts of the body, it would make sense that no place would be spared from the effects of capillary inflammation. As we age, every organ system in the body suffers the consequences that come from getting old. Why not put the bulk of the blame on the capillary cells that control the relationship of blood to end-organ function? Intuition would suggest that inherited genetic deficiencies and persistent environmental exposures would create capillary-cell stress, and thus make certain end organs more vulnerable to the risk of infection, vascular events, autoimmune disease, and cancer.

Borrowing from my own experience, optimizing capillary-endothelial-cell function specifically, and vascular-tree heath generally, would serve to protect end organs from genetic deficiencies and persistent toxic environmental exposures, as well as the subsequent consequences of aging.

It became evident that approaching disease and aging from a cause-and-effect relationship to the vascular endothelium produces two important principles, both of which have become central to how I practice medicine.

First, this approach produces clarity of how disease begins and why it progresses. This has become clear from advances in basic science as to just how much integrative function the capillary endothelial cells have to and from the blood and end organ. Rather than just passively diffusing nutrients, oxygen, and carbon dioxide to and from blood and end organs, these cells have developed specific functions that involve their morphology, immune support, blood flow, and clotting.

Second, tying health to the thorough understanding of the vascular tree and its cellular function creates a holistic approach to both treatment and prevention of disease. Allowing for genetic and environmental aberrations creates distinctions in how health care should be delivered to a given individual. Understanding the risks of vascular inflammation then produces a framework to guide behavioral changes, as well as treat with medications or supplements to mitigate inflammatory effects and maintain optimal endothelial-cell and end-organ function. This inside-out approach would then gain traction in limiting or preventing illness involving multiple end organs through a single common pathway. Could focusing on optimizing capillary-endothelial-cell function revolutionize health-care delivery and prevention of disease? I think so.

3

Endothelial-Cell Function and End-Organ Support

All the cells in the body simultaneously function separately together in order to form a complex and highly efficient human organism. The extent to which all cells function and work well together is the same extent to which the whole body functions optimally. Conversely, when these intercellular relationships break down, end-organ function declines, and total body health cascades in decline with it. Each cell, and hence each organ system, can adapt to changes that adversely affect their function to a point; but then, with further adversity, they can begin to decline, and then their decline in capacity to perform accelerates.

The innermost lining of all blood vessels in the human is composed of endothelial cells (see figure 1, in the appendix). As the arterial tree narrows and blood vessels decrease their lumen diameter, the smallest arteries specialize into capillaries. The capillaries are the workhorse of the arterial tree, as they manage the relationship of the blood nutrients to those required by the end organ, from the skin, to the brain, to the skeletal muscle, to the heart, and to all other systems. Endothelial cells line the lumens of all the blood vessels in the entire vascular system, and these cells have several different functions, depending on the caliber of the vessel and the end organ they serve.

Capillary endothelial cells function best when they are supplied with a rich and continuous source of oxygen from red blood cells, vitamins, minerals, cofactors, and other proteins and cells that both help protect their function and support the end-organ cells they serve.

The arrangements between the endothelial cells and end-organ cells can be complex, but, ultimately, end-organ function will depend on capillary endothelial cells to transport what is and is not needed, actively and passively, to and from the blood and the end organ in order to support their function.

- Depending on the end organ they serve, capillary endothelial cells can function as receptors for certain important proteins in the blood that the end organ may need, as well as in the transport of oxygen, fats, sugars, and amino acids.
- Endothelial cells can also signal and participate in the production of nitric oxide (see figure 2, in the appendix) and substances like it, in order to regulate smooth muscle tone of larger arteries and arterioles, thereby managing the volume and flow of blood to the end organ.
- Capillary endothelial cells can signal for and actively transport hormones to end organs that further affect how the end organ functions. In addition, capillary cells regulate their gap junctions (the small spaces between endothelial cells) and their receptors to limit or enhance the movement of important nutrients or inflammatory cells from the blood. (See figure 5, in the appendix.)
- A critical function of the capillary endothelial cell is to signal and regulate the complex cascades of cells and proteins that modulate appropriate immune response. (See figures 4, 10, and 11, in the appendix.) This form of surveillance both protects the end organ from itself (in order to prevent autoimmune disease and/or the establishing of a foothold by cancerous cells) and from influences outside of the end organ, such as neutralizing bacterial/viral exposures or chemical toxicities.

- Additional signaling can regulate processes that make the blood clot less (or, thin the blood). This can facilitate a smooth transition of blood through the capillaries and small arterioles by reducing adhesion and shear stress. These anticlotting processes can further improve the likelihood of efficient active and passive transport of oxygen, nutrients, and other constituents to and from the end organ.

When viewed in totality, it becomes astonishing how much power and control the capillary cells have to affect health.

How Endothelial Cells Form

At the moment of conception, the earliest sequences of development involve blood vascular cells that produce a vascular tree. These vascular trees form road maps to islands of cells that eventually are cued to further specialize, leading to capillary endothelial cells and specialized end-organ epithelial cells. Some of the earliest formation involves brain- and heart-cell development, leading to early pumping of blood to and from the newly developing organ systems. The development of capillary endothelial cells and their differentiation to suit specific end organs requires growth factors that are genetically predetermined. These factors stimulate endothelial-cell migration, replication, and specialization.

Endothelial cells, like all cells in the human body, are composed of many organelles and membranes. The two most important organelles are the nucleus (or brain of the cell) and the mitochondria, the part of the cell that produces energy, controls membrane mechanics, and signals other organelles through ROS (reactive oxygen species) production and other mediators. The nucleus helps organize and process signals that the cell receives and sends. Its DNA supplies the rest of the endothelial cell with blueprints for the maintenance of cell proteins. For example, when proteins in the mitochondria need replacing because of improper functioning, the DNA of the nucleus supplies some of the blueprint (along with mitochondrial DNA) to make the proteins that allow the mitochondria to function.

Again, like most cells, the endothelial cell makes energy with and without oxygen. However, what is surprising is that 90 percent of its energy production comes from processes that do not require oxygen. The mitochondria of capillary cells make the remaining 10 to 15 percent of their energy by utilizing oxygen. This fact is stunning, as I had previously thought that most energy production in capillary endothelial cells would be through the mitochondria and utilize oxygen. This has two important benefits: (1) the capillary-cell functions well without being dependent on oxygen from the blood supply; (2) the mitochondria in capillary cells function more as facilitators of sophisticated feedback loops to control the mechanics of membranes and other organelles in the capillary cell. They do this through feedback loops involving calcium ions, nitric oxide, ATP/ADP (adenosine triphosphate/adenosine diphosphate) ratios, and ROS production. These loops would not be possible if the capillary cells required the mitochondria to make most of their energy, as the signaling would become too extreme, from wider fluctuations of energy production.

The extent to which the nucleus, mitochondria, other organelles, and membranes function efficiently as a unit is the same extent to which endothelial-cell function is optimized. As endothelial cells age, the DNA of the nucleus and mitochondria becomes increasingly exposed to the toxic effects of free radicals (or reactive oxygen species [ROS]) in the cell. The free radicals can attach to DNA and disable it. When this happens, the blueprint that scripts signaling arrangements and protein synthesis, essential information that the cell requires as part of its function and maintenance, is disrupted, and in some cases, irreversibly lost. With combinations of defective DNA and toxic ROS, the aging endothelial cell can have across-the-board limitations that cause less response to the needs of the end organ. This toxicity will continue and can be unrelenting in the cell as aging inflammatory influences continue to assault the mitochondrial and nuclear DNA until they cannot function.

These losses subsequently expose the end organ to changes in oxygen, nutrition, and immune protection. Since this process is diffuse and involves the entire vascular tree, depending on environmental exposures and genetic vulnerability of specific end organs, aging and disease of these end organs will occur. As they age, the other less vulnerable end organs will follow suit. (Such vulnerability refers to environmental and/or genetic factors.) Therefore, the acceleration of aging, or lack thereof, becomes dependent on capillary-cell maintenance.

What Capillary Cells Do

Endothelial capillary cells divide into various functions, as described below.

Specialization-Barrier Support

The capillary cells evolve to specialized functions for the various end organs they serve. For example, in the brain, the capillary cells form very tight barriers between each cell, known as *tight gap junctions* (see figure 8, in the appendix). This helps maintain the blood-brain barrier in order to control what brain cells are not exposed to from the blood. For other organs, similar specialization occurs, and these are discussed in more detail in the next chapter.

Filtration

In the liver, intestines, kidneys, and bone marrow (see figures 3 and 9, in the appendix) the capillary endothelial cells have specialized to become more like a filter, and they have large intercellular gaps between them, as well as membrane pores of varying sizes, allowing for a variety of molecules and substances to abut up against the epithelial cells of the end organ, without the strict capillary cell patrolling that is required in the brain.

Controlling Smooth-Muscle Cells

The capillary cells also control the smooth-muscle cells that surround larger arteries and arterioles. These capillary cells actively secrete and signal molecules that influence the volume of blood flow that flows through them and is directly influenced by fluctuating requirements of end organs like the heart, lungs, and skeletal muscle. These molecules—such as *nitric oxide,* a smooth-muscle relaxer (see figure 2, in the appendix) or *endothelin,* a vascular smooth-muscle constrictor—control blood volume to capillary cells by causing the smooth muscle of arterioles and larger arteries to relax or constrict. Production of these molecules depends on numerous feedback mechanisms that involve the capillary cell's mitochondria and the way in which it interprets signals from the supported end-organ cells. How well they respond to end-organ demand is a reflection of capillary-cell health and plasticity (capacity to adapt to changing needs of the end organ).

Nitric Oxide

Nitric oxide has several important properties linked to it which are critical in staving off inflammatory pathways associated with chronic illness and aging. In addition to causing vasodilation, nitric oxide is associated with improved immune function, which includes both surveillance and response to foreign proteins from infections and cancer cells. With regular aerobic exercise, the release of nitric oxide by capillaries in skeletal muscle, heart, and lungs limits toxic free radicals in these cells, thereby limiting damage to membranes, DNA, and organelle surfaces. With exercise, the release of nitric oxide also facilitates the utilization of sugar and fatty acids for energy in these end organs, thereby reducing insulin resistance and diabetes. This mechanism of nitric oxide release is tied to capillary mitochondrial function, as nitric oxide production is mediated by mitochondrial-ROS feedback loops.

With a sedentary lifestyle, nitric oxide levels in capillary and end-organ cells of the lungs, heart, and skeletal muscle decrease, and, paradoxically, this increases insulin resistance, contributing to the onset of diabetes. This becomes a universal marker of aging. In combination with other vascular inflammatory risk factors, prolonged sitting increases inflammation, with subsequent breakdown of capillary-cell function. The cycle of inflammation also involves the endothelium of larger arteries, as they become subjected to permanent narrowing of their lumens from plaque development and membrane thickening. These processes produce net decreases in capillary nitric oxide and increases in endothelin. Reductions in the nitric oxide-to-endothelin ratio becomes favorable to more inflammatory signaling, and the cycle of progressive multiple end-organ futility is well under way.

Clotting

Besides regulating blood flow, capillary cells also control coagulation, or clotting of blood (thrombosis). These functions involve signaling mechanisms and secretion of molecules that can both prevent and promote thrombosis, depending on whether there are extenuating circumstances to normal capillary-cell or end-organ function. When capillary cells are healthy and happy, there is signaling for reductions in clotting, which facilitates the smooth passage of plasma constituents and blood through their lumens, without sticky residues. With less adhesive signals, and, subsequently, less clotting, there is improvement in capillary-cell membrane function. This facilitates the passive diffusion of oxygen and other gases, as well as active transport of amino acids, protein, and nutrients to end-organ epithelial cells.

When capillary endothelial cells are faced with end-organ injury, they can urgently transform their membrane surface to be pro-clotting. This is adaptive and would diminish blood flow to the site of the injured end organ. This would wall off the injury, limit the risk of infection, and allow the end-organ cells sufficient substrate for repair. Depending on their location from the end-organ injury, other capillary cells would block clotting activities. That is, they would cause migration of more blood volume, inflammatory cells, and mediators of inflammation to adjacent areas of the end organ in order to further support repair. Repair of the end organ from injury is therefore coordinated by subsets of capillary cells that, depending on their location to the injury, have opposite effects.

With aging, capillary cells lose their effectiveness to block the clotting process. This results in net increases to vascular inflammatory responses that are inappropriate for health of the end organ. This proclotting predisposition can result in complete occlusion of blood flow through capillaries, as well as small and large arteries. This can severely compromise end-organ function permanently. Maintaining capillary and large vessel anticlotting bias can have substantial benefit to protecting sudden loss of blood flow and subsequent compromise to end-organ function.

Moderating Inflammation

The processes of acute and chronic inflammation that affect the entire vascular endothelium are multifactorial, and can involve a variety of molecules and inflammatory cells, both in the blood and surrounding end-organ tissues. For example, when there is inflammation of a membrane from an inflammatory molecule like LDL cholesterol, capillary cells signal and encourage trafficking of specialized white blood cells, as well as platelets (known as clotting cells), in order to migrate to the toxic sticky cholesterol molecule. At this point, an inflammatory battle occurs between net forces that either promote or mitigate further inflammation. With net anti-inflammatory influences, damage from the LDL cholesterol can be neutralized by a few mechanisms, and the particle will be removed.

Depending on the integrity and health of capillary-cell function, net proinflammatory influences may occur and result in cascades of vascular inflammatory mediators to the LDL particle, which in turn create more injury and cause inflammation to mushroom. When injury is persistent and inflammation mushrooms, there is thickening of the endothelial-cell membrane and development of plaque on the basement membranes of larger arteries. This can severely limit blood flow through the vessel and negate any benefit that surrounding smooth muscle would have to compensate for the narrowing by plaque.

Immune Support

Capillary endothelial cells have a critical role in immune signaling and packaging of an inflammatory response to unwanted particulates, infectious agents, and/or cancer cells. Foreign proteins and abnormal cells are packaged so that they can then be clearly identified by other inflammatory cells and efficiently removed. This process of setting up removal is complex, requiring a rich mix of signaling and coordinating efforts of the capillary endothelial cell with cells and proteins of the immune system (found in the blood). Together, they work to complete the extrication of unwanted cells. The response must be precise, as too little, too late, too much, or not at all can all lead to disasters. With too much response, excessive scar tissue forms. With not enough response, disseminated infections or cancers can result. Failing to respond or responding too late will lead to even more dire outcomes.

Capillary cells perform several critical functions in optimizing immune support to end organs. In addition to facilitating the initial preparing and presenting of unwanted cells and other debris to the specialized white blood cells (macrophage cells) for elimination, they also provide effective trafficking and recruitment of other inflammatory molecules to these foreign proteins (see figure 11, in the appendix). In other words, as they dispatch these cells (macrophage and other white blood cells) to the protein or cell of concern, they also signal other molecules that complete the elimination of the unwanted molecule.

Depending on where the abnormal protein or particle is, capillary cells can cause both adherence to their membranes and active transport of white blood cells through their cytoplasm for purposes of eradication of unwanted particulates, infectious agents, and/or cancer cells (see figures 4 and 5, in the appendix). This means that they orchestrate the recruitment of the right kind of inflammatory cell, at the right time and place, in order to efficiently eliminate a properly identified intruder. Once the intruder is eliminated, it then becomes the function of the capillary cell to assist in cleanup of any lingering inflammatory response. This entails a reversal of anti-inflammatory signals in order to limit scarring at the place of response.

With aging, these processes become impaired. That is, too much, too little, or no inflammatory response becomes more common toward unwanted invaders. The door opens for chronic inflammation, more scar tissue, and/or dissemination of infections or cancer cells.

When it comes to managing the immune response, capillary endothelial cells, and to some extent, the small arterioles that feed them, become combinations of both an offensive and defensive coordinator, to borrow from football jargon. Immune coordination is comprehensive and involves signals to adjacent capillary cells, the blood, the end organ, and the larger arteries that feed them. This results in a holistic approach of multiple cell coordination in modulating comprehensive immune function. Malfunction at the capillary cell level cascades to adversely affect the rest of the cells and proteins involved in the immune process.

The capacity of capillary endothelial cells to perform the complexity of their function is generally defined by competent management of the permeability of their membranes to and from the blood and end organ. *Permeability* is defined as the active and passive exchange of molecules, including oxygen, into and out of the blood and end organ. *Active transport* is where the endothelial cell invests energy in transporting molecules in and out of the blood or to and from the end organ. *Passive transport* is where the molecule is allowed to move into and out of the blood or end organ through diffusion, or without the endothelial cell expending additional energy to do so. This commonly occurs with gases, such as oxygen and carbon dioxide. When functioning well, these cells appear to be directing a symphony of multiple moving parts as they coordinate a variety of molecular exchanges; at the same time, they act as security officers in mediating inflammatory responses to foreign invaders.

Abnormal Function

When there is disruption of end-organ function, whether from trauma or infection, the endothelial cells of the capillary beds to the end organ involved immediately send signals that result in either more or less blood flow, as well as factors that either promote or disrupt clotting. A second set of signals produces immune support, depending on the insult, with various types and concentrations of white blood cells; these signals also procure the benefits of other immune proteins found in the blood. This results in a comprehensive assault on the end-organ trauma or foreign invader, which facilitates isolation, containment, and destruction (of the invader), while at the same time producing influences that minimize scarring. The response to invaders mediated by the capillary cell is bidirectional; that is, the responders (inflammatory cells and proteins) can affect the end organ by coming from the blood, or the response can come as an SOS signal calling for more or less help from the end organ itself (such as infections involving lung, skin, or intestines).

With advancing age (the equivalent to increased genetic damage to cellular DNA), or with one or several vascular inflammatory risk factors present, the capillary cell's response is less robust, producing errors in both signaling and coordination, resulting in too much or too little blood flow, clotting, and immune response. The result, depending on genetics, environmental influences, and the end organ involved, could be the development of a stroke, heart attack, serious infection, excessive bleeding from trauma, or excessive end-organ scarring (fibrosis) from the insult.

Vascular inflammatory risk factors that adversely affect endothelial-cell function throughout the entire arterial tree include a long list that is growing annually (see graphs 1, 3, and 5, in the appendix). At the top of the list is advanced age, defined as greater than age seventy-five and associated with accumulations of increasing genetic aberration to capillary-cell nuclear and mitochondrial DNA, as well reductions in most antioxidants, which produce increases in free-radical concentrations in the cell. The speed of aging, tied to progressive genetic incompetence, is directly linked to increases in aggregate vascular inflammatory risk factors. As has been alluded to previously, this includes LDL cholesterol and triglyceride elevation, blood sugar elevation, excessive stress, high blood pressure, inadequate sleep, cigarette smoking, alcohol excess, drug abuse, malnutrition, and sedentary lifestyle. These risk factors, when persistent, set up the endothelial cell to fail (see graph 3, in the appendix). When they stack, the vascular inflammatory processes accelerate endothelial cell decline. Therefore, advanced age causes genetically induced endothelial cell deterioration, but the processes associated with vascular inflammation make it worse and further accelerate their decline.

When assessing vascular inflammatory risk factors (see graphs 1 and 5, in the appendix), any of these risk factors, if persistent, may produce a progressive, and at some critical point, terminal acceleration of endothelial-cell dysfunction. With most of these vascular risk factors, such as diabetes or cigarette smoking, the endothelial-cell dysfunction is diffuse and involves all the blood vessels of the vascular tree, and at some level, every organ system. This results in simultaneous deterioration of multiple end-organ function.

Increased deterioration of specific end organs from vascular inflammation often depends on genetic influences. For example, a diabetic with a strong family history of coronary heart disease will also have the same predilection to develop the same condition and would be at risk for a heart attack or sudden death. In other diabetics, the inherited risk may point more toward the development of kidney or liver disease. As vascular inflammatory risk factors persist and stack, the concomitant end-organ risks of infection, cancer, scarring, and death increase as well, with the greatest end-organ risk associated with inherited genetic predisposition or persistently toxic environmental influences.

From these discussions, it is implied that efficient end-organ function is only as good as the capacity of the corresponding capillary endothelial cells to function. The capillary bed of each end organ becomes the manager of the conduit that regulates supply and demand of essential support to and from the blood and end organ. Aging and vascular risk factors alter nutrient supply channels, limit response to end-organ needs, and create a risk of end-organ scarring, infection, and cancer. At a certain point of decline, capillary-endothelial-cell dysfunction causes an acceleration of these risks to end-organ decline and subsequent failure.

This acceleration may produce a sudden life-threatening event. Or, more commonly, as is seen toward the end of life, one organ system failure cascades to include multiple others. All five graphs in the appendix demonstrate this acceleration, with increasing age. Graph 2, for example, shows a second bisecting line that demonstrates irreversibility of progressive vascular inflammation, culminating with imminent death. The implication of accelerating decline leading to death correlates to a critical mass of endothelial-cell dysfunction, which, when reached, causes death to the human organism.

Conclusion

To summarize, healthy endothelial cells do not act alone but collaborate with adjacent capillary endothelial cells, the blood elements, the end organ served, and even distant organs and endothelial cells. The endothelial cells' signaling system integrates appropriate responses to the end organ served, as well as messaging endothelial cells in larger arteries and other end organs. These signals/messages are involved in immune function, blood flow and clotting dynamics, as well as nutrient packaging and oxygen/ carbon dioxide exchange. (Throughout the next several chapters, the specialized functions of the endothelial cells in individual organs will be described in greater detail.)

Aging can be defined as a progressive vascular disease involving the entire arterial tree and affecting the genetic capacity of endothelial cells to function. Aging is also associated with reductions in most antioxidants that combat free-radical damage. Aging influences increase or decrease, depending on containment of vascular inflammatory risk factors.

The next chapter will peer into the dark hole caused by vascular inflammation.

4

Signs and Symptoms of Vascular Inflammation Associated with End-Organ Dysfunction

Over the course of thirty-six years of practice, I have had a unique opportunity to watch people age, often witnessing a terminal event culminating in death. At other times, I have been in the position to manage multiple disease processes in critical-care situations that require complex management decisions and interventions. With the explosive growth of CT scans, MRI (magnetic resonance imaging), and ultrasound in the past twenty-five years, the diagnosis of medical problems has become more precise, leading to quicker, more effective interventions. At the same time, this has led to increasing complexity in decision making as more details emerge about illness.

As I have watched this unfold, patterns of illness defined by these tests repeat themselves and appear linked to capillary-endothelial-cell dysfunction and vascular inflammatory aging. In this chapter, I will discuss the symptoms of vascular inflammatory change and endothelial-cell dysfunction, and show how they directly tie to the ways in which end organs decline and fail.

Signs of Vascular Inflammation

Depending on genetics and environmental exposures, most of us in Western culture are well into the processes of vascular inflammation by the time we reach age forty. The table below shows the signs of inflammation, the addictive behaviors that often accompany them, and the consequences of not acknowledging the need to make behavioral/ lifestyle changes.

Signs of Inflammation	Addictive Behaviors	Consequences
• fifteen pounds or more of weight gain • irregular or no exercise • fast-food eating • increasing stress from work • conflicted family pressures • poor sleep habits	• indulging in overeating or sugar binging • prescription and nonprescription drugs • alcohol • tobacco • excessive shopping • gambling • even pornography	• high blood pressure • insulin resistance or adult-onset diabetes • high LDL cholesterol and high triglycerides • fatigue • weight-bearing joint pain • no time to exercise • no time to prepare healthy meals • medications required • denial becomes easier • problems become chronic and harder to change • complications produce serious end-organ declines

Not that it is ever too late in life to make behavioral changes to positively affect health, but the adage "the sooner the better" truly carries weight when discussing vascular decline and its consequences. Without behavioral change from age forty on, the progression of vascular disease is like a broken record of predictable and often destructive breakdown of multiple organ systems. What's worse, particularly in men, death can be sudden and premature.

On the other hand, by choosing to modify vascular risk, the alternative, although not guaranteed, is much brighter. Behavioral modification becomes a lifelong process that culminates in proactive and intentional changes. The true payoff comes with advanced age, as quality of life expands by decades to involve all organ systems (see graph 1, in the appendix). Advanced age can be viewed as the final exam of accumulative vascular risk, as combinations of inflammatory risk factors accelerate change throughout the course of eighty-odd years of living. Completely closing vascular inflammatory windows, as advanced age approaches, becomes the cornerstone in staving off adverse health outcomes and promoting quality of life. Thus, that becomes one of the purposes of this book: to preempt the deadly causes of vascular inflammation and then aggressively mitigate them for quality life extension.

In each circumstance, there is a direct connection between decline and the capacity of the capillary endothelium to maintain optimal function to their end organs' epithelial cells. The *epithelium,* or *epithelial cells* (as opposed to the capillary endothelium), refers to the cells of end organs that have evolved their functions for a specific line of work. For end-organ cells to function optimally, they must connect and interact with the capillary endothelial cells. This intimate exchange of signals and nutrients with capillary cells results in a seamless back-and-forth conduit between the end organ, the capillary cells, and the blood.

The potential breach in this relationship is complex but ultimately involves combinations of vascular blood-flow dynamics and immune surveillance, two critical functions that capillary endothelium control. None of these initial breaches in and of themselves appear life threatening or produce clinical symptoms, but they form the initial seeds that can contribute to the beginning of end-organ dysfunction produced by early capillary-cell inflammation. Recognizing the urgency to mitigate vascular inflammation before symptoms arise could have far-reaching benefits in limiting expensive complications involving a host of end organs later in life. The sooner in life this process begins, the better the long-term outcome. With age, all vascular inflammatory processes accelerate, leading to end-organ decline. Therefore, mitigating such consequences as becoming arthritic, edentulous, blind, deaf, and demented become quality-of- life game changers. The list also includes vascular inflammatory– related heart, lung, and kidney failure, as well as skeletal muscle atrophy, bone loss, and digestive malfunction. Intentional vascular inflammatory mitigation done as early as possible will pay compounding dividends later on (see graph 4, in the appendix).

Complications of these end organs are directly tied to the density of vascular risk. By that I mean the coupling of adverse risk factors will accelerate vascular disease progression over time (see graph 5, in the appendix). For example, a smoker who has diabetes and abuses alcohol will have a much faster accumulation of diffuse vascular inflammation and plaque, compared to someone who just has a single risk factor, such as an elevation in LDL cholesterol. So, as risk factors stack, vascular risk increases and accelerates. With this background, let's explore different end organs and how they can be affected by vascular inflammation.

Skin

Beginning at age thirty, just as vascular inflammatory processes are beginning to gain traction to affect capillary-endothelial-cell function, the skin begins to lose elasticity, and small wrinkles emerge. At first, these changes are largely imperceptible to the naked untrained eye. With the passage of more time, and as vascular risk becomes quantifiable, wrinkles progress, with or without ultraviolet (UV) overexposure from the sun. It is about this time that the skin starts to become dry, forms flakes, and begins to itch from dryness. Coinciding with these developments is the appearance of moles and other benign growths on the skin's surface.

After age fifty, and particularly with aggregate vascular risk, adverse changes begin to accelerate to skin morphology. Dryness, itching, and wrinkles continue to progress, and the skin begins to lose its thickness. These changes precipitate increases in bruising and skin burns. Further decline in capillary-cell function leads to easily identifiable immune deficiency of the skin. Skin cancers, autoimmune plaques (psoriasis), slow-healing wounds develop, as well as increases in bacterial, fungal, and viral skin infections. With the skin thinning and losing elasticity, vitamin D levels decline, and body-temperature regulation becomes impaired. With advanced age, there is typically an acceleration of these changes, with extreme dryness and predisposition to skin cancers of all types, vitamin D deficiency, and poor body-temperature regulation.

Skin biopsies often confirm atrophy of dermal thickness and thinning of the stratified epithelial-cell layers that form the outside barrier of skin architecture. Coinciding with loss of skin thickness to the dermis is aggregate loss of the density of dermal blood supply. These changes would suggest a cause and effect. As capillary-cell volume decreases and the dermal layer thins, the epidermis becomes more vulnerable to dryness, autoimmune disease, infection, and cancer.

Treatments of progressive skin disease can be expensive and can require continuous clinical surveillance. Plastic surgery, laser therapy, and injections for treatment of wrinkles and sagging skin aside, treatment of skin cancers, dryness, itching, infections, and slow-healing open wounds can torment both patient and health- care provider. In some cases, infections and cancers (melanoma or squamous cancer) can be life threatening. All of these conditions correlate with progressive capillary-endothelial-cell declines related to accumulation of vascular inflammatory risks.

Vision, Dental, and Hearing

Similar to what occurs in the skin, with accrued vascular inflammation, declines in visual acuity become noticeable from the midthirties. Besides lens refractory problems, progressive visual decline is associated with reductions in accommodation (the ability to adapt from dark light to bright light) and peripheral vision. Glaucoma and cataracts become more common, and macular degeneration becomes a serious threat as a leading cause of blindness.

Hearing-loss progression is often associated with ringing in the ears and loss of balance.

As periodontal gum disease progresses, infections in the gums increase risk for tooth loss, abscesses, and blood-borne infections that can affect heart valves and are linked to occlusion of coronary arteries.

None of these outcomes are pleasant; they are expensive to treat, and they produce substantial reductions in quality of life. As these changes occur, blood pressure, blood sugar, and blood LDL cholesterol levels are typically increasing (see graph 1, in the appendix).

In addition to increased incidence of blurred vision, cataracts, and glaucoma, evaluation of eye arteries through the ophthalmoscope will demonstrate narrowing of vessels and small hemorrhages that directly tie visual change to vascular inflammation. All of this incriminating evidence adds fuel to the fire, as exposed endothelial cells that line the vascular tree become increasingly compromised by inflammation. As large vessel membranes thicken and plaque forms (see figure 7, in the appendix), the capacity of the endothelium to perform at all levels of the arterial tree diminishes, and the end organs served are cut off from optimum function. On the flip side, protecting the arterial endothelium also protects the end organs served, improves their function, and delays age-related consequences (see graph 1, in the appendix). Blindness can be prevented, tooth loss can be diminished, and even hearing loss can be delayed.

Lungs

Lung health is also intimately tied to the vascular endothelial cells (see figure 6, in the appendix). As an example, Voelkel and Rounds, in a recent review, "The Pulmonary Endothelium: Function in Health and Disease," have provided valuable insight into how endothelial-cell dysfunction ties into two very common lung conditions, asthma and chronic obstructive pulmonary disease. Implied in their discussion is a direct correlation of particulate exposures over time, inflammation of lung epithelium and inability of endothelial cells to provide enough support to counter these influences.

By age forty, along with added weight, higher cholesterol levels, higher blood pressures, and insulin resistance/diabetes, lung function has also begun to deteriorate. Depending on additional concomitant risks related to tobacco or particulates, reductions in lung function by as much as 30 percent (or more) can occur, when compared to baseline lung function from the midtwenties. The decline can result from irritating particulate exposures over several years. With constant bronchial tree and alveolar inflammation from particulates, the endothelial-cell capacity to manage proper immune response to control the persistent irritation diminishes, as does the capacity to facilitate optimal oxygen/carbon dioxide exchange with alveolar cells. Chronic cough, shortness of breath, increased exertional fatigue, and chest pain are common symptoms related to these declines. Signs include increases in heart rate at rest and with exertion, as well as increases in respiratory rate with any activity. Bronchitis, asthma, and early emphysema frequently need persistent treatment with inhalers, steroids, and antibiotics.

The chronic incursion of smoke and particulates into the lung cavity creates problems for capillary endothelial cells on both their blood and alveolar sides. Patching the lung with the formation of scar tissue helps to limit inflammation but diminishes the capacity of the lung to perform gas exchange. With more scar tissue and declining lung function, capillary cells become limited in terms of their ability to manage alveolar and blood signals and/or gas exchange. This translates to compromises in immune function, blood clotting, and artery-dilating properties in lung tissue. Increasing vulnerability of scarred lung tissue to bronchitis, pneumonia, emphysema (COPD), shortness of breath with exertion, and cancer becomes commonplace. An endothelial/capillary cell basis for these changes is highlighted by Petrache and colleagues on research involving cigarette smoke, oxidative stress, and subsequent loss of capillary cell barrier support, which then lead to further lung-tissue compromise.

The capacity to limit these influences and maintain the function of the lung is tied to limiting environmental exposures, such as smoking. By doing so, not only is lung tissue spared from chronic irritation, but also vascular inflammatory risk is reduced and capillary-cell function is stabilized in lung tissue. When function is stabilized, managing the immune surveillance, clotting mechanism, and blood-flow dynamics to the lung alveoli are restored, even if some lung tissue has been compromised by scarring (see figure 6, in the appendix). By stabilizing capillary-cell function, even in compromised conditions, pneumonia risk diminishes, emphysema progression is minimized, and cancer risk can decline. The capillary endothelium orchestrates this by restoring a return to effective immune presence in lung tissue. This causes more-efficient immune-screening procedures in the lung air spaces and subsequent elimination of infectious invaders and cancer cells before they populate to cause serious trouble. Bronchitis cough and sputum volume diminishes, and symptoms of shortness of breath with exertion stabilize.

Figures 4, 5, and 10 in the appendix demonstrate possible mechanisms by which capillary endothelial cells affect immune function in lung epithelial cells. Through the processes of white-blood-cell adhesion and migration through their gap junctions, as well as active transport through their vesicles, proteins and white blood cells of inflammation are brought to and from the lung epithelium from the blood. When this process of immune surveillance is overwhelmed, cough and shortness of breath increase, frequently leading to adverse outcomes which include pneumonia, emphysema and cancer.

The stress test of lung capillary cells is their capacity to provide alveoli with increased blood volume that would produce more oxygen/carbon dioxide exchange. This would occur as a result of heart- and skeletal-muscle signals calling for increases in oxygen delivery to their cells as a result of increased workloads. As the heart pumps more blood because of increased oxygen demand from skeletal muscle, the lung capillary cells are sending signals and secreting molecules like nitric oxide, which will cause profound vasodilatation of the capillary cells' lumens in order to increase blood flow to the lung alveoli. The larger blood volumes result in increased exposure of alveoli to capillary cells, allowing for greater exchange of oxygen and carbon dioxide. Scarring of the lung from chronic irritation reduces the capacity of alveoli to respond to increases in blood flow with oxygen/carbon dioxide exchange. Shortness of breath with limited exertion and chronic fatigue are the result.

With advanced aging, emphysema or chronic lung disease of any type, shortness of breath, and fatigue increase and are associated with 25 to 50 percent or more reductions in all measurements of lung function, as compared to what would be expected in an individual of age twenty-five with normal lung function. Vascular inflammatory risk factors (see graph 1, in the appendix) can decrease these measurements more quickly, and stacking risk factors (see graph 5, in the appendix)—for example, smoking, high cholesterol, insulin resistance/diabetes, and hypertension, among others—can produce an accelerated reduction in anticipated test results. This occurs as a result of progressive capillary-cell dysfunction from the inside out (increases in LDL cholesterol and blood sugar) or the outside in (particulate exposures to lung alveoli).

Heart and Skeletal Muscles

As the vascular endothelia of heart- and skeletal-muscle arteries become progressively inflamed, chest pain, fatigue, shortness of breath with exertion, and skeletal-muscle atrophy occur. This often coincides with increases in weight, resting heart rate, and blood pressure, and becomes evident by age thirty-five to forty. Stress testing, imaging tests, and ultrasounds to evaluate heart function demonstrate increases in valve and artery calcifications and reduced muscle and valve function. These changes correlate well with increasing heart and skeletal-muscle dysfunction tied to vascular inflammation of the entire arterial endothelial system, with the capillary cells feeling the brunt of these adverse changes.

Advanced aging and vascular inflammatory change are intimately tied to the effective functioning of the heart and skeletal muscle. As in lung function, vascular inflammatory risks attenuate heart function by making capillary endothelial cells dysfunctional and limiting these cells from responding adequately to the sometimes dramatic increases in oxygen needed by the heart and skeletal muscle. With less capacity to dilate their lumens from nitric oxide production, symptoms of increased fatigue, shortness of breath with exertion, and chest pain occur. Increasing fatigue associated with muscle cramps and pain in skeletal muscle is also commonplace. Multiple vascular risks act in aggregate to accelerate heart- and skeletal-muscle decline by producing thickened capillary-endothelial-cell membranes, plaque in larger coronary arteries, and calcium on heart valves. As mentioned previously, these easily measured changes precipitated by capillary-cell dysfunction to heart muscle can lead to heart attack, arrhythmias, and heart failure, precipitating symptoms of breathlessness, chest pain, and fatigue. Sudden cardiac death can be just a step away.

Treating symptomatic conditions with medications, stents, bypass grafts, valve replacements, pacemakers, defibrillators, and blood thinners becomes a very expensive intrusion to quality of life, and may not halt the progression of disease or address root cause. But alas, dependency on these options can become the only avenue for survival, given enough vascular disease progression.

Pancreas, Liver, Kidneys, and Intestines

In the pancreas, liver, kidneys, and intestines, the capillary endothelia have developed unique morphology, which includes pores of various sizes in their plasma and basement membranes to provide for the functioning of these organs' epithelial cells. Managing blood-flow dynamics, signaling digestive enzymes, balancing clotting requirements, and limiting immune risk to foreign invaders, together, creates a complex vascular milieu of integration at the capillary-endothelial-cell level. When done correctly, absorption of intestinal nutrients is comprehensive and packaged to the liver (see figure 9, in the appendix) and pancreas seamlessly. From there, nutrients are converted to glycogen (stored carbohydrates), fat, proteins, and clotting factors. Energy end products are then shipped for storage to the liver or fat cells, or to other end organs where they are needed. Much of this processing and movement of constituents is coordinated by capillary endothelial cells signaling to and from the digestive organs, blood, and other end organs, such as the brain, heart, and skeletal muscle.

Other capillary cells specialize in processes that remove waste molecules. Elimination of waste and fluids while minimizing protein loss and regulating mineral (sodium, calcium, and potassium) homeostasis is optimized by the unique morphology of the capillary endothelium to the kidney epithelial cells, identified as *podocytes* (see figure 3, in the appendix). Capillary endothelial cells, along with podocytes, form the *glomerulus,* which is part of a collecting unit called a *nephron,* which in turn makes urine from blood-plasma waste products.

When things go awry, and capillary-cell function to these end organs is impaired from inside-out (metabolic) or outside-in (such as from abnormal intestinal bacteria) influences, anorexia, abdominal pain, fever, bleeding, diarrhea, bloating, nausea, vomiting, fatigue, and malnutrition result. Signs include weight changes (usually weight loss), increases in temperature and heart rate, and dehydration that can progress to life-threatening shock.

With persistent breaches to capillary cells, often beginning in midlife from vascular inflammatory influences, their capacity to assist end-organ epithelial cells diminishes, symptoms of illness increase. The liver, pancreas, intestinal tract, and kidney cells can come under stress from this compromise, and they often become inflamed. Symptoms emerge: end organs, such as the liver and pancreas, leak enzymes into the blood, and nausea, vomiting, bloating, intestinal bleeding, diarrhea, and abdominal pain increase. With increased kidney stress, proteins, blood, and white blood cells can be found in the urine. Depending on the persistence and intensity of the breach, permanent symptoms (nausea, diarrhea, abdominal pain) can occur and are frequently tied to increased risk for infection, cancer, and end-organ failure from scarring.

Even with advanced interventions to treat disease to these organ systems, lingering symptoms of pain, fatigue, nausea, bloating, diarrhea/constipation, and bleeding are common. Treatments and their follow-up are expensive, have their own set of serious side effects, and are often only partially effective in reducing symptoms of end-organ dysfunction. As spirals of capillary-cell dysfunction increase, end-organ damage from scar tissue and immune dysfunction occurs, with further increases in risk for infection, autoimmune disease, and cancer.

Immune System

As can be implied from this discussion, the cornerstone that marks optimal capillary endothelial-cell health is the comprehensive management of immunity by these cells. The immune system, and its arsenal of inflammatory white blood cells, blood proteins, as well as clotting and growth factors, encompasses a vast network that requires careful integration at the tissue level of all organ systems.

Even subtle missteps can produce cascades of inappropriate signaling that can culminate in too little or too much response to tumor cells, foreign particulates or proteins, and infections. This can culminate in exposure of any vulnerable end organ to excessive scar tissue, infection, autoimmune disease, or cancer. Initial symptoms of immune dysfunction are often vague, and include fatigue, malaise, and pain. Such symptoms are often mistaken for depression. Signs of immune dysfunction can be associated with fevers, recurrent infections, weight loss or gain, poor sleep and eating habits, and increases in stress.

Immunity involves the complex integration of aggregate inflammatory cells and proteins that have specific functions to eliminate from an end organ or blood plasma any cells and foreign molecules that don't belong. These cells' capacity to perform to a specific breach is orchestrated by signals from the capillary endothelium. Even small genetic defects involving any of the cells or proteins involved in the immune cascade can reduce capillary-cell effectiveness to perform this function. In addition, persistent and excessive toxic, metabolic, or environmental exposures can make capillary-cell adjustments to immune signaling difficult, thereby thwarting adequate responses to invaders. Therefore, competent immune surveillance has a lot of moving parts that require precision to perform well. For these reasons, optimizing capillary-endothelial function to manage the elaborate responsibilities of immune surveillance becomes the ultimate marker to good health.

Cracks in immune surveillance usually begin in the midthirties and are tied to threshold capillary-cell dysfunction associated with stress, weight gain, poor eating and sleep habits, as well as from genetic influences and autoimmune diseases, like lupus and rheumatoid arthritis, which occur with a much higher frequency in women. Intestinal bleeding and abdominal pain from autoimmune causes like Crohn's disease can also emerge.

With the passage of time, and with aggregate vascular inflammatory risk, capillary-cell dysfunction, and immune deterioration, cancer and infection in all organ systems increase. Infections most commonly arise in the urinary tract, lungs, or intestinal tract, and are associated with combinations of fever, abdominal or flank pain, bloating, burning with urination, nausea, and diarrhea. Lung symptoms from infection include fever, cough, shortness of breath, and chest pain. Cancer predilection also increases and can involve any organ system, with predilection often based on genomics (inherited DNA vulnerability). With advanced age, the cycle of progressive immune dysfunction increases further, and infection and cancer rates accelerate along with it.

Behavior has a profound effect on immunity. Along with advanced age, persistent stress, insomnia, poor diet, and lack of exercise, as well as chronic exposures to cigarettes and alcohol, all can produce inflammatory mediators and free radicals that contribute to progressive capillary-cell dysfunction and immune failure, resulting in increases in infections, cancer, autoimmune disease, and end-organ scarring.

Brain

It could be argued that the most dynamic development in the evolution of the capillary endothelium involves the cells that form a protective barrier to the brain, known as the *blood-brain barrier unit.* Coupled with adjacent helper cells (*pericytes*) and brain epithelial cells (*astrocytes*), the capillary cells of the blood-brain barrier maintain an exclusive bath of nutrients and oxygen, known as *cerebrospinal fluid,* to optimize the high-energy needs of brain cells. The capillary cells of the blood-brain barrier have developed several energy dependent levels of morphology that increase security from potential blood poisoning, and also make the cerebrospinal fluid safe for delicate brain cells. As such, the anatomy of capillary cells of the blood-brain barrier is exactly the opposite of the porous capillary-cell membranes of the intestines, kidney, liver, and pancreas.

Support of the blood-brain barrier and subsequent brain function requires a constant blood supply pumped through six large arteries at a rate of about one liter per minute. Any reduction in blood flow from thickening or narrowing of the large arteries to the brain (arteriosclerosis, or hardening of the arteries), or from heart or lung failure, can reduce blood flow (and oxygen) to the brain and trigger capillary dysfunction. When this occurs, optimal barrier support declines, brain function deteriorates, and symptoms of decreased mental acuity (brain fog), headache, fatigue, and sleep disturbances result. With the passage of time associated with aggregate vascular inflammatory risk, advanced age, and capillary-cell dysfunction, these symptoms can progress to dementia and other neurodegenerative diseases.

Metabolic vascular inflammatory diseases, such as *diabetes* and *lipidemia* (high LDL cholesterol and high triglycerides), or smoking cigarettes over a period of years, can trigger capillary-cell dysfunction of the blood-brain barrier. These persistent adverse metabolic and free-radical influences alter the capillary-cell mitochondrial energy and feedback-loop landscape, culminating in less-than-robust barrier support. With leaks of molecules into the cerebrospinal fluid, coupled with decreases in oxygen and optimal nutrients, the inflammatory morass quickly spreads to the brain nerve cells. Headaches, brain fog, sleep disturbances, and depression are early signs and symptoms of these changes.

With progression of capillary dysfunction, concentration difficulties couple with short-term memory loss. These changes make complex problem solving and learning new information difficult. With further progression, there are personality changes, as well as reductions in motor and sensory skills. These declines contribute to patterns of thinking that limit adaptation, produce social isolation, and increase risks for falling. Progression to dementia and dependent living becomes imminent.

With the passage of time, persistent vascular inflammation produces large vessel narrowing, clots, and occlusions which can result in an abrupt cutoff of blood to the brain. Because of high oxygen requirements, sudden loss of blood supply to brain cells quickly results in their compromise and death. The size of the occluded artery will determine the extent of brain loss. This is known as a stroke, ministroke, or TIA (transient ischemic attack). Symptoms can range from transient blindness or dizziness, to loss of function to an entire side of the body. Even coma and death from brain swelling can occur.

Over time, with some TIAs, small vessel vascular occlusions produce an aggregate impact to brain function. This can be identified as *chronic ischemic white matter change,* which is seen on imaging studies and correlates with evolving cerebral atrophy, or loss of brain-cell volume. In my own observations in over twenty years, having interpreted thousands of carotid imaging studies, reductions in brain volume appear linked to proportionate and progressive increases in membrane thickening and plaque buildup in the large arteries that supply blood to the brain. To accommodate for this loss of normal brain tissue, astrocytes of the blood brain barrier are signaled to make amyloid and tau scar tissue to fill the space created by brain-cell loss. These changes correlate with diminished cognitive capacity, which includes short-term memory loss, difficulty learning new information and performing complex problem solving, as well as reduction in motor skills.

Protecting blood flow to the brain by mitigating vascular inflammatory risk factors stabilizes blood-brain barrier function, as well as oxygen and nutrient support to brain cells. This can further stabilize signs and symptoms of progressive memory loss and loss of motor skills. Delays to dependent living occur, as dementia progression is minimized.

Advanced age and increases in aggregate vascular risk that contributes to declines in motor and cognitive function are also associated with increased risk for cancer, seizures, and infection. These conditions contribute further to acceleration of cognitive skills, as they impinge on and destroy normal brain tissue, and increase brain scarring. Reduced cognition, depression, headaches, fatigue, malaise, and loss of motor function all are common.

Maintaining the integrity of brain function can become a barometer to grade capillary-endothelial-cell functioning of the entire arterial tree. With reference to brain function, there is no tolerance of the brain to reductions in cerebral blood flow. In other words, brain function will decrease to the level that blood flow decreases. Therefore, healthy cognition is a proxy to the healthy capillary-cell function not only of the brain, but also all other organ systems. Early signs of diminished brain health, such as fatigue, headache, and brain fog, can be viewed as indicators of early capillary-cell dysfunction.

So how do capillary cells facilitate end-organ function? With end organs providing such a diverse set of functions, how do the capillary cells manage to meet those organs' needs? Even more important, while meeting these needs, how do capillary cells maintain a universal communication code that is understood by adjacent and distant endothelium and blood constituents, as well as distant end organs? The way in which capillary cells orchestrate all of this will be the basis of the next chapter, as we explore details in relationships between capillary cells and major end-organ systems. What should become clear as these details emerge is just how important capillary cells are to the integrity of end-organ function and total body homeostasis.

5

Endothelial Cells and Major Organ Systems

Now that we have an understanding of how capillary endothelial cells affect signs and symptoms of end-organ disease, this chapter will provide details about how the capillary endothelial cells have evolved to affect function in each organ system. In many instances, these cells have developed unique morphologies to their basement membranes in order to accommodate specific end-organ requirements, while simultaneously managing blood constituents on their plasma membranes as they apply to end-organ needs. Adopting their morphology to end organ-needs without changing their internal mechanics is a dramatic example of how capillary cells can manage end-organ function while also communicating with other capillary-endothelial and end-organ cells.

Skin

The skin is a unique organ system because of its vastness, as it covers and protects the internal organs of the entire human organism. The healthy skin is composed of several layers, with the outer layer composed of stratified epithelial cells that serve as a protective barrier, known as the *epidermis.* Underneath the epidermis, is the *dermis,* which is also composed of epithelial cells. The skin capillary cells are abundant here.

In addition to barrier support, the skin regulates many other body functions:

- The skin absorbs vitamin D, and also manages salt and water in order to regulate body temperature. This requires a delicate balance between managing salt and fluid loss through the skin on the one hand, and supplying adequate oxygen and nutrients to the dermis, the subcutaneous cells, and fat cells on the other. These dynamics are further influenced by changes in lean body mass (which increase or decrease skin surface area), activity levels, ambient air temperatures, and the presence of preexisting skin disease (age-related thinning of the dermis layer). In addition, the skin capillary cells receive signaling from distant sources in order to regulate heat loss from insults related to trauma, dehydration, or infection.

- When there is disruption of the skin from trauma, chemicals, or burns, several mechanisms are put into place through capillary cells that restore the skin barrier, prevent foreign invaders from coming into the bloodstream, and control subsequent scar formation. With normal skin healing, the scar is eventually minimized, or sloughed and replaced by new skin that resumes its previous function.

- The thickness of the dermis, which protects the epidermis and influences temperature regulation, is a reflection of capillary-cell function. Skin thickness, or lack of it, is associated with both advanced age and increased vascular inflammatory risk factors. The speed of wound healing, the capacity to produce or conserve sweat, the production of vitamin D by the skin epithelium, as well as the prevention of skin tumors and containment of infections, all are dependent on competent capillary-cell function in a full-thickness stratified skin epithelium and dermis. The same extent to which skin thickness is lost is the extent to which capillary-cell function has diminished.

- The capillary endothelium brings white blood cells, immune proteins, and clotting factors to the site of a cut or burn in order to induce an inflammatory response and begin the processes of healing. Other substances are then called upon to stimulate growth of new dermal and endothelial cells, and such growth completes the healing process. The capacity to signal, produce, and respond appropriately to changes in the dermis and epidermis requires the capillary cells to read and then signal either an increase or decrease in the immune response, depending on the timing of the healing process. Other influences—such as increases or decreases in clotting, and adequate oxygen diffusion and nutrient transport—all are required to create a satisfactory response that will cause healing. The response should not be too harsh, as this could result in too much scarring; but it should be strong enough to limit bleeding and infection.

- The dermal capillary epithelium can demonstrate dynamic adaptability to evolving changes in body mass. With substantial weight gain, the epithelium can mount exceptional growth characteristics in order to produce more capillary cells and blood vasculature to accommodate new and expanding skin mass. The increased surface area subsequently resets capillary-cell regulation of temperature and heat loss as fat volume increases. The combination of age, weight gain, and increases in skin mass, with concomitant reductions in epithelial and dermal thickness, increase the risk for skin slough from pressure and friction. Open wounds (*decubiti*) become common in high-pressure areas, and bacterial infection can create cellulitis and more skin breakdown. Obesity is coupled with diabetes and immune suppression, and the table has been set for skin infections to escape the surveillance mechanisms of capillary cells, find their way into the bloodstream, and then produce serious systemic infections, known as *sepsis*.

Given the right genetics and ultraviolet light exposure, combined with compromised capillary-cell function, skin growths escape surveillance, and increase. This applies to cancers of all types, including the deadly melanoma.

A key mediator in skin capillary-cell response is nitric oxide. This molecule relaxes the smooth muscle that surrounds arterioles and larger arteries to increase blood flow to skin capillary beds; as such, it is a major regulator of both body temperature and capacity of the skin to access effective immune responses. The capacity of capillary cells to produce nitric oxide defines their health. As capillary-cell function declines in the skin and the dermal layer thins, nitric oxide levels decline in proportion.

Summary

In summation, optimal capillary-cell function in the skin assists in the management of barrier function, which includes temperature and sweat regulation, vitamin D metabolism, wound healing, skin repair from trauma, and prevention of infections and skin cancer. As the skin layers thin, capillary-cell function declines, and all of these functions decline with it. The thinning of the skin and decline in skin function are tied to the effects of aging and aggregate vascular inflammatory risks. These changes serve as notice that protecting capillary cells and the arterial-tree endothelium from vascular risks can minimize skin disease as well as modulate effective skin homeostasis to other end organs.

Gums

Healthy teeth are dependent on healthy gums to support them. The gums, and the capillary vasculature support they provide, create a foundation for prevention of tooth decay and loss. The gum barrier limits bacteria, food, and viruses from invading the support structures of teeth, preventing these intruders from infecting tooth roots. Chronic inflammatory disease is associated with thinning of the gum line (like thinning of the skin dermis), and this can cause bacteria to enter the bloodstream. For this reason, it should not come as a surprise that gum disease is a direct reflection of capillary-cell dysfunction. It has been linked to a variety of cardiovascular conditions, including heart disease, hypertension, and diabetes mellitus. Maintaining healthy gums is critical to maintaining healthy teeth.

The trench work (no pun intended) for managing gum health is performed by the capillary endothelial cells and the ways in which they interact with gum epithelium. The supply of gum epithelium with nutrients, oxygen, immune cells and proteins from the blood provides the basis for optimal barrier support. If capillary-cell support for the gum epithelium fails and the gum barrier is breached, bacteria chronically penetrate the tooth roots, and cascades of vascular inflammation follow. This includes bacteria entering the bloodstream and attaching to heart valves (bacterial vegetation) and/or contributing to the production of coronary-artery plaque, which leads to coronary artery disease and heart attack.

In optimal conditions, barrier epithelial cell gum health is affected by combinations of capillary-cell support on one side of the gum epithelium and a symbiosis of beneficial bacterial mouth flora and saliva on the other side. The constant presence of bacteria to the gum epithelium makes these cells vulnerable to breach. For this reason, the capillary endothelial cells, through signaling combinations of clotting, blood supply (increases in nitric oxide production), and white-blood-cell trafficking, directly support the gum epithelium in the elimination of bacteria that penetrate the gum epithelium. The capillary cells further supply the gum epithelium with increases in oxygen and nutrients from blood when demands from the gum epithelium, related to mastication or changes in saliva/bacteria concentrations, require additional barrier support.

With persistent bacterial breach, tooth decay, periodontal disease, and abscess result. Over time, this can require invasive surgery (root canal or tooth extraction). Depending on the scope and duration of inflammation, gum disease may eventually cause the roots of most of the teeth in the mouth to become infected and require extraction. This can occur as early as the third decade of life in patients who have diabetes, smoke cigarettes, have poor oral hygiene, or abuse alcohol or drugs.

Central to adverse changes in the gum epithelium is the decline in capillary-endothelial-cell function. Capillary dysfunction correlates with thinning or atrophy of gum tissue, worsening of epithelial-cell barrier protection of teeth, and increased vulnerability to periodontal disease, tooth decay, and abscess formation. These changes are linked to advanced age and aggregate vascular inflammatory risks. In addition to mitigating those risks, other preventative measures include drinking more water, brushing teeth after meals, and flossing at least two times daily, all of which are also important to preventing gum inflammation.

What happens when there is a breach of bacteria through the epithelium of the gum? Like other end-organ breaches, think of the epithelial cells as an actor in a play and the capillary cells that line their membranes as the director. Within the capillary cells, the mitochondria are the producers. Capillary endothelial cells in the proximity of the bacterial breach will send signals to increase nitric oxide and blood flow to the area of the breach, in an attempt to open up the area to inflammatory cells and immune proteins. As they modulate an inflammatory response with more blood, white blood cells, and immune proteins directed toward the bacteria, other capillary cells are sending signals to limit blood supply and inflammation in order to wall off (contain) the response. Eventually, specialized white blood cells called *macrophages* will envelop the disabled bacteria and consume them.

Once the invader is eliminated, steps are then taken to clean up inflammatory debris in order to minimize additional inflammation and prevent scarring of tissue. If the breach is chronic and persistent, scarring and atrophy of the gum barrier occurs. Therefore, gum homeostasis is dependent on barrier control by capillary cells as they simultaneously serve the nutrient needs of the teeth.

What has become well established is the direct relationship of gum inflammation, atrophy, and periodontal disease, vis-à-vis capillary-cell dysfunction, and the subsequent cascades of vascular proinflammatory effects elsewhere. Inflammatory changes in gums and how they lead to vascular disease elsewhere is elucidated by Demmer and Desvarleux (see bibliography) in a review of periodontal inflammation. Gum disease sets off signals that can adversely affect endothelial cells in other organ system. That is, inflamed gums cause bacteria and the increased expression of inflammatory markers to leak into the bloodstream. This combination causes vascular inflammation to occur in arteries that have no functional connection to the gums. This can lead to plaque that critically narrows heart coronary arteries, which can then precipitate a heart attack.

Summary

Looking at the gums in the mouth is a good proxy for understanding what is going on within the vascular tree throughout the body. Poor periodontal health—as evidenced by gum loss, infections, abscess formation, and loss of teeth—is a strong indicator of advancing vascular inflammatory processes that correlate with impending heart disease from coronary-artery narrowing. Maintaining optimal gum health with teeth brushing, flossing, and advanced periodontal teeth cleaning not only maintains the health of teeth but also prevents vascular inflammation elsewhere in the body. Aggressively preventing and managing periodontal disease can have substantial health benefits in potentially limiting heart attacks and strokes.

Vision

Vision involves a set of highly specialized interconnected nerve cells that send electrical impulses to and from different parts of the brain to create vision. The visual process is also affected by the eyeball contents, which include unique fluids, the lens, various membranes, peripheral nerves and muscle tissue. While all of these are essential to vision, it is the capillary endothelium that assists, directs, and produces the scene that leads to the integration of function of the lens, fluids, and all these specialized cells. In this section, we will focus on the capillary endothelium of the cornea, as well as the small artery vasculature that emerges to supply the retina. Both the cornea and retina, along with their respective accompanying capillary endothelia, have evolved unique capacities to create the human visual experience.

Cornea

The cornea has two primary functions. It shields the human eye from bacteria, dust, and particulates, and, along with the lens, is a major contributor to visual clarity. Capillary cells of the cornea direct immune support to limit infections, remove particulates or debris, and wall off the effects of blunt trauma or allergic reactions.

The capillary cells, along with the corneal epithelial cells, function to keep the fluids that collect in the corneal *stroma,* which is a thick transparent layer of the cornea, clear and colorless. The capillary endothelial cells of the cornea do this by using energy to create a barrier to keep out certain blood constituents. They have a secondary function of actively pumping and filtering excess fluid out of the corneal stroma. By actively (i.e., with energy utilization, as opposed to passive processes of diffusion) managing this process, the capillary endothelium keeps the corneal stroma in a slightly dehydrated state relative to the blood.

This requires precise management of electrolyte and mineral content of the fluid, thereby minimizing precipitants and maintaining fluid transparency, which is critical to maintaining optimal visual acuity. Without optimal pumping, filtering, and management of electrolytes, the stroma would swell, become hazy, and begin to blur vision. Since these endothelial cells generally lack the capacity to regenerate, it is important to protect and prevent their loss. Vascular inflammatory risks, as well as aging, increase the disappearance of these cells, which over time increases both cloudiness and pressures in the corneal stromal fluid. Visual acuity declines, and blindness increases.

As stated, the capillary cells of the cornea direct immune support to limit infections, remove particulates or debris and wall off the effects of blunt trauma or allergic reactions. The signaling to different types of immune support, (white blood cells, immune proteins, and other mediators of inflammation), clotting, and blood-flow dynamics are all integrated simultaneously to coordinate and manage visual acuity, allowing for an optimal visual experience.

With aging and accumulative vascular inflammatory risks, the corneal endothelium becomes less effective in maintaining refractive clarity. This correlation of chronic oxidative stress from vascular inflammatory risk to corneal damage is implied in a study by Brown and associates (see bibliography) and suggests a strong relationship between capillary-cell dysfunction and loss of corneal clarity. Whether because of irreversible loss of capillary cells (thinning of the corneal capillary endothelium) in the cornea or increasing dysfunction in those that remain, the capillary cells pump less fluid out of the corneal stroma to maintain a dehydrated state. The cloudy fluid that results diminishes visual acuity. Expensive corneal transplants in conjunction with lens implants (for cataract buildup) offer relief for this condition, but they do not address the underlying root cause of endothelial-cell dysfunction. Whether transplanted or not, age and stacking of vascular inflammatory risk factors increase the need for corneal/lens transplant surgery and the requirement of early, frequent, and expensive interventions to prevent blindness.

In a sense, this surgery is the visual equivalent of coronary bypass surgery. Replacing the lens and cornea to restore vision is similar to bypassing coronary arteries of the heart in order to restore heart-muscle function. Without addressing vascular inflammatory risks and subsequent capillary endothelial-cell health, both of these surgeries only postpone for a few years the decline in heart and eye function. In contrast, with intentional vascular anti-inflammatory behaviors and treatments, the need to have these surgeries, or to repeat them, can be postponed by decades, and in some cases, indefinitely.

Retina

The capillary endothelium in the retinae actively participates in managing the blood-nerve barrier that seals the retina to an enriched bath of supportive nutrients, oxygen, and electrolytes, similar to the cerebrospinal fluid of the brain. The retinae are the primary clusters of highly specialized nerve cells that connect the eyeball to the brain. As such, the retinae are integral to the processing of visual impulses. Like the brain, the retinae are associated with a microvascular circulation of small arteries and capillaries that have a unique barrier-protective function. By utilizing higher amounts of energy, these capillary cells produce a blood-nerve barrier which maintains a restrictive bath of oxygen, nutrients, and some minerals that protects and supports optic nerve (retina) function.

For optimal support of the blood-retinal barrier and to facilitate the high-energy needs of the retinal nerve, capillary cells require a constant blood supply. Any persistent disruption of blood flow, such as from heart disease or vascular plaque narrowing of larger arteries downstream to retinal capillaries, can impact capillary function and result in retinal nerve epithelial-cell decline. Gaps in barrier function affect not only the bath but also the immune support that capillary cells give to retinal epithelium. Decay to immune surveillance of the retina is often associated with similar changes in the brain, as both organ systems are sensitive to persistent reductions in blood flow.

If blood flow declines, optimal barrier function begins to fail, and the high maintenance needs of the retinal nerve cannot be met. Decaying retinal nerve function soon follows. The cascades of retinal eye diseases which progressively impair vision occur. Combinations of advanced age and aggregate vascular risk produce capillary-cell dysfunction that accelerates retinal-nerve decline. The macular degeneration that results is often irreversible.

To understand the subtle process of capillary-endothelial-cell dysfunction involving the retina, the best evidence of cause and effect have come from adult-onset diabetics. What has become clear is that even with subtle increases in fasting blood sugar, known as *prediabetes* (defined as fasting blood sugars between 100–125 mg/dL), there is a correlation to initial capillary-endothelial-cell dysfunction. The relationship between prediabetes and capillary-endothelial-cell dysfunction has been reviewed and summarized by S. Grundy (see bibliography). Concluded in the discussion is that abnormalities in simple carbohydrate (sugar) metabolism produce enough vascular inflammatory influence to affect retinal-capillary function, which then adversely affects retinal-nerve health. Insulin resistance deranges the metabolism of all cells but is particularly lethal to endothelial cells. In addition to changing energy mechanics, free-radical production increases in these cells, which can further limit mitochondrial and membrane performance.

When capillary cells fail, barrier function deteriorates, capillary cells become more porous, and potentially toxic molecules penetrate the blood-retinal barrier. Depending on the magnitude of the breach, several other adverse changes to barrier function may occur. Like the ailing captain losing control of his ship, the sick capillary cell loses the capacity to control processes that optimize vision, by allowing influences that reduce necessary barrier and nutrient support to retinal nerve cells.

Breach can be acute or chronic; it can involve overwhelming influences from the blood (bacterial infection, blood sugar elevation), or external influences, such as blunt trauma or penetrating infection to the eyeball. Regardless of type, breach causes increases in inflammatory mediators. The health of capillary cells serving the retina will determine how the breach is managed. Acute breach, with optimal capillary function, should result in resolution over days to weeks, with little residual scar tissue (blurred vision).

In chronic breach, such as with persistent vascular inflammatory risk (diabetes, tobacco use, LDL cholesterol elevation, etc.), the changes associated with capillary-cell dysfunction often involve progressive declines over decades. The initial effects on the capillary cell involve their mitochondria. Once mitochondrial function has been altered in capillary cells, either by reductions in oxygen or changes in energy substrate, their signaling capacity to membranes and organelles decline, and ROS (free-radical exhaust from energy production or lack of production) composition becomes more toxic. This translates to net increases in inflammatory mediators and toxic free radicals, and potential declines in membrane and organelle function in capillary cells. Barrier/immune function and maintenance of the bath to retinal epithelium and subsequent function of the retinal nerve all become unreliable. The relationship of endothelial-cell decline to mitochondrial dysfunction and the aging inflammatory cascades that follow is highlighted by work from A. Csiszar (see bibliography).

Protecting and maintaining mitochondrial function of capillary cells to retinal epithelium is central to the quality assurance of capillary-cell function. A vicious cycle of dysfunction, starting with capillary cells, has been initiated by persistent vascular inflammatory mediators. Progressive, and in some cases irreversible, blindness from retinal disease results.

Why are free radicals so sinister? Not all free radicals produce negative effects. Some actually serve in feedback loops to support healthy capillary-cell responses to infection or trauma. Others are easily metabolized or reduced in the presence of sufficient antioxidants and do not cause harm to cell function.

The more virulent free radicals have uneven or unpaired electrons that have a strong affinity to find a partner proton. These electrons may find their mates (positively charged minerals or trace metals, for example), and then attach to a constituent in the blood, a capillary-cell membrane, nuclear DNA, or other organelle, and cause damage.

What happens next is what can make a toxic free radical dangerous. The attachment can produce a chain reaction of more free radicals and damage, which can escalate like the effect of a cluster bomb. The chain reaction can lead to a toxic dance of inflammatory cascades that can produce a tenacious goo to the membrane, which could allow for and/or attract more toxic inflammatory response. The damage that results can be irreversible to membrane function.

Once toxic free radicals seize control of the endothelial cell, they alter mitochondrial function, and with it, all membrane and organelle function of the cell. They are also associated with shortening of the protective nuclear cap and cross-linkage of DNA. The term *oxidative stress* describes the quantity of toxic free-radical risk to cells.

Antioxidants are found in abundance in some fruit, most vegetables, and herbs. Advanced age and accumulated vascular inflammatory risk produce across-the-board reductions in antioxidant levels in capillary and end-organ cells. Supporting antioxidant levels becomes a central theme in limiting free-radical damage. In the case of capillary-cell retinal function, reducing oxidative stress by maintaining antioxidant levels and mitigating vascular inflammation risk limits macular degeneration.

Summary

To summarize, visual acuity and eye health are directly related to capillary-endothelial-cell function. Capillary-endothelial-cell function provides barrier and immune support to visual clarity. Persistent disruption of capillary function can set up cascades of inflammation, leading to retinal diseases and blindness, with adult-onset diabetes serving as a model for these changes. As with the skin and the gums, the functioning of the retina and the maintenance of visual acuity are linked to capillary-cell function. Preserving capillary-endothelial-cell function of the eye through appropriate vascular anti-inflammatory interventions will likely have beneficial effects to limit visual complications associated with corneal or retinal-nerve dysfunction.

Lungs

The primary site of gas exchange for oxygen and carbon dioxide in the lungs is the *capillary-endothelial/alveolar cell interface* (small epithelial cell sacs in the lung that receive oxygen and remove carbon dioxide). The managers and coordinators of this process are the capillary endothelial cells. The microvasculature of the lung endothelium is similar to other endothelial cells throughout the body, in terms of coordinating exchange of nutrients, clotting, blood flow, and immune function, but in the lungs the morphology of these cells has evolved to allow enhancement of the passive diffusion of gases to and from the blood. The capacity of capillary cells to increase or decrease blood flow by relaxing or constricting adjacent smooth-muscle cells, found around arteriole endothelial cells, is key to controlling fluctuations in systemic oxygen demand. This capacity is controlled by nitric oxide production in capillary cells (figure 6 in the appendix)

Gas exchange in lung capillary endothelial cells is facilitated by permeability. *Permeability* in lung capillary endothelium is dependent on calcium homeostasis. *Calcium homeostasis* controls potassium and sodium flux on all surface membranes and establishes what is known as *electromechanical gradients* to these membranes. These gradients can push or pull molecules into and out of capillary cells, and can assist in diffusion of oxygen and carbon dioxide to and from lung alveoli and into and out of blood.

Calcium homeostasis in capillary cells is controlled by their mitochondria and involves feedback loops participating in energy production. Calcium management of membrane permeability, in combination with increased nitric oxide production, creates a dynamic response to increased oxygen demands by increasing both permeability and blood flow in lung capillary beds. With rigorous exercise or physical labor, cardiac output can double, and the permeability of capillary cells of the lung alveoli to accommodate large increases in blood flow for increased oxygen/carbon dioxide exchange is essential.

Another important function of lung capillary cells is managing an appropriate immune response to inhaled particulates or intruders. Lung alveolar cells can be bombarded by inhalation of particulates or noxious molecules that can stimulate excessive inflammation of lung tissue. This can be compounded by other factors, such as altitude, volume of infectious or particulate exposure, presence or absence of other gases or particulates in the breathing environment, or previous scarring of lung tissue. Examples would include air pollution (carbon monoxide, toxic particulates), parasites, viruses, bacteria, or fungi. With the presence of lung scarring, particulates, infection, injury, increasing altitude, or carbon monoxide gas, the inflammatory response generated by the capillary cell to the alveolar epithelial cell must be strong enough to mitigate the intruder, but not so strong as to seriously impair the exchange of oxygen and carbon dioxide or create excessive scar tissue. The capillary cell must wears two hats at the same time. It must maintain and support gas exchange while coordinating an immune response, which paradoxically could adversely affect gas exchange. Inadequate response and chronic bronchitis or pneumonia associated with more serious oxygen debt (*hypoxia*), occurs. The wrong type of response, and wheezing (asthma) or mucus plugging occurs. Too much response, and permanent lung scarring can result.

The burden of maintaining capillary and alveolar cell function involves intentional changes in human behavior. Whether from chronic cigarette smoking or exposure to inhaled particulates, such as dust or air pollution, the endothelial cells labor with the immune resources at hand in order to mitigate and eliminate unwanted exposures. Over time, the persistence of particulate exposure, such as tobacco smoke, will take its collective toll on the alveoli issue. From combinations of chronic inflammatory exposures coupled with exhausted immune support, a chronic inflammatory scar response, also known as pulmonary fibrosis, emphysema or chronic obstructive pulmonary disease (COPD) replaces normal lung tissue.

Summary

To summarize, the capillary endothelial cells of the lung have a very demanding, multipronged function, as they respond to complex cues in order to increase or decrease blood flow to alveoli for gas exchange. In addition, membrane permeability is always in flux, in order to facilitate gas exchange and signal appropriate immune responses to and from blood and lung tissue to mediate particulate and other inflammatory exposures. This requires a quadrangle of signal response from lung capillary cells to involve blood immune proteins, lung alveoli, and specific white blood cell mediators.

Heart

The heart muscle contracts continuously, with only a second or less of rest between contractions. Depending on oxygen and energy signals from the skeletal muscle and/or changes in workload, the heart muscle may be called upon to contract from forty-five to two hundred beats per minute. The efficiency of the heart pumping depends on several factors:

- cardiac muscle tone (mitochondrial density in heart muscle)
- the blood pressure the heart must pump against
- the effectiveness of heart valves to close and open completely without leaks or obstructions
- the heart muscle's electrical system
- the coronary arteries that provide the blood supply to the heart muscle

Structure

The heart has three main infrastructures to support pumping. The first major infrastructure is the specialized capillary cell. To support wide fluctuations in workload, oxygen and nutrients delivered to the muscle cells from capillary cells become a limiting factor to optimal performance. This is because the muscle cells rely on large fluctuations of oxygen (carried by blood) to make energy from their mitochondria in order to support variable workloads. The capillary cells facilitate this exchange. In contrast to capillary cells where only 10 percent of cellular energy comes from mitochondria (90 percent from anaerobic metabolism in the cytoplasm), hardworking heart-muscle cells produce 90 percent of more or their energy from their mitochondria.

Although capillary mitochondria provide only 10 percent of capillary-cell energy requirements, what they control in that process pivots them as the dominant force in managing fluctuations in cardiac-muscle performance. The mitochondria in capillary cells do this primarily through feedback loops that increase or decrease the production of nitric oxide, the potent smooth-muscle relaxer which increases blood flow through the capillary beds that support heart-muscle cells. Changes in nitric oxide levels in capillary cells directly support changes in heart-muscle oxygen/energy demand. In providing increased oxygen to heart muscle, the capillary cells do not have to increase energy production in their cells nearly to the degree that heart-muscle cell mitochondria do. Thus, capillary cells facilitate increased heart-muscle work, without taking away more oxygen from the blood for their own purpose. The capacity to respond in dramatic fashion to heart-muscle contractility, and subsequent oxygen demand with increases in nitric oxide production, defines the uniqueness of heart capillary endothelial cells.

Capillary cells in the heart, as in other end organs, facilitate other important effects to heart muscle. For example, capillary cells adjacent to heart muscle can have different responses to the same set of stimuli. Some capillary cells may promote an anti-inflammatory response to a certain trigger, while other capillary cells send signals to increase inflammation to the same trigger. This can occur, for example, in the setting of preexisting coronary-artery narrowing from plaque. As plaque narrows the larger coronary arteries, increased workloads from heart muscle can produce ischemic muscle injury pain, known as *angina pectoris*. Angina occurs when heart-muscle cells do not get enough oxygen to support contraction. This injury to heart muscle, from lack of oxygen supply, produces different kinds of response from capillary cells, depending on where they are located in reference to the injured heart-muscle cell. If oxygen debt is not relieved, either through less workload or more blood flow, a heart attack (*myocardial infarction*) can result.

Besides capillary cells and nitric oxide production, a second major infrastructure for heart-muscle support is comprised of the three major coronary arteries that supply all the blood to the heart-muscle cells' capillary beds. These three coronary arteries are large vessels that originate just above the heart's aortic valve annulus. They are very responsive to the effects of nitric oxide and endothelin (smooth-muscle constrictor), as the endothelial cells of these arteries are lined by a thick layer of smooth-muscle cells. Although the endothelial cells of these coronary arteries both manufacture and respond to nitric oxide and provide barrier support, they are not wired to respond to diffusion and transport of oxygen and nutrients to heart-muscle cells from the blood. Yet their basement membranes are vulnerable to inflammatory influences involving LDL cholesterol free radicals and inflammatory debris. This results in plaque buildup and narrowing of their lumens to permanently limit blood flow to upstream heart-muscle capillaries. This narrowing becomes the foundation for angina, when heart muscle cannot get enough oxygen, in spite of SOS signaling and increased nitric oxide production from capillary cells upstream from the compromised coronary artery.

The third major infrastructure of heart muscle is comprised of the nerve cells that support a cohesive integration of muscle-cell contraction. These cells are all programmed differently in order to facilitate a coordinated effort of muscle-cell contraction. The nerve cells require their own set of capillary cells to supply them with oxygen and nutrients, as they facilitate increased or decreased rates of muscle-cell contraction. With capillary-cell dysfunction, nerve cells die and electrical support to heart muscle disintegrates. Without it, heart rhythm and synchrony are lost. Heart muscle may not contract at all, or contract irregularly or ineffectively, potentially resulting in extreme compromise to overall heart function.

Deterioration and Dysfunction

Gradual deterioration of capillary-endothelial-cell function can result in subtle but steady declines of the heart muscle's capacity to perform. This occurs in a predictable way when the internal workings of the capillary endothelial cells become suboptimal to accommodate fluctuations in heart-muscle cell work capacity. It is made worse when the capillary cells can't get what they need from plaque narrowing of larger coronary blood vessels that reduce blood flow to them upstream. The capillary-cell dysfunction can be acute or chronic, but it is almost always related to changes in the capacity to deliver increased oxygen and nutrients to muscle cells when higher demands call for it. Depending on the magnitude of capillary breach, large swaths of muscle can be involved, which can eventually cause serious decline in effective heart function. Symptoms increase and compromise life quality, no matter how much invasive bypass surgery or catheter stent intervention occurs.

Besides losing blood flow from large arteries, over time, capillary cells develop free-radical damage to their DNA, mitochondria, membranes, and other organelles. This damage, which is often irreversible, adversely affects their performance as membrane gradients, leading to defective protein synthesis and blocked feedback loops, and other mechanisms of signaling are lost. Capillary-cell function becomes a shell of what it once was, and with it, the heart muscle and nerve cells its supports wither and become compromised to the same degree.

There are no reliable screening tests to evaluate the early and dangerous changes to capillary-cell function, although research is aggressively pursuing different noninvasive testing options. Being able to measure change in capillary-cell function is problematic in all organ systems. The lack of screening becomes a major dilemma in preventative care. The early changes in capillary-cell function are the ones that are most reversible, yet they cannot be adequately evaluated in clinical practice. This represents a major void, as current research models require damage to these cells sufficient to treat disease rather than prevent it.

Measuring and preventing capillary-cell dysfunction in heart muscle is therefore indirect. Useful tools include:

- Measuring/estimating heart muscle's maximum performance (MET, VO2 Max-see glossary for description) from a standardized exercise stress test, with or without cardiac ultrasound, becomes the yardstick for identifying the sum total of capillary-cell function to heart muscle as it applies to large-vessel coronary blood flow.
- Preemptive management of vascular inflammatory risk factors (see graphs 1 and 5, in the appendix) then becomes critical to improving and maintaining capillary-endothelial function to heart muscle, and, subsequently, to other end organs.
- Teaching and facilitating behavioral modification, with adjustments made to sleep, stress, addictions, diet, exercise, medications, supplements, socialization, and spiritual awareness. When intentional, these can enhance endothelial-cell function and serve as a fundamental basis for preventative health care.

Summary

The function of heart-muscle cells to respond to changes in workload is dependent on capillary-cell production and release of nitric oxide; this in turn causes more blood flow (and oxygen delivery) to capillary cells, which then feeds these nutrients to hardworking heart cells. The extent to which nitric oxide can be released by capillary cells is the same extent to which heart muscle can perform. Capillary cells can produce and release substantial amounts of nitric oxide to increase oxygen to heart muscle without utilizing additional oxygen to accomplish this. This allows heart muscle to get full benefit to the increases in blood flow. Changes in the capacity of heart muscle to perform can be estimated by the MET and can serve as a proxy to assess conditioning and determine an age quotient. Advanced age and aggregate vascular risk that produce large coronary-artery narrowing and occlusion from plaque formation can severely limit the capacity of capillary cells to deliver necessary oxygen and nutrients to heart muscle. In total, they contribute to acceleration of capillary-cell decline and reductions in effective nitric oxide production and release by these cells.

Gastrointestinal System

This gastrointestinal system is identified as a long, tubular, continuous, flexible pipe whose purpose is to accept foodstuffs, break them down, absorb what is essential, and remove as feces what is not. This process is supported by capillary cells which respond to specialized epithelial cells that perform different functions in the process of absorption and elimination. The long tube is broken down into different parts, depending on function and location, which include the *esophagus, stomach, duodenum, jejunum, ileum,* and *colon.* They in turn are further supported by the *liver, pancreas,* and *gallbladder.*

The location of the capillary endothelial cell along the intestinal tube, as well as the kind of food presented, will determine how capillary endothelium signals, interacts, and coordinates with the intestinal epithelium. To serve this function, capillary endothelial cells of the gastrointestinal system have evolved their outer membranes to become more porous, or *fenestrated,* compared to the more defensive and barrier-protective capillary cells of the brain or retina of the eye.

Digestion

The first part of the long flexible digestive tube is the esophagus. When food or drink is swallowed, it enters this very long and straight muscular tube. With the help of gravity, and with strong rhythmic contractions of both skeletal and smooth muscle, food and drink is propulsed into the stomach, where processes of food breakdown begin. In the esophagus, capillary cells promote simple barrier control, and supply oxygen and nutrients to skeletal and smooth-muscle cells in order to aid in contraction and subsequent propulsion of food down the esophageal tube to the stomach.

Because of the rich mixes of simple and complex carbohydrates, proteins, and fats entering the stomach and intestines, the capillary endothelium in these areas has evolved vesicles and other sophisticated transport vehicles to quickly package food constituents through their basement membranes, for purposes of entering the *enterohepatic circulation.* The processing of proteins, carbohydrates, and fats by capillary cells arriving from the intestinal epithelium requires speed and precision.

Besides managing food processing, capillary cells are also involved in extensive immune surveillance as they scourge and respond to the surrounding epithelium for abnormal bacteria, viruses, toxins, or cancer cells. In addition to immune support, they facilitate increases in blood supply through nitric oxide mechanisms in order to facilitate food packaging as well as control the delicate balances of blood clotting.

Immune access/surveillance has an additional wrinkle in the intestines, as bacteria are constantly awash against the epithelium throughout this long digestive tube. The relationship of bacteria to epithelial and endothelial cells is symbiotic, as the bacteria, along with enzymes produced from both the pancreas and the intestines themselves, participate in the breakdown of food into simple molecules as part of the preparation for transport through the epithelial cells, the capillary cells, and then to the liver and pancreas via the enterohepatic circulation. Maintaining the right type and quantity of bacteria in the right place in the intestinal lumen requires expert marksmanship. The capillary cells participate in this surveillance by assisting the epithelial cells throughout the intestine in managing bacterial populations (in part by optimizing the release of inflammatory white blood cells, when needed, for rebalancing bacteria populations), and also by assisting in the management of epithelial-cell production of secretions which further enhance absorption. When this management goes awry, intestinal overgrowth of harmful bacteria, yeast, or parasites can occur. This can disrupt the absorption process and cause abdominal symptoms and malabsorption.

Capillary cells also assist the epithelial cells in food-related stimulation of enzymes, acids, and proteins from the liver and pancreas via the blood. They also diffuse oxygen and provide nutrient support to epithelial cells in order to facilitate their function. As mentioned, their basement membranes provide active transport through vesicles and pores, allowing protein, carbohydrate, and fats to find their way to the liver.

Digesting food has become more complicated in the modern Western world, with added-on/engineered sugared/refined food processing, hormones, insecticides, mercury and heavy metal poisoning, and the use of various chemicals to preserve food. This diet, as it gets presented to the stomach, looks different to the epithelial and capillary cells than the whole, natural, unpreserved food eaten in generations past. These modern highly processed foods increase stress on all the cells involved in absorption, and predispose humans to early endothelial- and epithelial-cell dysfunction. Not only do refined simple sugars, toxic chemicals, saturated fats, and subsequent loss of good bacteria throughout the intestine produces problems with clean absorption of packaged nutrients, but the by-products of this pollution returning from the liver and fat cells (elevated blood sugars, fatty acids, LDL cholesterol) produce further impairment in the capillary cells capacity to function, vis-à-vis the intestinal epithelium. A vicious cycle emerges with toxic highly refined diets that affect capillary-cell function from the outside in and then from the inside out.

Over time, usually beginning by age forty, as vascular inflammatory processes have begun to establish themselves, impairment of capillary-cell/epithelial-cell function can result in the beginning of a breakdown of intestinal function. In addition to intestinal overgrowth of so-called bad bacteria, acid indigestion, predilection for ulcers and bleeding, and the emergence of autoimmune diseases occur. Popular colloquialisms have been used to describe some of these changes, including "leaky gut" syndrome, IBS (functional or spastic bowel), and gluten sensitivity. Other serious conditions also emerge, including malabsorption syndromes and inflammatory bowel diseases (ulcerative colitis and Crohn's disease). With more passage of time, progressive capillary-cell dysfunction decreases immune surveillance, and colon cancer appears with increasing frequency. Stresses to other end organs involved in the digestive process also occur, including the emergence of fatty liver, hepatitis, and pancreatitis (from many different causes), and symptomatic gallbladder stones (*cholecystitis*).

Efficient Absorption

Efficient absorption of nutrient matter from the intestinal epithelium into capillary cells in the stomach and intestines is accomplished by *vesicular transcytosis* (Figure 10 in the appendix). This activity of the capillary-cell basement membrane creates small shopping bags to pick up nutrients and actively carries them into the blood on their way to the liver. As the capillary cells do this, they are also sending messages and producing nitric oxide to increase blood flow and limit clotting activities in the intestinal tract.

Capillary cells of the liver and pancreas have also evolved unique morphology to accommodate their relationship to these end-organ epithelial cells (see figure 9, in the appendix). This includes the presence of larger pores, and even gaps, in their basement membranes for facilitating quick delivery of packaged nutrients to liver cells.

The liver functions to make proteins and clotting factors, as well as to both produce and then package molecules that can be used for energy. These energy units can be stored in the liver (in the form of glycogen) or moved to be stored in fat tissue, where they can be retrieved for use by other end organs (in the form of fatty acids).

The processes of packaging these energy units is further refined with assistance from the pancreas. The pancreas produces insulin and digestive enzymes in order to improve utilization of sugar molecules in all cells, including the liver.

Immunity

The porous nature of capillary cells throughout the intestinal system creates vulnerability to exposure of end organs to increased risk for infection. Standing guard and acting as a capable assistant for immune surveillance with the capillary cells in the liver are the *Kupffer cells* (Figure 9 in the appendix). These cells are specialized white blood cells, which, when signaled from the liver capillary cell, will migrate and attack bacteria, viruses, or other blood constituents that may harm the exposed liver cells. The urgent and appropriate response to an unwanted invader requires a close symbiotic relationship with the capillary cell to coordinate activity. Inadequate signaling or response from the Kupffer cells is often the cause of liver cells becoming infected with viruses or other conditions which can eventually lead to chronic hepatitis, cirrhosis, and liver cancer.

Just as in other organ systems, the capillary-cell function throughout the gastrointestinal system involves multitasking several functions at one time. With reference to the liver and pancreas, all these responsibilities can deteriorate with their dysfunction.

- If their capacity to perform diminishes, the end organ is compromised. For example, if the capillary cells of the liver do not work closely together with the Kupffer cells, or are not signaling comprehensive immune responses, the liver cells become vulnerable to infection and inflammation.
- In other instances, capillary-cell dysfunction in the pancreas, through faulty or inadequate immune signals, can allow for exposures of pancreatic cells to potentially toxic molecules, which, depending on the volume and length of exposure, can inflame them, producing pancreatitis, cysts, infections, and cancer (with persistent exposure).
- With persistent capillary dysfunction, the pancreas becomes vulnerable to scarring, producing compromise in pancreas epithelial cells that can result in diabetes and malabsorption. Although these conditions may have genetic predispositions, it is capillary dysfunction that "aids and abets" the process.

With the exception of type 1 (juvenile) diabetes and some autoimmune diseases, where onsets are typically in adolescence and favored by genomics, most dysfunction of capillary cells in the gastrointestinal system begins at age forty or older. This dysfunction correlates with the emergence of vascular inflammatory changes that have evolved for several years (see graphs 1 and 4, in the appendix). The same culprits that have been discussed previously and that produce inflammation, in aggregate, produce declines in capillary-cell function, leading to impairment in intestinal capacity to digest and absorb food properly. Hypertension, high cholesterol, insulin resistance/type 2 (adult-onset) diabetes mellitus, obesity, inactivity, inadequate sleep, excessive stress, and various addictions (drugs, alcohol, cigarettes, food) are all part of the processes that have established themselves to cause vascular disarray. The correlation of these emerging vascular inflammatory markers of capillary dysfunction to the timing of symptomatic gastrointestinal disease cannot be ignored.

Summary

To summarize, capillary cells have evolved a close symbiotic partnership with their end-organ epithelial cell brethren from the intestines, esophagus, stomach, liver, gallbladder, and pancreas. The unique porous morphology of these capillary cells creates quick access to nutrients but also creates risk for unwanted infection. For this reason, immune surveillance has been further enhanced, with capillary cells developing relationships with different types of specialized white blood cells. Competent capillary-cell function involves facilitating the packaging and transport of nutrients from the intestines, supporting the needs of the end-organ cells with oxygen/enzymes from the blood, as well as limiting access to malignant cells or unwanted bacteria and viruses by providing competent immune surveillance. The changes that occur in gastrointestinal function in middle age appear to correlate closely with diffuse inflammation of the vascular endothelium, brought on by well-known vascular inflammatory conditions. Mitigating these influences should protect gastrointestinal function and serve as a backdrop for prevention of gastrointestinal disease.

Urinary System

Kidney and genital function offer another example of how the capillary cell has evolved to optimize function of these vital organs. In the kidney, the endothelial cells have developed, along with kidney epithelial cells, into a filtering unit known as a *nephron.* Within the nephron are specialized capillary and epithelial cells that filter blood to make urine; this is called a *glomerulus* (see figure 3, in the appendix). The glomerulus can best be described as a group of porous capillary cells that abut up against foot-like epithelial cells, also known as *podocytes.* By supporting the podocyte, the capillary cell filters blood plasma to make a filtrate. The filtrate then is further ultrafiltered through the podocyte's membranes to make urine.

The most critical step in this process is the type of filtrate the capillary cell sends to the podocyte. If contaminated with proteins, white blood cells, and other inflammatory debris, the podocyte's capacity to make urine diminishes, and the nephron becomes dysfunctional. When done correctly, the ultrafiltered urine has passed through four membranes in the glomerulus (see figure 3, in the appendix); this urine is clear, and contains no bacteria, crystals, protein, sugar, red blood cells, or white blood cells.

This filtering process of the glomerulus is the primary mechanism of eliminating toxic chemicals and end products of metabolism from the body. This filtering and extracting of waste, as well as the recycling of other molecules back into the blood, requires a competent glomerular capillary cell. Coordinating these processes with the blood and kidney podocyte, while at the same time managing immune surveillance, clotting, and blood-flow dynamics, requires a fully intact capillary cell internal structure of organelle and membrane function. Missteps in membrane permeability from capillary cells create unnecessary exposures of inflammatory filtrate to the podocytes of the glomerulus, which, over time, leads to scarring and dysfunction.

With emergence of persistent vascular inflammatory risk (usually at age forty, but earlier in some cases), capillary-cell dysfunction allows for increasing inflammation to the filtering membranes of the podocyte cells. With a decline in podocyte function, adverse clinical cascades lead to fluid retention, and the buildup of toxic molecules in the blood will follow. Along with fatigue and pain, excessive protein and sugar spillage in the urine increases, as blood sugar and blood pressure increases and edema fluid accumulates in the legs and dependent areas. As immune surveillance decays, infections, autoimmune disease, and kidney cancer increase in frequency. With persistent inflammation, scarring of the glomerulus occurs and can progress to cause kidney failure that requires dialysis.

Capillary-cell blood flow through the kidney glomerulus is regulated by many intravascular influences, including the renin-angiotensin system, and dysfunction in this system abnormally increases blood pressure and produces even more vascular inflammation from shear damage. With advanced age and aggregate vascular inflammatory risk, this system becomes biased to produce more angiotensin II, which causes persistent increases in blood pressure and shear stress.

Summary

To summarize, the capillary cells of the kidney glomerulus, besides filtering plasma, also manage the volume of blood flow through the nephron and set the table for the podocyte's final filtering stage to make urine. In addition, they fortify immune function to the podocytes and other epithelial cells of the kidney filtering system. Producing and distributing vasodilators (like nitric oxide) or vasoconstrictors (like endothelin) in response to changes in blood volume, as well as anticipating and effectively handling immune challenges at the glomerulus, become central to how effectively the podocytes ultrafilter the plasma to make urine. Optimizing capillary-cell health through vascular anti-inflammatory behaviors, medications, and supplements will improve the filtering function of the podocyte and protect effective kidney function.

Reproductive Function

The capillary endothelium also plays a central role in sexual response and reproductive function for both sexes.

Males

The capability of the penis to perform erectile function is dependent on elaborate sacs of capillary cells known as the *corpora cavernosa.* These large spaces, or sacs, are connected by muscle and elastic fibers and lined by capillary and small-vessel endothelial cells. With proper stimuli, the capillary endothelium read and direct a complex set of signals, ultimately leading to the production of nitric oxide and other molecules which assist in increasing blood flow to the penis architecture. The spaces are filled with blood, almost as if participating in a hydraulic lift, creating an erection. Once the sexual response is completed, they cause an about-face, coordinating the rapid removal of blood from the penis. Part of the sexual response involves signaling to nerves and muscle in the penis, as well as optimizing responses to the brain to create sensations of pleasure.

Capillary endothelial cells in the testes, found in the male scrotum, have evolved to assist and respond to the production of sperm from specialized epithelial cells in these organs. In this case, capillary-cell coordination of blood-flow dynamics and testosterone concentrations, as well as the facilitation of end-organ response to hormones from the brain, all are effectively applied to produce sperm and the semen (fluid) that protects them.

With aging and aggregate vascular inflammatory risks, capillary-cell dysfunction produces erectile dysfunction, which limits the male sexual response. Medications that produce an improvement in erectile dysfunction, such as Viagra (or sildenafil), have been developed. Their mechanism of action offers a real clue as to why erectile dysfunction occurs. Central to this mechanism of action is its effect on penis capillary cells in the corpora cavernosa. By facilitating the capillary cell to produce and increase nitric oxide levels, blood flow to the penile corpora cavernosa is increased.

The production of nitric oxide, and the response it facilitates in the penis, is impaired from advanced age and persistent vascular inflammation, just as occurs in other end organs that are heavily dependent on nitric oxide levels, such as the heart and skeletal muscle. With progression of aggregate vascular inflammatory disease, even medications to increase nitric oxide levels cannot overcome the increasing dysfunction of the capillary cell, and erectile dysfunction becomes refractory to treatment.

Because of the cause-and-effect relationship of erectile dysfunction to capillary-cell dysfunction and vascular disease, erectile dysfunction has emerged as a major risk factor associated with coronary (heart), skeletal muscle, peripheral vascular, and cerebrovascular disease. What has become obvious is that management of erectile dysfunction requires management of vascular inflammatory disease, as such dysfunction directly correlates to capillary-cell health.

Male menopause. Testosterone supplementing for male menopause is in its infancy, but is now widely used to treat symptoms of increased fatigue, depression, mental fog, loss of muscle mass and libido, and erectile dysfunction. Similar to the effects of female hormones in women (which will be discussed below, in the subsection on females), in some cases, testosterone supplements have produced dramatic improvement in male symptoms and a so-called new lease on life. Unfortunately, studies are beginning to emerge which dampen the long-term prospects of testosterone treatments. Just as with longer-term estrogen use in women, testosterone treatment is associated with increases in prostate cancer, heart attack, and sudden death. Tied to these events are increases in LDL cholesterol and hypertension.

What makes testosterone treatment difficult to sort out for men is that its use is frequently associated with increased energy levels (exercise), improved diet and sleep hygiene, as well as other vascular anti-inflammatory improvements to health (better stress management). It would appear that testosterone treatment may jump-start better behaviors, leading to a net improvement in vascular anti-inflammatory effect. That said, the long-term use of testosterone, like that of estrogen in women, is fraught with increased risk, involving serious vascular thrombosis and prostate cancer.

Summary

There is a direct link between erectile dysfunction and capillary-cell dysfunction related to reductions in blood flow to the penis from reduced nitric oxide levels. Much of male menopause can also be attributed to and mitigated by improving aggregate vascular inflammatory risk. While testosterone therapy may jump-start energy levels and improve skeletal-muscle mass and libido, its long-term use may increase vascular inflammation and clotting risk to heart and brain; it may also increase prostate cancer occurrence. A smarter and more prudent approach to sexual health is through maintenance of capillary-cell health, which influences the capacity of a male to sexually perform. This is harder to do, as it places the burden of responsibility for improvement squarely on lifestyle choices rather than taking a shot or popping a pill. When it comes to sex, many men would rather not commit to healthy vascular lifestyle choices if they have the choice of taking a pill. On the other hand, comprehensive mitigation of aggregate vascular risk provides meaningful improvement to erectile dysfunction, particularly when adopted earlier in life. This is a much more attractive long-term strategy to mitigate the genital-urinary issues that inevitably occur as men age.

Females

In women, clitoral stimulation leading to orgasm has a very similar mechanism of blood engorgement, as compared to the male penis. Central to clitoral engorgement of blood is the production of nitric oxide by the capillary and small-vessel arterioles in response to tactile and pleasant emotional stimulation. This sets off a cascade of chemical messages involving clitoral nerves and muscle, as well as the brain, resulting in the engorgement of blood into the clitoris. Although climax in females appears to involve more aesthetics of the brain than in males, the clitoral capillary-cell function is pivotal in the process.

In terms of ovary health, the capillary cells and their response to and from the blood and ovary end-organ cells involving blood flow and hormone triggers are central to the effective coordination of monthly egg production, pregnancy, and the monthly menstrual cycle. In addition to providing nutrients to the ovary epithelium to support egg cells, the capillary cells coordinate the appropriate flow of blood to the sex organs, and facilitate signaling conduits for successful sex-hormone delivery and production to and from the blood and ovaries. This facilitation has no margin for error, as the timing and concentrations of hormones from ovary to brain and back again facilitate successful sexual response, storage and release of eggs, pregnancy, and menstruation when pregnancy does not occur. When capillary-cell function is optimal, this process is seamless.

When capillary endothelial cells of female sex organs become dysfunctional, many different types of ovarian and reproductive concerns arise, which can be related to increased pelvic pain, too much or too little menstruation, and limited success with intentional pregnancy. Secondary concerns involve capillary-cell-related immune dysfunction, producing increased risk for infections, cysts, and cancer of the ovary or uterus.

In polycystic ovary syndrome (PCOS), a condition with a genetic predisposition, there is disruption of normal monthly menstruation, as well as increased pelvic pain, all of which is associated with the development of multiple cysts on the ovaries. The condition is increasing in frequency, and it can be directly linked to endothelial-cell dysfunction in the ovary. This relationship has been studied by Carmina, Lobo, and colleagues (see bibliography), whose timely research connects PCOS to endothelial-cell dysfunction related to increases in oxidative stress from vascular inflammation tied to diabetes and obesity. What has become clear is that PCOS is correlated to being overweight and having increased insulin resistance/diabetes, stress, depression, and high blood pressure, all of which increase vascular inflammatory risk and affect capillary- and endothelial-cell health. A novel approach to PCOS treatment would be to implement a treatment strategy that makes reductions in vascular inflammatory risk factors the primary focus. This would include behavioral modification for purposes of weight reduction, sleep hygiene, regular exercise, and reductions in sugar and saturated-fat intake. This strategy of limiting vascular inflammation could result in a return of monthly menstrual cycles, reduction in pelvic pain and cyst density, and, ultimately, a lessening of the potential of experiencing longer-term risks, such as ovarian cancer.

By improving vascular inflammatory risk, capillary-endothelial-cell immune surveillance improves, and PCOS is mitigated.

Menopause. Another application of the cause-and-effect relationship of capillary cells to female end-organ function involves menopause. This is a universal condition in all women, where there is a cessation of normal menstruation, often associated with hot flashes, memory loss, osteoporosis, insulin resistance/diabetes, impaired sleep, increased pain syndromes, weight gain, dry and wrinkled skin, loss of scalp hair, fatigue, and depression. The development of menopause usually occurs from ages forty-five to fifty-five, but there are some women who experience symptoms as early as age thirty-five, and others who may not experience symptoms until age sixty. The timing and intensity of menopause symptoms may have genetic predispositions, but they correlate with the emergence of aggregate vascular inflammatory risk factors and subsequent capillary-endothelial-cell dysfunction.

So how are menopause symptoms best managed? Current practice utilizes short-term female hormone replacement (for four years or less). The risks of taking female hormones for longer periods of time, or with advanced age, have become well known and include breast cancer, blood clots in the legs and lungs, as well as increased risk for stroke and heart attack. Taking different types of estrogen/progesterone may produce less harm when taken for longer periods, but these relationships need further clarification. Perhaps hormone replacement using natural plant-based molecules in smaller doses may be a better long-term fit. Much more research on the matter must be done to ensure safety in long-term hormone replacement.

What can be said about menopause is that the deleterious symptoms associated with the condition (hot flashes, insomnia, memory loss, weight gain, insulin resistance/diabetes, and hypertension) can be minimized by vascular anti-inflammatory management that produces improvements in endothelial-capillary-cell health. Engaging in regular exercise and reducing simple sugars in the diet, while at the same time accentuating whole-food intake to include fresh vegetables and herbs, can be very helpful in limiting the intensity and duration of symptoms. In addition, behaviors involving weight control, sleep hygiene, stress reduction, as well as appropriate treatment of blood pressure, LDL cholesterol, diabetes, and depression, all become mandatory in managing menopause- related increases in vascular risk. A lifestyle, as opposed to a drug or hormone, approach to menopause is supported by the Physicians Committee for Responsible Medicine and further complemented by research performed by Kronenberg and Fugh-Berman (see appendix).

With direct intervention of vascular inflammatory risk, symptoms of menopause decrease. Whereas it has become clear that long-term use of female hormones increases cancer and stroke risk, being intentional about reducing vascular inflammatory risks has no downside risk; and it would have the pleasant upside of maintaining sharp cognition as well as supporting skeletal and muscle tone.

Summary

To summarize, the capillary endothelial cell plays a critical role in the management of genital and reproductive functioning. These cells, as in other organ systems, have adapted to function as a facilitator to end-organ epithelial cells in the management of a complex array of signals and mediators to and from the blood in order to assist in the proper functioning of monthly menstruation and pregnancy. In some cases, the capillary cells' primary function is facilitating changes in blood flow to the end organ, as in the sex response to climax. In others situations, the capillary cells function primarily as a filter, and in still others, they provide a strong barrier support. Finally, to other end organs, such as the ovaries and testes, they facilitate function by primarily supporting hormone, nerve, and brain signaling. In each instance, the capillary cells' anatomy has been modified, and internal feedback loops have been adjusted, in order to optimally perform these functions. Comprehensive mitigation of vascular inflammatory risk ensures that capillary-cell outer membrane anatomy and permeability are maintained and these feedback loops remain intact, which then provides optimal support to the end organ. This improves the likelihood of longer-term end-organ function, limits symptoms when end organs are programmed to shut down (ovary), and decreases risks for infection and cancer that occur with advanced age. Clinically, this type of preventative health care would translate to fewer urinary tract infections, less pelvic pain, fewer menopause symptoms, and reductions in cancer and abnormal bleeding. Mitigating these adverse consequences can be substantial, as they often accelerate with the onset of male or female menopause.

Skeletal Muscle

Skeletal muscle supports the bones, tendons, ligaments, and cartilage of the body, and as such, facilitates posture and movement. Skeletal muscle expands dramatically in adolescence and typically increases in mass through age twenty-five. Unless exercised or utilized consistently, skeletal muscle atrophies, and with that, so does the support given to bones, tendons, ligaments, and cartilage. With aging and aggregate vascular risk, skeletal muscle can atrophy faster; therefore, maintenance of muscle tone becomes mandatory. Maintaining muscle tone and mass indirectly maintains bone and joint function, and can limit falls, worsening of posture, and the pain and stiffness caused by arthritis.

There is no other organ system in the body where capillary-endothelial-cell function is required to facilitate such dramatic increases to end-organ function as in skeletal muscle. When exercised or worked to maximal intensity, the skeletal muscle requires dramatic increases in oxygen and nutrients in order to facilitate energy production for contraction.

In the resting state, skeletal muscle requires very little energy for support; hence its blood supply diminishes to basal levels. With exercise or with exertion, the capillary endothelial cell must ramp up quickly to signal for more blood flow to the working muscle, in order to provide oxygen and nutrient (glucose/pyruvate, fatty acids, protein) support to satisfy the dramatic increase in the needs of the working muscle.

When skeletal muscle is poorly toned, the capillary endothelium must work harder to get even more blood to flow to the affected muscle, since flabby untoned muscle has fewer mitochondria (energy producers) near its contracting elements. In skeletal muscle, the capillary cells have adapted their membranes to accommodate the dynamic explosion of increased energy that skeletal muscle requires with maximum work. Besides increasing blood volume, oxygen, and nutrients to skeletal muscle through increased nitric oxide production, capillary cells can make new blood vessels to accommodate the persistent increase in oxygen need. This increases the density of capillary support to the affected skeletal muscle. This process, called *angiogenesis,* facilitates persistent increases in blood flow to muscle, which eventually allows the affected muscle to make more mitochondria to facilitate improved skeletal-muscle contractile tone. Genesis of new endothelial cells to make new capillaries to expand blood supply becomes critical in managing sustained demands for oxygen in maximally exercised muscle. This response, along with muscle tone, determines the intensity and duration that skeletal muscle can be exercised. Said another way, the capacity of the capillary cells of skeletal muscle to migrate, reproduce, form new blood vessels, and secrete nitric oxide (NO) defines the capacity of skeletal muscle to exercise maximally.

NO arterial dilation with subsequent skeletal-muscle contraction comes into play with exercise. For example, with aerobic (continuous movement) exercise, there is a strong signal from skeletal muscle to capillary endothelial cells to produce nitric oxide (see figure 2, in the appendix) for purposes of increasing oxygen and nutrients in order to accommodate contractile elements in skeletal muscle. The extent to which the capillary-endothelial-cell nitric oxide response allows for increased blood volume to supply oxygen and energy substrate is largely the extent to which skeletal muscle can exercise maximally.

As might be expected with aging, the nitric oxide response to exercise decreases and becomes a major factor contributing to reduced exercise capacity. The reasons for this involve changes in capillary-cell function, limiting the capillary cells' capacity to respond to muscle signals and produce nitric oxide.

Summary

To summarize, in skeletal muscle, the capillary-cell endothelium provides three key support systems to maximize oxygen delivery to muscle cells. The first is to form new capillaries by moving vascular endothelial cells to areas of muscle *hypoxia* (oxygen debt) and then dividing to form new blood vessels. The second involves the gap junctions and membranes of capillary cells which have evolved transport vesicles to assist in the active transport of nutrients directly from blood to muscle. The third concerns capillary-endothelial-cell capacity to respond to sudden skeletal-muscle hypoxia, which determines effective performance of the skeletal muscle and is dependent on the capillary cells' capacity to signal and produce nitric oxide. When capillary-cell function deteriorates, skeletal muscle atrophies, and the aggregate support the muscle gives to bones, joints, tendons, ligaments, cartilage, and posture declines concomitantly. What is more—the same factors contributing to capillary-cell dysfunction in muscle are also similarly affecting these other skeletal support structures. Vascular inflammation therefore creates deterioration of all these support structures in tandem.

Brain and Spinal Cord Function

Capillary endothelial cells have evolved in a very special way to protect and serve the most complex of all the vital organs: the brain. Whether capillary cells function to signal shifting blood flow from one part of the brain to another, perform clotting and immune surveillance, optimize nutrient/oxygen support, or provide barrier protection from toxic blood plasma constituents, the capillary cells to the blood-brain barrier empower the capacity of the brain nerve cells to function.

Capillary endothelial cells provide the core for a lattice of cells that work together as a unit known as the *blood-brain barrier* (see figure 8, in the appendix). The capillary cells partner with epithelial cells (*astrocytes*) of brain connective tissue, as well as other cells (*pericytes*), to function as both a pump and a barrier to keep some molecules from the blood out and others in, in order to create a bath that provides exactly what the delicate brain cells require. This bath of clear colorless fluid is known as *cerebrospinal fluid.* Maintaining the cerebrospinal bath requires energy from capillary cells to actively pump, or keep molecules from the blood out of this fluid.

The *gap junction,* or the space between capillary cells of the blood-brain barrier, has evolved to function in the exact opposite way as those spaces between capillaries in the gastrointestinal system. Rather than transporting an abundance of different plasma constituents into the blood, gap junctions of the blood-brain barrier capillary cells restrict movement of large swaths of plasma, including many proteins, water-soluble molecules, as well as red and white blood cell and platelets. The dramatic changes of membrane and gap-junction function are a testament to how the capillary cells can adapt to specific needs of different end organs.

The capillary cell plasma and basement membranes can easily accommodate diffusion of oxygen into, and carbon dioxide out of, the brain bath. The diffusion of these gases is critical to the health of the nerve and glial cells (connective tissue or structural-support cells) of the brain, as these cells require substantial amounts of a constant energy supply (derived from oxygen) to function. Oxygen and glucose (pyruvate) become the essential ingredients for nerve-cell mitochondria to make energy efficiently. Because of constant demand for oxygen and pyruvate, blood flow to the brain must be constant and optimal. Any reduction, and adverse consequences to nerve-cell metabolism will occur.

In contrast to all other tissues in the body except red blood cells, brain cells do not use fatty acids for energy. Rather, when glycogen (the storage form of glucose) is depleted, the brain will use ketone bodies for energy in their mitochondria. Ketone bodies are made only in the liver, and they can be used by the brain, skeletal muscle, and heart for energy. Whether glucose (pyruvate) or ketone bodies are used to make energy from oxygen in nerve cell mitochondria, the by-product, carbon dioxide, must be removed quickly through the blood-brain barrier by the process of diffusion. The extent to which oxygen, pyruvate, or ketone bodies are not supplied is the same extent to which brain capacity becomes limited, and nerve cells, parenthetically, atrophy and die.

The capillary cells of the blood-brain barrier also produce a metabolic barrier; that is, they produce specific enzymes in coordination with the astrocyte cells that metabolize toxic proteins and other substances that must be removed in order to protect brain tissue. In addition, there are mechanisms in place to prevent circulating antibodies (a type of immune protein) from acting as free radicals to nerve-cell membranes. Preventing immune proteins from binding to nerve cell membranes becomes critical to limiting inflammation to nerve cells. That said, there are times, in acute infectious or traumatic crisis, where movement of inflammatory white blood cells and proteins across the blood-brain barrier is essential to manage these events.

The capillary cells of the blood-brain barrier have been modified at the pituitary gland, hypothalamus, and choroid plexus (specialized cells in the brain ventricles that secrete cerebrospinal fluid). Whereas the choroid plexus produces the brain bath, the remainder of the capillary cells forming the blood-brain barrier support the maintenance of this fluid. At the hypothalamus and pituitary gland, barrier support is less developed and less defensive to blood constituents, as compared to the rest of the brain. The capillary cells are more porous, which allows for immediate access of these midbrain structures to feedback hormone molecules from distant end organs. This is required for regulation of temperature, thyroid and adrenal function, growth, sleep, and sexual function.

This barrier can be flexible in the sense that when the brain is disrupted from infection, trauma, bleeding, neurotoxins (cyanide), seizures, or sudden oxygen deficiency (stroke), the barrier protection can change dramatically. To manage the acute breach, constituents are allowed to infiltrate the bath from the blood at a rapid pace, which can either wall off the breach and support the brain; or, depending on the scope of the breach, can alternatively cascade further damage to the brain from additional inflammation, swelling, and scar tissue.

Depending on the size and scope of breach, scarring could result in irreversible loss of nerve cells. The capillary endothelium manages this breach, with the help of astrocyte cells. If capillary cells have become dysfunctional from either advanced age or aggregate vascular inflammatory risks, the bias is toward more inflammation to the brain, resulting in scarring, nerve-cell death, and chronic residuals from the breach, such as motor or sensory loss, cognitive decline, or seizures. Once lost, the brain nerve cells are lost permanently.

Chronic neurodegenerative diseases, including dementia, are often linked to loss of blood flow through the six large arteries supplying the brain, and subsequent capillary-endothelial-cell, blood-brain barrier dysfunction. As mentioned elsewhere, vascular inflammation from vascular inflammatory risks can narrow any of these six vessels, either in diffuse fashion, with membrane thickening, or with a focal obstructive plaque. Both of these conditions increase with aggregate vascular risk and advanced age, resulting in net reductions in blood flow to capillaries, the blood-brain barrier, and, subsequently, the nerve cells of the brain. When brain cells are chronically affected by lower pyruvate/oxygen/ energy supplies and more oxidative stress, capillary-cell, blood-brain-barrier, and subsequent nerve-cell function declines. Nerve cells atrophy, and at some critical point, they die. Cognitive decline is the inevitable result. These cascades of vascular inflammation can be preempted by lifestyle intervention, including social and spiritual fulfillment as evidenced in a review of this subject matter from Middleton and Yaffe (see bibliography).

Because the brain requires virtually 100 percent of all the blood volume pumped to support its function, declines in cognition can be linked to even subtle reductions in blood supply to the brain. As blood flow continues to diminish from large-vessel vascular inflammation, capillary-cell capacity to support the blood-brain barrier and nerve cells defaults. With aggregate reductions in oxygen support caused by decreased blood flow, brain-cell atrophy occurs, with the shortened axons and dendrites of these cells replaced with amyloid deposits, which are made from and facilitated by the capillary endothelium and adjacent glial cells.

Though the capillary cells can try to produce new blood vessels to increase oxygen and nutrients to starving brain cells, this is a site-specific resolution and will not address obstructive plaque-related reductions of blood flow downstream from the larger blood vessels to the brain. Therefore, although producing new capillaries to support more oxygen to brain tissue is well intentioned, the strategy is flawed because of irreversible hard plaque narrowing downstream of large vessels that cannot support more blood flow. Decreased blood flow to the brain from large-blood-vessel narrowing, no matter how the capillary cells respond at the blood-brain barrier, produces adverse change to brain function. Where and how much blood flow declines, coupled with genetic predispositions, will determine the cause and type of the neurodegenerative/cognitive decline that can result.

Progressive narrowing of one or more of the six large vessels providing blood to the brain is caused by persistent and aggregate vascular inflammation punctuated by advanced age. We've discussed the causes throughout, so it should be apparent by now how important it is to reduce vascular inflammation.

Changes in Memory

Clinically, the progressive nature of vascular inflammatory processes, leading to capillary-endothelial- and nerve-cell dysfunction and subsequent decline of cerebral function, are demonstrated by imaging studies. Early changes of vascular inflammatory processes are seen consistently in the white matter (axons connecting the gray matter of the cortex to the midbrain, or *hippocampus*) of the brain. These long axon connections from the gray matter to the hippocampus are integral in the formation of memory, both the retrieval of information and the learning new information. With axon damage, the capacity to retrieve, learn, and adapt to new information declines. This loss in the capacity to retrieve recent memory information becomes a critical piece to the initial changes that occur in an aging brain, which can spiral to dementia.

As more white matter is lost from progressive vascular inflammatory disease, memory loss progresses. Learning new information or adjusting to new environments becomes very difficult, if not impossible. The phrase "set in your ways" is how behavior is labeled, and is associated with increasing dependency, falls, and social isolation, as activities of daily living become more difficult. Those with the most severe memory loss may remember only childhood recollections, and are also suffering from marked reduction in motor and sensory skills, leading to falls and fractures. With severe loss of memory, associated with marked cerebral atrophy on imaging studies, perception and judgment of reality is lost, delusions surface, sleep is disrupted, and twenty-four-hour dependency on others for basic needs has been established.

The early changes in memory correlate with brain-imaging descriptions of *ischemic white matter changes* or small areas of *infarcted axons*. In aggregate, they represent the composite of small brain strokes. The volume loss created by these and subsequent loss of brain gray matter produces cerebral atrophy. The extent of cerebral atrophy will often correlate with severity of memory impairment and cognitive decline.

With ischemic-white-matter changes and corresponding short-term memory loss, the brain is well on its way to becoming less plastic and less responsive to visual, acoustic, and motors cues. The familiar becomes more comfortable than learning something new.

Being aware of these changes often comes late, and when identified, most dementia has already progressed to alarming levels.

Other Diseases

Reductions in blood-brain barrier function associated with capillary-cell dysfunction may also play a role in autoimmune diseases, such as multiple sclerosis (MS) or amyotrophic lateral sclerosis (ALS, or Lou Gehrig's disease). In these settings, capillary-cell immune control has been lost, which allows inflammatory proteins from the blood to find their way into the cerebrospinal fluid, where they can attach to and inflame nerve cells. This attachment produces a chain reaction of inflammatory response, as the immune system thinks that the nerve cell is now a foreign substance, and it must therefore be urgently eliminated. When the body tries to eliminate its own cells, this is called *autoimmune dysfunction.* When it involves axons of nerve cells in the brain, it is called *multiple sclerosis.*

The immune dysfunction is complex, and is triggered from combinations of genetic and environmental (blood-borne viruses) influences that can either be the cause or effect of capillary-cell dysfunction. Mitigating vascular inflammatory risks limits the effects of these influences to capillary cells of the blood-brain barrier.

Breakdown in capillary-cell function of the blood-brain barrier can also have adverse immune consequences involving infection and cancer risk. With impaired capillary-cell function and reductions in effective immune signaling, cancer cells, bacteria, viruses, parasites, or fungi may establish footholds in the brain meninges, leading to serious infections and/or the development of cancer. Even with early treatment with antibiotics and invasive surgeries, excessive scar tissue can result in seizures, loss of memory and/or motor skills, and a limited life span. With advanced age, infection and brain cancer rates increase. Prognosis for any meaningful recovery, even in the best of circumstances, is poor.

Summary

To summarize, preserving capillary-endothelial-cell function is the first and most essential step in preventing the cascades of decline leading to the epidemic of dementia and other causes of cerebral decline. The capillary endothelium of the blood-brain barrier has evolved a sophisticated tool set to assist in maintaining a unique bath that optimizes brain function. Capillary-cell function at the blood-brain barrier is dependent on a constant healthy blood supply supported by the six major arteries feeding the brain. Maintaining capillary-cell function through vascular anti-inflammatory lifestyle modifications, as well as through medications, supplements, and brain stimulation, will limit the adverse consequences linked to vascular inflammation. If comprehensive, adverse genetic, environmental, metabolic, and advanced-age-related risk can be neutralized, and will result in the ability to protect cognition.

Conclusion

As we have seen, capillary endothelial cells can adapt very well to the diverse needs of, and in some instances, the adverse changes to the end organs they serve. They do this while also paying attention to changing signals to and from the blood, distant end organs, and other endothelial cells—and managing/coordinating all the necessary resultant responses. Multitasking signals and adapting to changing responses are the cardinal features of successful capillary-cell functioning. Figure 12 in the appendix summarizes many known ways that capillary cells directly affect the function of multiple end organs. Implied in this figure is how dynamic capillary cells are to the functioning of the organ. It is clear that they are not passive instruments, but rather orchestrators in transmitting how and what blood does to end-organ function.

Adaptability of capillary-cell membrane morphology is a major headline to facilitate the function of end organs. Their outer membranes (plasma and basement membranes) and gap junctions may be tight and compact or thin and porous. In some places, there may be transport vesicles to speed processes of delivery; in others, electromechanical gradients may block movement of blood constituents. In some places, external membranes have large gaps where the capillary cell exposes itself to the end-organ cell. And in many places, immune surveillance is assisted by "hiring" cells to assist them in their protective role to the end organ.

In spite of major morphological membrane and gap-junction changes, the internal coding to which capillary cells respond does not change much from one end organ to the next. That is, the composition and function of the organelles and constituents of cytoplasm, how much energy there is, and where that energy comes from do not change much from capillary cells of the brain to those of the skin. The internal similarities of all capillary cells in the body, and how they code, implies the evolution of a highly advanced skill set of internal checks and balances that protects the function of these cells and produces a consistent signaling relationship with the body's immune system, as well as with other endothelial cells and end organs.

The similarity of internal dynamics of endothelial and capillary-cell function to all end organs also explains why vascular inflammatory risk factors affect the entire vascular tree in a similar fashion. Aging (the equivalent of increased cellular genetic damage and reduced antioxidants) influences and aggregate vascular inflammatory risk never affect just one set of capillaries or one organ system; rather, symptoms tend to emerge in one organ system that is the most vulnerable, often based on adverse genetics or environmental influences. Thus, one aging end organ often leads the pack, but in reality, all capillary cells and end organs are following suit.

The next chapter will focus on vascular inflammatory testing. While directly measuring capillary-cell function is still not reliably possible, a variety of indirect methods can be used to assess vascular health. The extent to which vascular risk percolates over time gives a quality peek into capillary- and endothelial-cell health. Assessing capillary health with these methods only tells us how bad things are in the vascular system. There are no reliable tests currently available to tell us just how normal their function is. Until reliable noninvasive tests become available—where we can say that capillary-cell function is normal or not normal—assessment remains indirect and involves a variety of parameters. In the meantime, we can qualify and quantify vascular risk by documenting metabolic risk, exercise performance, membrane thickening, calcium buildup, and plaque formation in arteries, and then correlating this to end-organ dysfunction, lifestyle choices, and blood inflammatory markers.

6

Testing

By this point, we can see that the capillary endothelial cells perform critical functions for every major organ. Maintaining health with age becomes predictable by maintaining good vascular health. This chapter is about measuring degrees of end-organ failure and how that applies to age and aggregate vascular risk factors. On this basis, we can come away with a good sense of how we measure up in limiting disease risk and aging consequences.

As I have stated, there is no single test, in blood testing or imaging studies, that is specific and accurately reflects endothelial-cell function, but a host ofblood tests and imaging studies can give indirect assessment of endothelial health. However, using these tests to screen for vascular health is currently not possible, unless paid for out of pocket, because insurance companies require a disease diagnosis prior to authorizing most of these more expensive imaging or ultrasound tests. The great irony is that when symptoms emerge to the point where a disease is evident, endothelial-capillary-cell dysfunction has advanced, often to levels requiring urgent resuscitation.

However, blood tests can demonstrate an association of inflammatory markers with the likelihood of endothelial-cell dysfunction and subsequent vascular inflammation. The following behaviors, blood tests, imaging studies, and stress testing should be considered when evaluating vascular health, with or without known disease or symptoms.

Clinical Assessments

Stress

Excessive and persistent stress, and its capacity to increase levels of adrenal steroids and catecholamines (epinephrine, norepinephrine), can, as a result, increase vascular inflammation and produce capillary-cell dysfunction. Signs and symptoms that emerge from the release of these molecules into the blood include high blood pressure, palpitations, fluid retention, and increased anxiety. LDL cholesterol and blood sugar elevations are common. Behavioral maladjustment to stress, which contributes to cause or is an effect, include imbalances in activities of daily living, often resulting in social isolation, increased anger or depression, sleep deprivation, and various addictions. Measuring stress has proved difficult in clinical practice, as there is no such test as a stress-o-meter. Measuring catecholamines or adrenal steroids in most instances, has not proved helpful, as measurements at a given point in time do not provide a direction or pattern of change. Since there is no single screening test to evaluate stress, indirect measurements, including a detailed history of stress inducers, and screening blood work can be helpful.

What makes stress difficult to assess is how stress is perceived from one person to the next. That is, one person's stress can be another person's cure. Some people thrive in situations that appear to be stressful, where that same environment would harm another. Everyone has a different type and volume of environmental hazards that produce stressful outcomes. Therefore, stress and its measurement must be assessed on an individual basis.

Once assessed, in most cases, mitigating stress requires behavioral modification. This can prove beneficial in motivating individuals to process other necessary changes that are also required to further reduce vascular risk and subsequent endothelial-cell inflammation. Stress treatment is often multipronged and requires multiple different types of interventions. Treatment interventions can include a change in jobs or living situations, developing a better diet and exercise program, and eliminating addictive behaviors as much as possible. Sleeping a consistent seven hours nightly should be addressed, and treatment protocols for depression should not be overlooked. All of these adverse habits and behaviors work in aggregate, are tagged to stress coping, and need to be unwound.

This process of behavioral modification is more difficult than giving a patient a pill to treat high blood pressure or elevated cholesterol. Addictive or maladaptive behaviors often cannot be changed with recommendations from a health-care provider. There are slips and slides in treatment, and relapses are common. Complex stress cases can require a team approach which includes psychologists, psychiatrists, and medications to assist in the behavioral-modification process. In other instances, retraining for a different job or moving to another living environment is required. In some cases, the cause of stress can be traced to a medical problem which needs to be treated with appropriate medications or other interventions. Treating stress takes dedication, patience, and perseverance from both patient and health-care provider.

Sleep

Sleep is critical to capillary-cell function. Managing the sleep process effectively becomes a critical element to reduce vascular inflammatory risk and subsequently restore capillary-cell function. Like stress, sleep deprivation or other sleep pathology, is associated with increases in stress hormones, high blood pressure, diabetes mellitus, obesity, and the metabolic syndrome. Inadequate sleep also causes daytime stress, with increased daytime drowsiness, loss of focus, anger flares, and memory lapses, leading to poor job performance and increased risk for accidents.

Sleep can be adversely affected by stress and various medical and psychological conditions, including excessive noise and light, work schedules, obesity, thyroid disorders, various heart and lung conditions, diabetes, prostate enlargement, cancer and cancer treatment, pain, infections, medications, depression, dementia, and psychosis. Lack of sleep and its complications need to be sorted out diligently, and it takes time to assess and treat this properly. Assessment requires the practitioner to take a thorough history, physical examination, fasting blood work, and in some instances, an overnight sleep study.

Overnight sleep studies can be very useful in quantifying apnea, hypoxia, and insomnia as causes of sleep disturbance, and can result in specific treatments to improve sleep. These tests can now be performed effectively in a home setting, thereby eliminating the difficulty of adjusting to a one-night institutional setting, the anxiety of which can distort test results. Since many of the conditions listed above are tied to organic brain conditions like dementia, abnormal sleep patterns are being increasingly recognized as either a cause or an effect of these conditions. Sleep testing for those who can tolerate it, combined with subsequent treatment, can have positive clinical impact on several underlying organic brain impairments, including dementia, psychosis, and depression.

Getting seven to eight hours of consecutive deep sleep, without frequent trips to the bathroom or other nocturnal disruptions, should be the primary goal of sleep treatment. Subsequent diagnosis of apnea with sleep testing then becomes a secondary goal for additional sleep benefit.

Blood Pressure

When taken properly with a calibrated blood-pressure cuff around the proximal arm (between the shoulder and elbow), blood-pressure readings provide critical information about vascular inflammation.

As blood pressures increase, shear forces within the vascular lumens of large vessels increase, creating more friction, which increases inflammation to the lining of these vessels. The lining cells of the lumens of the vascular tree are composed of endothelial cells. Shear stress, particularly in places where a large artery bisects into two smaller ones, can over time produce inflammatory thickening of endothelial-cell membranes. This thickening makes matters worse by causing the vessel to narrow and make the lumen less responsive to the smooth-muscle cells that encircle the endothelial cells of the artery. Blood volume through larger arteries is controlled by their smooth muscle. With smooth-muscle constriction, lumens narrow, and blood pressure increases. With persistent elevations in blood pressure, shear forces increase, and vascular inflammatory consequences follow.

The combination of increased shear stress from endothelial-cell-membrane thickening and persistent smooth-muscle constriction causes loss of compliance in the lumens of large arteries to small arterioles. The persistent smaller bore of these vessels cascades inflammatory influences by increasing the velocity of blood flow through their lumens. Unless mitigated by reductions in blood pressure, vascular inflammation spirals, and blood pressure relentlessly increases. Persistent inflammation leads to obstructive plaque development in large arteries, subsequent capillary-cell dysfunction upstream, and serious multiple end-organ decline.

Plaque development can be accelerated by other vascular inflammatory risks, and can lead to constricted blood flow through these larger arterial blood vessels (see figure 7, in the appendix) or to the formation of aneurysms. *Aneurysms* actually cause arterial blood vessels to dilate pathologically, creating a ballooning sac of blood that can penetrate the arterial wall and eventually rupture the vessel. Aneurysms can cause bottlenecks of blood flow to develop. These bottlenecks put more pressure on the vessel wall, which causes more thinning and dilatation of smooth muscle surrounding the vessel. This sets the artery up to fail, usually by rupturing, which frequently culminates in sudden death. Aneurysms are more common in long-term smokers who also have hypertension.

Blood-pressure screening can be found in many different venues. As such, quality assurance as to an accurate measurement can be lacking. To be considered reliable, blood-pressure readings should be taken by a cuff wrapped around the arm above the elbow. The actual blood-pressure reading should be taken at least twice to make sure that the measurement is consistent. Without consistent readings, blood-pressure screening can be misleading.

In a health-care provider's office, the blood pressure should be taken in each arm at least once to make sure there is no discrepancy between pressures in both arms. Differences in blood pressures in both arms can be a sign of more serious trouble in the vascular tree, and this may call for imaging evaluation.

Normal adult blood pressures can range from 100 to 130 mm/Hg systolic to 60 to 85 mm/Hg diastolic. Pressures above or below these levels can have adverse consequences and may need intervention.

The higher the blood pressure reading, the more risk there is to the arterial tree, the integrity of the endothelial-cell membranes, and subsequent constriction of the smooth-muscle cells around them. In effect, high blood pressures create a progressive inflammatory response from shear stress, resulting in increasingly higher blood pressures and more vascular risk.

When pressures persistently exceed 140 mm/Hg, an all-out assault to control blood pressure should occur, as these levels imply increasing vascular inflammation and endothelial-cell dysfunction. Accordingly, salt intake should decrease, and dedicated efforts to lower LDL cholesterol, stop smoking, exercise, and lose weight should be instituted. Improvement in sleep quality and stress reduction can also help in the management of hypertension (high blood pressure). In many cases, these modifications can be enough to keep blood pressure under control for years. When blood pressure is consistently measured over 140 mm/Hg, blood-pressure medication should be added as part of treatment. Coupled with intentional and comprehensive lifestyle interventions, the opportunity has now been created to produce the best possibility of reversing high blood pressure and limiting vascular inflammatory influences.

In some cases, when behaviors have been persistently modified, blood pressures can fall to levels that may result in eliminating some or all of the medications used in treatment. These changes reflect reversal in endothelial-cell inflammation and dysfunction, and are associated with net improvements in compliance (elasticity) of the arterial tree. These improvements typically coincide with weight loss, regular exercise, control of blood sugars and cholesterol, as well as reductions in tobacco use and alcohol. Blood pressures often decrease in proportion to aggregate changes in vascular inflammatory risk factors. As vascular inflammatory diminishes, reducing or eliminating blood-pressure medications can be done safely and can be a used as an indirect measure of aging reversal.

High blood pressure and other vascular inflammatory risks are not in a vacuum. Each risk factor can affect the other. That is, stress, lack of sleep, blood sugar elevations, and smoking cigarettes all perpetuate high blood pressure. Inadequate sleep and excessive stress may also increase the risk of diabetes, elevate LDL cholesterol, and increase risk for the metabolic syndrome. The point here is that these risk factors occur in aggregate, feed off each other, and further extend the processes of vascular inflammation. Modifying all of these risks together as part of a package only makes sense if victory is to be obtained in limiting progressive vascular inflammatory influences.

Assessing the Heart

Regular exercise is a cornerstone in modifying vascular inflammatory risk. Measuring the capacity to exercise, both at baseline and also serially, serves as a very useful marker in assessing vascular endothelial health. A number of protocols and procedures have been developed over the past forty years to help aid in this assessment. These tests not only diagnosis heart-/lung- and skeletal-muscle-related disease, but also serve as a benchmark for safe activity levels and exercise prescription.

Exercise stress testing, with or without the use of 2-D echocardiography (heart ultrasound), is effective in evaluating coronary artery disease, heart rhythm disturbances associated with exercise, as well as serving to measure the overall capacity of heart, lung, and skeletal muscle to perform. As discussed, exercise stress testing, when coupled with measuring VO2 Max (the measured amount of oxygen utilized with maximum exercise) or simply estimating the MET (metabolic equivalent) using a standard exercise format. As such, it can be hypothesized, that changes in serial measurements of MET in a given individual can be used as an estimate of net vascular influences and aging progression or regression. Without serial measurements, comparing the actual exercise MET to the predicted MET that would be expected with maximum exercise at age twenty-five creates a ratio of change and can be used as an estimate of aging progression. Age twenty-five is used as the baseline, as this approximates a fully mature adult who has attained maximum heart, lung, and skeletal-muscle development.

As an example, if the actual exercise MET obtained in a given individual is 60 percent of that expected from a predicted exercise MET at age twenty-five, it can be hypothesized that there is a 40 percent reduction in exercise capacity, and this reduction can then reflect the same percentage increase in aging. Serial stress testing and MET measurements in a given individual can provide a measuring tool that can mark increases or decreases in aging dynamics over time. It can be hypothesized that the extent to which an exercise intensity level can approximate that which could be expected at age twenty-five is to the same extent aging has been hazed!

Screening exercise stress testing, although not traditionally covered by insurance, can be used as a prescription for safe exercise intensity. This is important, as too much exercise, particularly when starting a program, can be dangerous. Skeletal-muscle injury, heart rhythm disturbances, and even sudden death can be serious problems occurring as the result of an overly zealous exercise program. When exercise testing is coupled with 2-D echocardiography, the test becomes even more sensitive in assessing heart performance. The ultrasound of the heart (2-D echocardiogram) also accurately assesses heart structure, including the heart valves, the size of the four heart chambers, and the effectiveness of heart muscle to contract. Exercise stress testing, with echocardiography, can be used in evaluating exercise capacity when preexisting heart disease is expected, a heart murmur or arrhythmia is identified, or there is a strong family history of premature heart disease.

Imaging Studies

Over the last twenty years, imaging studies have become commonplace in diagnosing cardiovascular disease, having become both more sensitive and specific, as imaging quality has improved. For the most part, screening imaging studies have not been approved for preventative health-care practice. Ultrasound images over the past forty years have improved dramatically as well; they are safe, generally less expensive, and can be used serially to assess changes in vascular inflammation, without radiation risk. Carotid ultrasounds, which evaluate the arteries in the neck that provide blood to the brain, can check for artery plaque and membrane thickening, and can be used as a barometer for estimating large-vessel endothelial membrane inflammation throughout the body.

What makes carotid imaging useful, in addition to evaluating the circulation to the brain, is its ability to assess vascular flow in an area where there is increased shear force. Shear force typically increases when a large vessel bisects into two smaller vessels. In the neck, the common carotid artery bisects into the internal and external carotid arteries. Where this bisection occurs, there is increased shear force, or pressure, in the lumen as blood flow is divided into two smaller arteries. This increased pressure, or shear, in the lumens of smaller arteries creates a predilection for inflammation that results in endothelial-cell-membrane thickening and eventual plaque buildup on their basement membranes. Shear forces increase further as blood pressure increases and can occur in any blood vessel that bifurcates. Therefore, carotid imaging may serve as an estimate of shear damage from vascular disease in all large bifurcating arteries.

Shear inflammation is more critical in the carotid arteries, however, since any reduction in blood flow caused by membrane thickening or plaque formation will subsequently have an adverse effect on brain function. With advancing age and stacking of vascular inflammatory risk factors, it is not uncommon for these vessels to show rapid and progressive inflammatory narrowing that can tie directly to increasing cognitive deficits. Modification of vascular inflammatory risk factors can dramatically slow or even stop this process.

It was the serial evaluation of carotid scans and heart ultrasounds, in hundreds of patients over twenty-five years of studying these scans, that became the driving force for me to understand the relationship between carotid inflammation/ narrowing and subsequent reductions in blood flow to the brain, along with corresponding decreases in brain volume (known as *cerebral atrophy*) and reduced cognitive function. These changes were not just "normal changes related to aging" but were part of a vascular inflammatory process causing large-vessel narrowing. This subsequently produced reductions in blood flow to the brain that directly influenced brain and cognitive function.

What became vitally important was to pay close attention to the early changes of carotid-artery-membrane thickening. These early changes, rather than being dismissed as natural processes of aging, should rather serve as a baseline for large-artery vascular inflammatory change that was likely occurring in a similar way throughout the body. As such, this became a teaching tool to urgently motivate patients to modify vascular inflammatory risk. When evaluated serially, as with exercise testing, success or failure of that risk could be measured by changes in membrane thickness or plaque size. In some cases, regression of one or both occurred, with rigorous reduction in vascular inflammatory risk. Aging had been hazed.

By modifying risk and keeping carotid-artery lumens open, saving critical brain volume—and, subsequently, its function—was on the line. Conversely, not doing so will result in a missed opportunity to save and protect optimal brain and blood-brain-barrier endothelial-cell function.

The following imaging studies are commonly used to assess vascular inflammation:

- **Ultrasound imaging** of the carotid arteries therefore becomes a simple test to estimate vascular inflammation in bifurcating arteries to the brain, as well as through the entire vascular tree. When this connection is made, the gravity of endothelial-cell-membrane thickening on carotid imaging becomes more profound, and the urgency to modify vascular risk is clarified.

- **Magnetic resonance imaging** (**MRI**) of the carotid arteries is more sensitive in evaluating obstructive plaque and is used in preparation for invasive carotid interventions, including stent placement or endarterectomy. These imaging techniques are much more expensive and do not offer substantial amounts of additional information about the early changes of endothelial-cell inflammation; therefore, they are not all that useful as screening tests.

- **CT imaging of the heart** can be useful in determining a coronary calcium score (density of plaque score) and as a proxy to coronary angiograms to quantify coronary-artery-vessel narrowing. The *coronary calcium score* offers an excellent snapshot as to how much vascular hard-plaque inflammation has already occurred in the large vessels supplying heart muscle. As such, this test, when done serially, serves as a sensitive barometer of vascular inflammatory progression in a given individual. CT imaging of the coronary vessels to quantify coronary-artery narrowing is usually reserved for those at high risk for critical coronary artery disease with progressive symptoms, where stress testing or nuclear imaging has proved equivocal. Furthermore, as with carotid MRI imaging, it is expensive, increases radiation and contrast-material risk, and adds little additional benefit in screening for early vascular inflammatory disease.

Limits of Imaging Studies

The imaging studies discussed above can accurately assess vascular inflammatory changes of membrane thickening and plaque development of large arterial vessels, but they cannot directly evaluate the smaller blood vessels or capillary endothelium, which are the true business cells between blood and end organ. Since all endothelial cells of the arterial tree work as a unit and are affected by each other, plaque narrowing of larger vessels, with subsequent declines in blood volume through these vessels, will have adverse effects on endothelial cells upstream, including capillary cells. As such, imaging studies provide direct evidence for large-vessel vascular disease and only indirect evidence for capillary-cell dysfunction.

Other Screenings

Screening the abdominal aorta for aneurysm and the leg arteries for artery plaque, with combinations of ultrasound and Doppler arteriograms, can be helpful in assessing vascular inflammation for those who smoke or have diabetes, as well as for formulating an appropriate exercise prescription. At times, these screens can be lifesaving, but in most cases, they merely offer confirming evidence for progressive narrowing of large arterial vessels from plaque buildup. In most cases, the abnormal findings correlate with membrane thickening and plaque development seen on carotid ultrasound scans. Therefore, it is not uncommon to have patients develop memory loss and other cognitive declines from decreasing carotid-artery blood flow, in association with reduced capacity to exercise from decreased blood supply to leg muscles.

CT or MRI imaging of the abdomen and pelvis are expensive procedures, have accumulative radiation risk for bone cancers and contrast-material risk to kidney function, and, therefore, have no role as a screening tool or in serially following plaque progression. On the other hand, inexpensive ultrasounds of the abdomen can screen for and serially follow large plaque development of the aorta; they can also screen for and serially follow aneurysms. Kidney dimensions can be easily determined and serve as a proxy to renal-artery narrowing (as renal arteries narrow, kidney dimensions decrease).

A simple screening urine analysis, employing the dipstick method, can also be used to estimate the integrity of capillary-endothelial-cell function as it applies to the kidney's glomerulus (see figure 3, in the appendix). Increased protein or red blood cells on a dipstick urine analysis can correlate to increasing capillary-cell dysfunction in the glomerulus and is frequently seen in diabetics. It can be also associated with rising serum creatinine levels and decreasing kidney function.

Blood Tests

Of all the current methods of assessing endothelial-cell function, blood testing currently offers the best chance to preemptively evaluate and then follow inflammatory vascular risk. A variety of tests are currently available, with more on the way. Most of these tests are inexpensive, are drawn the next day after fasting from midnight, can be followed serially, and can serve as a benchmark for assessing vascular risk and establishing plans for prevention.

Two of the most important screening tests for vascular inflammation are the fasting blood sugar and LDL cholesterol level. With aging, inactivity, obesity, and the typical Western diet of highly processed, sugar-dense foods, insulin resistance increases. This is associated over time in a given individual with progressive increases in fasting blood sugars and LDL cholesterol levels. As these levels increase, arterial-membrane thickening and plaque development in large arteries occur, leading to diffuse endothelial-cell dysfunction throughout the arterial tree and the capillary cells, resulting in the subsequent deterioration of end organs.

Blood-Sugar Tests

Normal fasting blood sugars have a narrow range of 75–99 mg/dL. When fasting blood sugars persistently exceed 100 mg/dL, the processes of vascular inflammation associated with *insulin resistance* (the capacity of cells in the body to utilize simple sugars for energy) have begun. Simple or refined sugars are *monosaccharides,* composed of up to seven carbon molecules that are easily metabolized to *glucose* and then *pyruvate,* which is then used for energy production or stored in the liver as *glycogen.* This rapid breakdown of simple sugars to glucose creates the sugar rush, which puts stress on the liver and pancreas to process the surge in volume. The packaging of increased sugar volume almost always gets transferred to fatty-acid storage in adipose cells (fat cells). Simple sugars are found in all snack foods, breads, juices, many dairy products, and desserts, including ice cream and cookies. With this in mind, elevations in fasting blood sugars of greater than 100 mg/dL have become commonplace, with up to one-third of all adults in the Unites States having evidence of insulin resistance or diabetes. Elevated fasting blood sugars adversely affect the metabolism of all cells—including capillary cells—increase LDL cholesterol and free-radical levels, and, therefore, have become a fundamental marker and indirect measure of capillary-endothelial-cell dysfunction.

In the early stages of insulin resistance, there are typically no specific symptoms associated with it, except for perhaps vague pain or fatigue. The processes of early vascular inflammation from insulin resistance are stealthy and can brew for years before obvious signs and symptoms emerge. Unfortunately, when symptoms do emerge, the diffuse vascular inflammatory processes involving the entire arterial tree will already be under way, resulting in significant capillary-endothelial-cell dysfunction involving multiple end organs.

Since insulin resistance leading to type 2 diabetes mellitus (adult-onset diabetes) is epidemic in Western culture, and increases dramatically with advanced age, testing fasting blood sugars in all adults is mandatory in assessing vascular health. If fasting blood sugars are greater than 100 mg/dL, adding the HbA1C (which measures the persistence of blood sugar elevation over time) is clinically prudent. If both of these tests are abnormal, red flags are raised, and then aggressive efforts to treat are implemented. Such efforts initially involve modification of diet, sedentary behavior, and insufficient sleep. In some cases, medications may be required. The process of progressive insulin resistance is both insidious and relentless, and major efforts should be made preemptively to reduce all refined sugar in the diet. Dietary-sugar vigilance, along with exercise, weight loss, and proper sleep, becomes a critical practice cornerstone in managing insulin resistance/diabetes and its deleterious effects to the vascular endothelium and capillary cells.

Cholesterol Tests

Cholesterol levels are obtained by a fasting blood lipid panel, and these panels generally include *LDL cholesterol, HDL cholesterol* (good, anti-inflammatory cholesterol), and *triglycerides* (another inflammatory fat when elevated in the blood). There is still controversy in the literature as to what constitutes across-the-board healthy levels of the different cholesterols.

LDL cholesterol. Inflammatory cholesterols always involve LDL (low-density lipoprotein) cholesterol, which is why most people are familiar with "bad" LDL cholesterol. The worst of the LDL cholesterols are the oxidized (exposed electron) small-particle LDL (also known as Ox-LDL, *oxidized low-density lipoprotein*). This particle is highly inflammatory, and increases with age and aggregate vascular risk. Other cholesterols that are known to be inflammatory and that can be determined with additional testing include *lipoprotein (a), very low density cholesterol* (VLDL cholesterol) and *apo-lipoprotein B-100 cholesterol.* In addition to these, elevated serum triglycerides are categorized as another type of inflammatory fat molecule.

When any or all of these inflammatory cholesterols/fats are elevated in the fasting state, they produce inflammation to all the endothelial cells of the arterial tree by adversely affecting their metabolism. They also can act as toxic free radicals that can injure membrane surfaces and damage organelles, including the DNA of the nucleus and mitochondria.

Because all of these inflammatory influences are well-known contributors to the cause and effect of vascular disease, aggressive efforts should be undertaken to lower inflammatory cholesterol levels. Ideally, intervention should be preemptive, and should occur before symptoms emerge or large-vessel plaque development is identified. Although treatment guidelines are constantly in a state of flux, the importance of early treatment using diet, exercise, and medication to prevent the devastating effects of inflammatory cholesterols to the arterial circulation is essential. Becoming personally aware of the blood levels of all of these inflammatory cholesterols, particularly if family history points to early-in-life vascular events, is important in clarifying vascular risk and initiating treatment strategies. Being preemptive and preventative requires good data. Knowing your cholesterol numbers gives you a heads-up in modifying risk earlier. The capacity to follow blood sugars, HbA1C, and LDL cholesterol levels serially is very useful for vascular inflammatory management.

Another useful test in evaluating LDL cholesterol can be particle size. This test is more expensive and not commonly obtained in cholesterol screening, but it provides useful information about the virulence of LDL cholesterol. The smaller the LDL cholesterol particle, the more inflammatory it becomes. If LDL cholesterol levels are measured as normal, but the preponderance of the LDL cholesterol measured is small particle, vascular inflammatory risk to the endothelium would still be present. With advanced age, diabetes, or certain genomics that predispose to premature vascular events (heart attack, stroke), there are increases in the small-particle LDL cholesterol. Being informed on a one-time basis about LDL particle size, particularly if falling into one of the three categories, can be a very useful in assessing LDL risk.

Triglycerides. Elevated fasting serum triglycerides are associated with inflammatory responses that thicken the arterial endothelial-cell membranes and contribute to plaque development of larger arteries, affecting all endothelial-cell function. Elevated blood triglycerides increase insulin resistance and influence energy precursors used in endothelial and end-organ cells to make energy. As with any vascular proinflammatory marker, elevated triglycerides contribute to plaque development in large arteries and cause subsequent capillary-cell dysfunction upstream.

Elevated serum triglycerides are also associated with adult-onset diabetes, low thyroid hormone levels, as well as liver and pancreas disorders. As such, lowering them requires a thoughtful approach to associated clinical conditions. Like fasting blood sugar and LDL cholesterol, triglycerides can be measured serially as part of a routine lipid panel.

HDL cholesterol. Elevated triglycerides can also be tied to low HDL (high-density lipoprotein) levels. (HDL is the so-called good cholesterol because it is anti-inflammatory.) Having low HDL levels compounds the likelihood for premature plaque development. Higher blood levels of HDL cholesterol are vascular anti-inflammatory, and are thought to have an antioxidant effect on Ox-LDL cholesterol. While having low HDL cholesterol is considered a serious vascular inflammatory risk factor, efforts to increase HDL cholesterol have not been clearly associated with reducing vascular-related injury. Further investigation as to how the HDL cholesterol limits inflammation is required before firm recommendations can be made about increasing HDL levels.

As with the LDL molecule, HDL particle size matters. Increasing HDL levels without increasing HDL particle size may be key to understanding lack of HDL benefit, since large-particle HDL appears more vascular anti-inflammatory than small-particle HDL.

Other Blood Tests

Some other blood tests that can be useful in assessing inflammatory risk include *homocysteine* and *highly sensitive C-reactive protein* (HSCRP) levels. Elevated homocysteine levels are associated with increased endothelial-cell membrane injury, membrane thickening, and large-vessel plaque formation, and, as such, are considered a risk factor for vascular disease and endothelial-cell dysfunction. Reducing these levels has proved difficult, but adjusting diets to reduce weight and taking high doses of folic acid and vitamin B6 (pyridoxine) can produce reductions of up to 25 percent or more. The relationship of homocysteine and treatment to vascular inflammation can be reviewed in a journal article published in *The Lancet* almost twenty years ago by Spence and Peterson.

In spite of cause and effect of elevated blood homocysteine levels to large-vessel plaque development, it has been difficult to prove the vascular anti-inflammatory benefits in relation to reducing homocysteine levels. In spite of this difficulty, it should not dismiss attempts at diet changes, weight loss, and vitamin supplementation in an effort to lower these levels. Taking higher doses of folic acid and pyridoxine, if monitored by a health-care provider, should not produce serious side effects.

The highly sensitive C-reactive protein (HSCRP) can serve as a barometer to measure the effectiveness of total vascular anti-inflammatory effort. When measured serially and trending lower, it gives patient and provider assurance that measures taken to lower vascular inflammatory risk are working. Unfortunately, HSCRP levels can be elevated for other reasons, such as autoimmune, cancer, and infectious causes. However, even with these false positives, HSCRP levels can serve as a useful marker for evaluating and treating vascular inflammation. Using the HSCRP as a final exam in assessing the effectiveness of a vascular anti-inflammatory program, and following these levels serially over time, can correlate with regression or progression of vascular inflammatory risk.

Conclusion

A variety of additional tests are currently being used in research laboratories to assess early vascular inflammatory changes involving arterial endothelial cells. Although promising, to date, these tests lack clinical utility. In some cases, they are invasive, may not produce consistent results, and are expensive. What has become clear is the need for precise, inexpensive endothelial-cell testing that can be used to identify risk in the earlier stages of vascular inflammation, before soft-plaque buildup and membrane thickening have occurred. If accomplished, preemptive interventions for primary prevention will produce better preemptive clinical results.

Once imaging or ultrasound has identified thickening to the endothelial membranes of the carotid arteries, calcium buildup indicative of hard plaque in the coronary arteries, or a balloon-like dilatation of the abdominal aorta, the processes of serious vascular inflammation have become well established and will likely progress to produce symptoms. Proving vascular inflammatory risk before membrane thickening occurs is key to providing impetus for primary prevention. These imaging tests, although ordered late in response to symptoms and usually associated with serious preexisting vascular inflammatory disease, offer the best attempts we currently have at our disposal to quantify vascular inflammatory risk.

Currently, our best chance at early preemptive preventative care of the arterial tree and capillary cells comes from blood testing of known vascular inflammatory risk factors. When utilized in conjunction with family history, an inflammatory profile emerges that provides impetus to early behavioral modification, and in some instances, medication and supplements, to both prevent vascular inflammatory processes and improve arterial-tree, capillary-cell, and subsequent end-organ health. When coupled with stress testing and MET measurements, carotid ultrasound scans, echocardiograms, and coronary calcium scores, the accumulated data offers the best assessment of vascular inflammatory risk currently available, as well as a safe exercise prescription and estimate of age progression.

Once vascular inflammatory risk is assessed, a thoughtful approach to therapeutic options must then be planned. The future bodes well for noninvasive testing of capillary-cell function. When this testing becomes reliable and inexpensive, one more tool will be available to make pronouncements about vascular health. Until then, indirect methods measuring well-known vascular inflammatory risk factors are the mainstay of assessment. Once measured and assessed, the process of mitigating vascular inflammatory risk then unfolds. The next chapter lays out a multipronged approach, beginning with important behavioral modifications as the foundation for vascular and capillary-cell health.

7

Therapeutics

Successful therapeutics involve interventions that nurture endothelial-cell function throughout the arterial tree; as such, these are both adaptive and antiaging. Taking medicine to lower cholesterol, while at the same time eating fat-laden steaks or smoking cigarettes, will not provide meaningful vascular anti- inflammatory benefit. Trying to exercise after eating a donut or being hungover from alcohol is a prescription for failure. Only when done in combination with other vascular anti-inflammatory behavior will these efforts bear fruit. When done as part of a comprehensive vascular anti-inflammatory plan, measurable success in a short period of time is possible.

The interventions in this chapter will cause reduction of inflammation of the endothelium of the entire vascular tree, stabilizing blood flow to capillaries and improving capillary-cell function. End-organ function may then find new life as vascular inflammation is lifted. Advanced vascular disease limits the return of capillary function, but its progression can also be affected and capillary-cell function accommodated. It is never too late to make the effort.

Exercise

It can be argued that exercise, or persistent intentional movement, is the foundation on which all other vascular anti-inflammatory therapeutics are built. As might be expected, with consistent exercise, endothelial-cell health improves, which then cascades to improve health in multiple organ systems.

Here are some of the many benefits of exercise:

- improves multiple organ systems in the body
- improves muscle tone, bone health, and energy levels
- promotes an overall feeling of well-being
- improves sleep quality
- improves mood and decreases need for antidepressant medication
- helps prevent dementia and other neurodegenerative diseases
- stimulates the immune system to prevent infection and accelerate wound healing
- lowers insulin resistance, thereby reducing blood sugar levels and predilection to diabetes
- lowers the risk of some cancers
- improves blood cholesterol levels by raising the good cholesterol (HDL), while lowering the bad cholesterol (LDL) and serum triglycerides
- improves lung and heart function
- reduces the risk of dependency and maintains activities of daily living for longer periods (with advanced age)
- reduces emergency-room visits, hospitalizations, and the number of medications required to control blood pressure, diabetes, and cholesterol levels
- can substantially reduce health-care costs
- maintains productivity in individuals for decades longer than those who do not exercise

Prolonged sitting or lying in bed has the opposite effect of exercise, as it accelerates vascular inflammation and promotes influences to increase aging and death. Exercise, particularly with advancing age, must be done carefully and discussed with a primary-care provider in order to prevent injury. With age, injury, joint or muscle pain, adjustments to movement become essential in maintaining a regular exercise plan.

There are two types of exercises: aerobic and anaerobic. *Aerobic exercises* are continuous sustained exercises—like walking, jogging, or biking—that stimulate and strengthen the heart and lungs, and increase the body's ability to use oxygen. *Anaerobic exercises* comprise intermittent movement, focusing on strengthening muscle which supports bone mass, tendons, and ligaments, and prevents skeleton decay. A weight-training program is a common example. We need both types of exercise.

A critical element of successful exercise is the ability to listen and pay attention to signs the body is giving the brain about how it is responding to a given movement. Listening to the body's language involving increases in pain, light-headedness, or excessive shortness of breath helps us to understand whether the exercise may be excessive and harming more than helping. *The persistence of these symptoms should not be ignored, as there can be substantial variations in a given individual insofar as what these symptoms mean and how they should be handled.* Having a good relationship with a knowledgeable health-care provider should provide insight into what symptoms are acceptable or unacceptable. Misinterpreting symptoms can have serious and even fatal consequences. An experienced personal trainer or exercise expert familiar with an individual's limitations can also be of assistance to develop an individualized exercise program. No two people are alike where optimal exercise prescriptions are concerned. However, that does not mean that exercise can't be enjoyed when done properly.

Exercise requires a thoughtful plan based on an individual's capacity to perform. At the very beginning of an exercise program, the exercise bias should be to underperform, starting out slowly to avoid injury of a muscle or joint. For those who cannot weight bear consistently, using an exercycle (stationary bike) or exercising in a pool may be an alternative. *Symptoms of chest pains, dizziness, unusual fatigue, or excessive shortness of breath should not be ignored, and should be reported to the trainer and health-care provider.* Also, the onset of headaches, nausea, or persistent pains in joints or muscles with exercise should be reported.

Though we often start to exercise with good intentions, people make three mistakes when they begin an exercise program:

1. Personal expectations, previous experience, and perceptions about exercise make people think they can perform like they did years or even decades before. This thought pattern usually triggers injury, as most people over time have gained weight, have reduced skeletal-muscle mass and tone, and have developed weight-bearing arthritis. In addition, medical problems, such as hypertension, diabetes mellitus, or even ischemic coronary disease have emerged, and these influence exercise performance. This is why the initial goal for exercise should be modest and based on current health. Modest, consistent exercise improves muscle tone and performance. Develop a balanced and consistent plan of safe movement, predicated on your capacity and health circumstances.

2. People stop exercising entirely if there is a pain in the ankle, knee, hip, back, elbow, or shoulder, resulting in frequent long stretches of no exercise. Exercising through joint pain is not advised, and if pain persists for days, you may need to see your doctor to rule out other causes. But every day is important when it comes to exercise, because consistent movement is an important intervention. Different types of exercise can work around most localized muscle or joint pain. For example, if jogging or walking is aggravating knee pain, you can switch to an elliptical machine, a pool aerobics class, or a stationary

bicycle, instead of stopping and starting jogging every time pain goes away and comes back. The new aerobic movement can be continued, and musculoskeletal symptoms from repetitive walking or jogging can be mitigated. You can also adjust by changing out old shoes, using arch supports, limiting downhill walking or jogging, and not jogging on asphalt or cement surfaces. In other cases, just modifying the exercise plan to walk or jog on alternate days while finding a different exercise on alternate days can be enough to prevent weight-bearing joint pain. Alternative exercises should be done at the same intensity of the primary exercise that is being changed out.

3. A third mistake involves the exercise mix. Aerobic (continuous movement) and anaerobic (intermittent burst movement, which can include resistance training) exercise should each be performed as part of a daily routine, and mixed in with some stretching and balance movements. Thirty minutes of aerobic exercise, such as walking, jogging, swimming, or machine work (elliptical, stepper, treadmill), followed by fifteen minutes of light weight-resistance training of the major muscle groups is ideal. Stretching, yoga, and balance (tai chi) can be added, and are beneficial to support posture, gait, and balance. Intensity of exercise should be monitored closely, and symptoms like palpitations (pounding in the chest), dizziness, excessive shortness of breath, chest pains, or severe increases in muscle or bone pain should be reported to a health-care professional or experienced trainer. Exercising for more extensive periods of time has not been shown to further improve vascular health. In some situations, prolonged exercise can increase injuries and cause other more serious outcomes.

For those with significant preexisting heart, lung, or arthritic conditions, exercising for only a few minutes a day may produce excessive fatigue or pain and substantially limit exercise capacity.

Length of daily exercise is important. As stated in a review by Jonathon Myers in *Circulation* (see bibliography), exercising for just ten minutes daily can produce some vascular health benefits, even for those who have limited capacity. Carefully increasing the effort over weeks, to fifteen to twenty minutes of exercise daily, can produce further benefit. Any breathlessness or continued pain needs to be monitored with a doctor, and exercise should be attenuated when symptoms become significant.

The most common reason for not exercising is procrastination followed by finding time to exercise. Extensive traveling, working twelve-hour shifts, having young children to take care of, or having other work agendas and family obligations put restraints on time and motivation to exercise. To find time often involves adopting changes in sleep patterns, which can be stressful. Finding time to sleep seven to eight hours, and then getting up an hour earlier to exercise in the morning when it can be cold and dark, can be difficult for anyone initiating an exercise program. Carving out time for exercise at the lunch hour can also be difficult for those who live in urban environments, have meetings to attend, or have other obligations at lunchtime. Late-night exercise is generally not recommended, as insomnia can occur from the stimulation of exercise. Finding time to exercise can prove to be very challenging, yet exercise is the most important vascular anti-inflammatory intervention. Making time to exercise requires planning, but the effort is well spent because of how important exercise is.

The good news is, exercise does not require joining a gym or a sports club, although some people find that having a specific place to go to for exercise becomes an important motivator to exercise. While exercise is repetitive and involves a routine, adapting to different exercise environments can be beneficial. For example, if your job involves overnight travel and takes you out of your exercise routine, or a vacation takes you to a place where there is no gym or swimming facility, being flexible to alternative types of exercise becomes important. The point is that exercise should be done consistently, regardless of the context and venue. It should become as important as eating three quality meals, getting seven hours of uninterrupted sleep, and twice daily brushing and flossing of the teeth.

Not exercising at a gym or health club means there is no need to purchase expensive health equipment. Depending on budget and the exercise plan that works for each individual, this may include one piece of equipment to sit on, such as a stationary bicycle or an elliptical machine, and a set of light weights, such as five- to twenty-five-pound barbells. If choosing to walk or jog for exercise, a pair of shoes that support the arches of the feet becomes important, and should be changed out at least every six months to avoid weight-bearing joint injury and pain. Occasionally, using ankle or knee supports is necessary to prevent painful joints with exertion. Preventing further injury or pain with splints or braces can become very important when trying to exercise consistently.

Even if it's difficult to do much exercise, stretching, particularly with advanced age, can have significant health benefit. This may serve to maintain flexibility, limit stiffness, and prevent additional injury when attempting to exercise. Balance exercise is also very beneficial in the elderly, and can limit falls and subsequent risk of broken bones by decreasing unsteadiness of standing and walking. Simple exercises such as balancing for several seconds while standing on one leg and then the other can be helpful. Being able to stand on one leg in various positions (tai chi) is a more advanced application involving the same principle. For those who don't have good balance, there are exercises that can be done while sitting down which still will increase strength.

If choosing to add light weights to exercise shoulders, arms, chest, legs, and buttocks, such exercise should be geared to an individual's abilities, and under the auspice of a trainer. When performed consistently, bone density, muscle mass and strength, posture, and gait all are maintained, and arthritis pain is mitigated. Anaerobic exercise, for most individuals, should not require more than fifteen minutes to perform. Technique is important to prevent injury, and light weights utilizing several repetitions are beneficial for most. Simple squatting, with or without weights, with proper technique, can effectively tone and support the large muscles of the legs and buttocks. Shoulder and arm exercise involves simple pressing of light weights above the head or chest while lying on the floor or on a bench. One or two sets of these exercises at ten to fifteen repetitions each, using light weights, should take about fifteen minutes and should not produce excessive fatigue, breathlessness, or muscle pain.

Sometimes, alternating exercise of different muscle groups to different days can be helpful. For example, exercising the shoulders and arms on one day can be followed by exercising the legs and buttocks on the next day. When beginning an exercise program, expect sore muscles for the first few days, as these tissues adapt to increased workloads. These pains should eventually go away, as muscles become toned and performance improves. Over a period of a few weeks, most will notice improvement in well-being and energy levels. These changes are bona fide signals that meaningful endothelial anti-inflammatory benefits to exercise have occurred.

Nurturing the vascular endothelium through regular exercise can be considered the cornerstone for giving new life to these cells that line the arterial tree. By doing so, capillary health improves, end-organ function is restored, and the first step of comprehensive preventative health care is realized. Even with these accrued benefits, exercise alone will not achieve optimal results unless it is coupled with other vascular anti-inflammatory behaviors. Vascular anti-inflammatory treatment must be multipronged.

Sleep

The processes of sleep remain a great mystery in terms of understanding of good mental health, but sleep is a critical foundation of vascular anti-inflammatory prevention and maintenance of capillary-endothelial-cell function. Sleep has different depths, or stages, during which we rest and dream. The deeper levels of sleep, including dream sleep, are restorative to the brain, as deep sleep eliminates metabolic residuals that affect how the brain performs. Deep sleep resets the brain to work optimally during consciousness (i.e., the waking state). When one night of acute sleep deprivation occurs in an otherwise healthy person, dream sleep increases the next night to compensate for inadequate brain cleansing the night before. Maintenance of a good sleep pattern is associated with multiple vascular anti-inflammatory benefits, including stress reduction, less weight gain/obesity, lower blood pressure, and lower blood sugar levels.

Any behavior that results in an individual having fewer than seven hours of continuous sleep will increase vascular inflammation in that person. It does not matter what the reason for the behavior is; chronic interruption of sleep and/or inadequate sleep quality induces physiologic and metabolic consequences that produce vascular inflammation.

The Role of Habits and Age

Unfortunately, bad habits that reduce sleep quality can be learned at young ages when the processes of sleep are taken for granted. Many of us don't develop good sleep habits. Staying up late at night for any reason, drinking excessive amounts of alcohol or caffeinated beverages, and even cramming for final exams all are behaviors adopted as part of accepted culture routines—rites of passage to adulthood. Many of these bad habits continue through adulthood, and then they are compounded by other worries and distractions of work and family life, which only make uninterrupted sleep even more difficult.

When younger (generally under age thirty), in the absence of alcohol, stimulants, and/or excessive social stimulation, it is fairly routine to fall asleep when tired, on demand, and to sleep for eight hours, uninterrupted. Extraneous noise, light, and even the time of day or night frequently does not impact sleep. This sleep includes quick induction (fewer than fifteen minutes needed to fall asleep) as well as abundant levels of sustained deeper unconsciousness and dream sleep.

As we age, particularly after age forty, quality sleep gets harder to maintain. We worry more, and so we take more stress to bed. The increasing burdens of life cause lighter sleep and create more middle-of-the-night awakenings. Weight gain increases snoring, as well as the risk of sleep apnea and reflux GERD (acid indigestion). There tends to be more bathroom visits to urinate. Falling asleep, after being awake, becomes harder as thoughts often turn to worries. All of these changes are made worse by the inheritance of the bad habits we learned as young adults when sleep was taken for granted.

Insufficient sleep is compounded by what we do next. Instead of falling back to sleep after an interruption, many of us would rather just get up, watch television, surf the Internet, or read. These activities are frequently associated with snacking. The net result is insufficient sleep, weight gain, and brain fog, with more fatigue and drowsiness during the day. Vascular inflammatory risk escalates if these behaviors become chronic. The corresponding changes in well-being can be subtle and not easily tied to poor sleep habits.

For insomnia, we often knee jerk to alcohol and sleep aids. While many may argue in favor of the short-term use of sleep aids, the long-term use of any sleep aid or alcohol to induce sleep is mired with adverse consequences to sleep quality, including diminished dream or restorative sleep. The cycle is completed in the morning hours of the following day, when increased brain fog from the use of these sleep aids requires excessive caffeine intake, which carries its own set of risks.

Various Sleep Problems from Age

Advanced age is correlated with several adverse behaviors that interfere with sleep continuity. This includes delays in falling sleep (induction), less time spent in restorative dream sleep, and more frequent interruptions to sleep, including sleep apnea and/ or frequent trips to the bathroom. Once awake, it becomes much harder to fall back asleep.

The sleep deprivation that results increases fatigue, pain, and brain fog, as well as adversely affecting blood sugar, blood pressure, cholesterol, and weight. The early-morning fatigue and brain fog causes knee-jerk use of caffeine and sugar in order to wake up and get started, which can further escalate blood-pressure and blood-sugar risks. Poor sleep habits in the elderly are highly correlated to increased dementia, reduced motor skills, and other neurodegenerative diseases.

In addition to these habits, other changes associated with age interfere with the benefits of sleep.

- Anatomic changes in the neck and throat occur with aging, and this can adversely affect sleep. The soft tissue in the back of the throat begins to sag or become redundant, and the cartilage in the nose thickens. Both of these changes can result in increased snoring, sleep apnea, and reduction in air flow to the lungs, producing hypoxia. This problem can be very serious, as combinations of hypoxia and decreased restorative sleep can lead to heart attacks, heart rhythm disturbances (such as atrial fibrillation), strokes, excessive daytime drowsiness, and eventual dementia. The treatments for sleep apnea can be cumbersome, but they can also be helpful to limit the cascades of adverse influences caused from sleep apnea. These treatments include oxygen, appliances fitted into the mouth, and CPAP (continuous positive airway pressure) machines that deliver predetermined pressures through the mouth and nose to keep these airway passages from obstructing during sleep.

- With increasing weight gain, there can be episodes of acid reflux into the esophagus, which can produce symptomatic heartburn and even aspiration of acidic gastric juice into the lung. This may cause the sudden onset of wheezing, shortness of breath, and cough. If acid-reflux conditions persist and are not treated, esophageal cancer, chronic bronchitis, pneumonia, and COPD (chronic obstructive pulmonary disease) can result.

- Excessive amounts of pain from musculoskeletal conditions can interrupt sleep and should be treated preemptively to prevent nocturnal awakenings. Too much, or even too little, thyroid hormone in the blood can affect the capacity to both fall and stay asleep, and this hormone level should be checked as part of sleep screening.

- Menopause and the development of hot flashes can severely impact sleep and should be addressed in a meaningful way.

- Untreated depression can affect sleep adversely, and treatment strategies should be implemented.

- Napping during the day exacerbates poor sleep habits at night, and if persistent, can increase dementia risk. Persistent sleep deprivation, at any age, spirals vascular inflammatory risks and nurtures capillary- and endothelial-cell dysfunction. Frequent daytime napping is a harbinger of aging acceleration and increasing dementia.

Solutions

Because of all these adverse cascades involving sleep disturbances, maintaining effective sleep requires proactive intentional behaviors.

- Go to bed at the same time each night.
- Limit influences that tend to stimulate (exercise, watching a scary or violent movie, and so on).
- Sleep in a quiet room.
- Eliminate alcohol and caffeine for several hours prior to sleeping.
- For those with overactive bladders, restricting fluid intake to 12 ounces after four o'clock in the afternoon can decrease evening bathroom requirements. Avoidance of diuretics (medications

that cause increased urination) at night, as well as foods that cause heartburn, can also be helpful.

- Raising the head of the bed by just a few inches to avoid gastric acid reflux can also be helpful to avoid reflux-related cough and GERD symptoms.
- For those who snore extensively and wake up fatigued in spite of eight hours of sleep, getting tested for sleep apnea can be very important.
- The careful short-term use of sleep aids may be required for sleep induction after a thorough search, with the help of a health-care provider who has eliminated other medical reasons for insomnia.

As stated, regardless of cause, persistent insufficient sleep contributes to vascular inflammation and accelerated aging. Consistent sleep of at least seven hours in every twenty-four hours is essential; for multiple reasons, with advancing age, this requires an intentional approach. Ensuring quality sleep may require several treatment strategies involving several organ systems and multiple behaviors. Sleep quality can be a moving target, with adjustments in intentional behavior necessary. When quality sleep is mastered, the process becomes an ally to vascular health and can be considered a sensitive marker in assessing aging progression.

Social/Spiritual Connectedness

Being isolated or alone, without a family, work, or spiritual connection, can produce substantial stress and has been associated with increased depression, suicide, and alcohol and drug abuse. How social isolation contributes to these behaviors and subsequent vascular inflammatory consequences are summarized by a review article from Burt Uchino (see bibliography). These conditions, either alone or in aggregate, contribute to increased vascular inflammatory processes tied to increases in stress hormones, hypertension, diabetes/insulin resistance, higher LDL cholesterol levels, drug and alcohol addiction, insufficient sleep, excessive fast-food consumption, and sedentary lifestyle.

Most humans do not do well living isolated. We require a variety of connections to help us find purpose, set goals, and develop a direction in life. Connections can serve different functions: some involve mutual interests, others require emotional intimacy, and still others entail following a spiritual path.

Central to a social/spiritual connection is caring. Caring can come from almost anyone, from any walk of life, who has an interest in helping another, preferably without any strings attached. Caring should not be based on quid pro quo ("if I give you this, then you will give me that").

It is generally recognized that socially well-adjusted people are happier, experience less depression, and exhibit less addictive behavior. For the most part, couples married for many years are happier and more contented than individuals who aren't in successful relationships—and people in happy long-term relationships live longer too. Those who go to church or practice their faith regularly have more contentment and live longer than those who don't.

Being socially/spiritually connected is often associated with other healthy behaviors. Whether social isolation is a cause or effect of depression or chemical dependency can be difficult to distinguish, but it probably is not important.

Implied in social/spiritual connectivity is an increase in well- being that can be associated with finding purpose and improved motivation to pursue healthier living habits. Linked beneficial vascular anti-inflammatory associations include better sleep, less fast-food eating, regular exercise, and job/work satisfaction that results in less work stress. As an example, connecting social enrichment to improved activities of daily living in those that are both frail and elderly was demonstrated in an observation study by Greaves and Farbus (see bibliography).

Also tied to social and spiritual well-being are reports showing improvement in immune function, with fewer colds, infections, and lost sick days from work. Other reports have linked social contentment to lower blood pressures and blood sugars, as well as reductions in blood markers of inflammation. Implied in these improvements in immune function are reductions in arterial-tree inflammation and dysfunction of capillary cells, with subsequent improvements to immune protection of end organs.

It becomes clear that having a mix of relationships with different textures of interpersonal exchange contributes to emotional and physical behaviors that protect against vascular inflammation and subsequently enhance endothelial vascular-tree function. With social/spiritual contentment, anti-inflammatory behaviors increase, vascular inflammation decreases, end-organ function improves, and aging is hazed.

Water

Water is essential for all life. It composes 48 percent of adult female body weight and 58 percent of adult male body weight. Because of its abundance in the human body and the loss that occurs through sweat and urination, water must be continuously replaced for optimal health. Of all the fluids that are available to drink, water is the most vascular anti-inflammatory. It should be as pure as possible, free of contaminants, excessive minerals, sugar, and/or engineered additives. Drinking water is optimal for capillary and end-organ cell health, with daily volume adjusted as needed, based on prevailing medical conditions and activity levels.

There is no consensus as to how much water to drink, and different medical conditions, body size, activity levels, and atmospheric conditions may require increased or decreased water intake. However, there is general agreement that at least 1,500 to 2,000 milliliters of water (six to nine 8-ounce glasses per day) should be consumed daily. This amount can easily double if working in hot dry conditions for extended periods of time. In general, people of smaller stature or who have preexisting heart, liver, or kidney disease should drink less water.

- When water intake is diminished over extended periods of time, the vascular system can become compromised. There can be significant changes in electrolytes and blood pressure, which can affect the capacity of the vascular system and capillary beds to support skeletal muscle. Generalized weakness and increases in mental confusion can result.

- Dehydration can occur, which, if mild, can be compensated by capillary cells of the skin sending signals to shift blood away from the skin and toward the internal organs in order to avoid loss of water and salt from perspiration through the epidermis (skin). The kidney nephron will also act to conserve intravascular fluid by concentrating the urine.

- In the elderly, and in those with chronic liver, kidney, and heart disease, or poorly controlled diabetes, complications from too much or too little water intake can occur quickly, as the endothelium of the skin and other end organs lack the capacity to adequately respond. Therefore, titration of water/ fluid intake must be more precise to compensate for diminished responses.

Other Fluids

Other fluids do not provide the health benefits that water does. In adults, and in moderation, coffee, grape juice, tea, and alcohol can provide vascular anti-inflammatory benefits, and are linked to preventing or improving different medical conditions. All of these drinks have risk, though. Caffeine can be addictive and may cause palpitations. Grape juice has large amounts of sugar and can make diabetes worse. Alcohol can also be addictive, may have adverse effects to peripheral nerves, and can increase the risk of some cancers. Being intentional about the amount of intake of these beverages becomes critical in managing vascular health.

Coffee and tea. Recent evidence suggests that drinking even one to two cups (12 to 16 ounces) of coffee before one in the afternoon can improve focus and concentration and likely has positive attributes to capillary endothelial cells. This intriguing relationship has been studied in Alzheimer's disease and is reported by Fillit and colleagues (see bibliography). If consumed over a period of years, there may be a protective effect to prevent dementia and neurodegenerative diseases, such as Parkinson's disease. On the other hand, drinking more than two cups per day may increase insomnia, tremors, anxiety, headaches, palpitations (heart rhythm disturbances), and high blood pressure. Caffeine can also act as a weak diuretic and increase urination, thereby increasing dehydration. Therefore, when dehydrated, caution must be used not to rely on iced tea or iced coffee. Adding sugar to coffee increases vascular inflammatory processes and contributes to the likelihood of overeating, weight gain, and blood-sugar elevations. Sugar substitutes, unfortunately, do the same thing.

The same can be said of tea. Drinking one or two cups of tea daily, particularly green tea, has antioxidant health benefits that affect immune health and translate into improved endothelial-cell function. Drinking more than two cups of tea daily, or adding sugar, can result in the same adverse health issues as drinking coffee.

Milk. Drinking milk has become a hotly debated topic in recent years. In those who are not lactose intolerant and do not have a milk allergy, drinking a glass or two (16 ounces) of milk daily provides protein as well as absorbable levels of calcium and vitamin D. Vitamin D is an essential vitamin that is required for numerous intracellular functions. With aging, vitamin D levels decrease, and bones become brittle. Drinking milk can help mitigate both conditions.

The problems with cow's milk centers around how it is pasteurized, what the cows were fed to produce milk, and what percentage of fat in milk is considered healthy. Milk quality is only as good as the quality of grain and grass the cows eats. Allergies and problems with milk digestion may be in part a problem with what cows are eating and how milk is pasteurized.

The bigger metabolic debate is how much fat in cow's milk is optimal. When fat is removed from milk, sugar calories, as a percentage of total calories in milk, increase substantially, and when absorbed, this results in a sugar rush to the liver. On the other hand, when fat is not removed from milk, the percentage of saturated fat that it contains is high, and this increases risk of weight gain and elevated LDL cholesterol and triglyceride levels. The compromise is to drink 1 to 2 percent (fat) milk, as this provides a better balance of protein, sugar, and fats, while decreasing the concentration of saturated fats per serving. Alternatives to pasteurized cow's milk are gaining momentum, but they are expensive and offer no proven additional benefits. Nevertheless, milk, no matter where it comes from, that has less saturated fat and sugar is preferred.

Fruit juices and colas. Fruit juices and colas are another popular choice, but they should be avoided. The packaging of these artificial drinks is disturbing, with many added preservatives designed to increase shelf life but with no health benefits. In the case of fruit juices, most have added sugar (particularly fructose) or have too much sugar per serving. These juices can worsen insulin resistance and diabetes, are addictive, and contribute to obesity. If possible, juice should be fresh squeezed (as in orange or grapefruit juice), with pulp included and in small quantities. Colas have the same problem as fruit juices, but in addition, have many more artificially added preservatives, which can act as free-radical poisons that produce even more inflammation and disrupt cellular function. Combinations of sugar, sugar substitutes, and preservatives in colas compound vascular inflammation at several different levels involving capillary-cell function; these beverages should be avoided. Neither colas nor highly processed fruit juices support healthy endothelial cells, and they contribute to diabetes, sugar addiction, obesity, and probably some cancers (pancreatic).

Alcohol. Alcoholic beverages must be used with caution. Besides contributing to addiction, alcohol, which is a simple sugar, can contribute to worsening diabetes. While consuming small amounts of alcohol could support endothelial- and capillary-cell function at some level, larger mounts do the opposite. In other words, alcohol has a very narrow therapeutic window of benefit that is easily crossed. Overimbibing does lead to accelerated vascular inflammation.

Anti-inflammatory vascular benefits of alcohol have been found to help brain and heart health when used in small quantities: 1 ounce of spirits, 3 ounces of red wine, 4 ounces of white wine, and one 10-ounce beer, daily for men and every other day for women. A balanced position paper on the risk and benefits of alcohol is reviewed by O'Keefe and colleagues (see bibliography). Implied in their discussion is that alcohol use can be dangerous due to addiction and tolerance of its effects with a tendency to drink more over time. Even when drinking in small quantities, there can be increased risk of falls, muscle weakness, adverse prescription-drug interactions, as well as digital (hand and foot) nerve numbness and muscle pain. In those with fatty liver or chronic hepatitis, any alcohol can make these conditions worse.

In summary, adequate daily fluid intake of pure water, supplemented with small amounts (8 to 16 ounces) of tea or coffee, makes good vascular anti-inflammatory sense. In adults, all other fluid intake must be viewed with discretion and understanding of risk and benefit. With advanced age, the window for imbibing other beverages is even narrower. As taste is acquired, drinking pure water becomes refreshing, and it satisfies thirst without side effects or adverse interactions. As up to 58 percent of our body composition is water, it only makes sense that it be replaced and not substituted by juices or colas.

Whole Foods

When I was a young boy our family took an annual summer trip to a small town in Iowa to visit my grandmother. We went by car, and after we arrived at Grandma's house and knocked on her door, she and the aromas coming from the kitchen would greet us. I came to identify these aromas as unique to Grandma, specific to how and what she cooked. That first Saturday night dinner after arrival was always imprinted on me. It was so tasty. We would sit together as a family, with grandma presiding, crowded around an old rectangular table, from the center of which all the aromas emanated. We ate the best food I have ever eaten, and it made the ten-hour trip well worth it.

Grandma would make most everything from scratch, from bread to biscuits, to casseroles and desserts. She also preserved fresh fruit and vegetables for winter storage, using tightly sealed jars with carefully measured concoctions of salt, sugar, vinegar, and water. She then stored these in her basement. My adventure in Grandma's house would start when she would ask me to go down the dark creaky narrow steps to her musty basement to find jars of preserved pickles, onions, plums, or tomatoes. As I went down the stairs, my imagination would run wild with every creak in the old stairway, but, eventually, with adrenaline pumping from being on high alert to the mysteries of the shadows in this dark place, I would find the labeled jars and quickly make my way back up the stairs. These trips to the basement at Grandma's house were the highlight of the vacation. I became intrigued by what I brought up from the basement. The preserved pickles and tomatoes tasted so good. Why did Grandma have a monopoly on making tomatoes, pickles, and plums taste better than what was available at home? The answer was complex but started with "advances" in processing and packaging.

Grandma's preserving methods were not passed on to my mother, as refrigerators and large multipurpose supermarkets with canned and prepackaged food became commonplace, replacing the much-smaller mom-and-pop corner markets in most neighborhoods. With rows of prepackaged and processed frozen and canned foods to choose from, the time-consuming processes of preserving fruits and vegetables became unnecessary to successive generations.

As the pace of life quickened, a quick trip to the grocery store for almost any prepackaged food item became the preferred method of obtaining perishables. Over time, larger supermarkets offered even more prepackaged and processed food. This food was cheap, easy to prepare, and often came with added salt, sugar, and other additives to enhance taste.

With more-extensive food processing, increased use of engineered chemical preservatives, as well as large amounts of white flour, salt, engineered sugars, and saturated fats, became widespread. Modern processing practices allowed for a longer shelf life, increased number of food choices, and cheaper production. Food company profit margins soared with the combination of longer shelf life and the increased demand for the addictive, heavily salted and sugared prepackaged food. The combination of salt, sugar, sugar substitutes, and chemical preservatives resulted in a tasty and highly profitable product line, but such food was also addictive and without other nutritional benefits. Consumption inevitably produced substantial increases in obesity, hypertension, and diabetes, while not supplying the vitamins, minerals, or fiber found in fresh produce.

In the early years of the food-processing industry, there was little concern about what the long-term impact of processed and refined food would have on health, let alone vascular health. Over the span of just one generation, these mass produced and chemically processed foods became the preferred way of eating most meals in most Western countries.

Fresh fruit, vegetables, water, and "whole food" were on their way out, as their short shelf life and the perception of time and work required to prepare them for meals made them a choice of last resort. Far more interesting to the mass public was the addicting quick fix of prepackaged salty, sugary foods and colas. A perfect storm of major risk factors for vascular inflammation and endothelial-cell dysfunction was set into place, and the general public was clueless.

In contrast to life as my grandma knew it, the faster pace of mobile living precluded interest in planting and tending to a vegetable garden, let alone preserving food through more natural techniques. What was overlooked, however, was that the processing techniques of food companies, in contrast to Grandma's methods, leached out valuable proteins, vitamins, complex carbohydrates, and fiber. They were replaced with engineered chemical preservatives and synthetic vitamins. With the intentional addition of excessive sugar and salt, habitual overeating occurred, and this was advertised as an innocent indulgence that we deserved. Obesity was not tied to salt and sugar, but, rather, to the consumption of fats. A vicious cycle of food addiction, weight gain, and sedentary lifestyle produced spirals of serious health complications, as capillary-cell function to all end organs became crippled. The seeds to an epidemic of stealthy vascular inflammation were sown.

What made matters worse were the other behaviors connected to eating highly processed fast food. Physical activity decreased, as interest in television and Internet surfing increased. Sleep habits worsened, and alcohol/drug/tobacco use increased. All of these behaviors worked together to cause more vascular inflammation. What becomes clear is that modern culture created a compilation of behaviors that release us from many of the routines of our ancestors that were beneficial to vascular health. They have been replaced with more leisure to do what we want. Much of what we do with this extra leisure time is destructive to the arteries and capillaries that tend to our end organs.

As consumer groups began to complain about the empty calories in prepackaged food, food-processing companies added back in engineered vitamins and minerals. In addition to vitamin- enriched white bread, baked goods, and cereal, widespread genetic engineering of fruit and vegetables occurred. The goal here was to create fruits and vegetables of greater size, with fewer seeds, more flesh, and thinner skins. These practices did little to enhance the food value of the created fruits and vegetables. Meanwhile, the preponderance of white flour meant breads with more sugar and less fiber per serving. Packaged cereals also had a tremendous amount of sugar and little fiber. All of these products required artificial vitamin enrichment.

At about the same time, livestock, poultry, and farm-grown fish were being mass produced in large production farms, receiving combinations of engineered growth stimulants, hormones, and other additives in their feed that would both hasten their growth and make the fish or animal larger, to result in the production of more meat at slaughter. Allowing animals to graze on open pastures quickly became a dinosaur, as evolving large agricultural companies emphasized speed of growth and volume of meat/ poultry/fish output. The effect of the modernization of packaged food was abundant, easily stored, cheaper food. What we now understand is that there are no short cuts to quality. The whole food that was grown, the meat and poultry that were raised, the fish that were caught in the smaller venues of previous generations were all of better quality. And the simple techniques of my grandmother produced better-tasting, higher-quality preserved food than those of the large processing companies.

My grandma's preserving process used simple ingredients, which included small amounts of salt, vinegar, herbs, and sugar in jars filled with water. In a small plot of ground (at most twenty by twenty feet), she grew corn, onions, tomatoes, squash, cabbage, cucumber, carrots, and other vegetable staples. A trellis over her kitchen window harbored a large grapevine. From that garden, she would eat fresh in the summer and fall, and preserve more than one hundred jars per year of what she could not eat or give away. Her simple methods preserved food value without chemicals, maintained taste, and did not leach out vitamins or fiber. Although the basement may not have been the perfect place to store her canned goods, I cannot recall anyone getting sick as a result of her preserving techniques or storage practices. For Grandma, gardening was just part of living, and the food produced an extension to her kitchen as well as tasty, healthy staples for the winter.

Modern processing techniques were devised as a method of making large volumes of food safe for human consumption, according to government standards, by eliminating bacteria, viruses, fungi, and toxins from the food, as well as preventing food from spoiling. Unfortunately, this resulted in grains, breads, snacks, and cereals that were leached of their fiber and vitamins and replaced with sugar or sugar substitutes (high-fructose corn syrup), salt, and chemical preservatives. This has led to a spiral of unanticipated consequences associated with overeating and other behaviors that increase vascular inflammation. Instead of making life better, the unintended consequences have caused an epidemic of metabolic diseases that have contributed to aging acceleration, not to mention the massive amount of money it costs to treat these conditions. We have paid a steep price for easy food fixes.

To clarify, *whole foods* are not manufactured, processed, or refined. They are fresh and grown from the ground, tree, or vine without toxic sprays, or growth stimulants. They contain the right (natural) mix of proteins, fats, complex carbohydrates, and sugars, as well as vitamins and minerals, to ensure optimal balancing of the body's metabolic machinery. Care should be taken when purchasing eggs, meat, poultry, and fish to understand the methods of how they were produced and raised. With appropriate diligence, we can purchase natural whole foods that can limit risks of processing and refining.

What my grandmother taught me also has some merit. Most of us have lost our desire to garden and grow our own food and then to more naturally preserve what is left over. I believe it is in our best interest to rekindle our knowledge of farming and grow some of our own food. This would entail understanding the processes for harvesting and preserving food naturally. Eating whole natural fruit, herbs, and vegetables produces cornerstone benefits to the arterial tree, the vascular endothelium, and the end organs they serve—plus, it smacks aging head-on.

Sugar

Most people who have tried to become healthier know that our food supply is inundated with sugar. As noted above, it is used in processing and preserving food, so we have an abundance of it. Because sugar is both addictive and limits the effectiveness of the brain's satiety center in the hypothalamus to sense feeling satisfied when eating, the result can be devastating for weight control and to vascular inflammation. How sugar and fat feeds back to the brain to affect appetite and increase risk for obesity is highlighted by Ahima and Antwi and extensively reviewed in a series of edited articles in *Neuropharmacology* by Heal, Smith, and Jones (see bibliography). When excessive sugar calories are consumed, feedback loops from the intestines create misguided cues to fool the brain's satiety center. With that thought in mind, it is worth understanding a little more of what we mean when we talk about "sugar," because it has many names.

Sugar is a simple carbohydrate which can be a *monosaccharide* or a *disaccharide.* Disaccharides are produced from combining two monosaccharides. For example, sucrose (table sugar) is a disaccharide produced from combining glucose and fructose. Lactose (the sugar in milk and dairy products) is a disaccharide that is made from galactose and glucose. Disaccharides like sucrose are easily converted to glucose, which is then reduced to pyruvic acid; this, along with fatty acids and ketone bodies, are utilized to make energy in all cells.

- Lactose is a disaccharide composed of glucose and galactose.

- It is found in milk and dairy products, and is a common ingredient for baked goods and infant foods. Galactose is also found in some pectins (fruit fiber) and is not as sweet as fructose or glucose.

- Maltose is a disaccharide composed of two glucose molecules. It is often used as a food additive.

- Sucrose (table sugar) is a disaccharide composed of glucose and fructose. It is processed and refined and is not found in nature. The concentration of refined sugar and its effects on metabolism make it dangerous.

- Fructose, a monosaccharide, has a very sweet taste, and so it has been used in food packaging as an additive to enhance sweet taste. It has also become a major ingredient in pastries and desserts. High-fructose corn syrup is a very common ingredient in food processing, and it has developed notoriety in recent years for contributing to addictive eating that has resulted in obesity and diabetes. In short, like sucrose, fructose can be very addictive.

Once ingested, the simple sugars, such as sucrose and fructose, are easily absorbed and surge to the liver. The pace of the surge can be stressful to the liver and pancreas, causing what is known as a *sugar rush*. This can cause a burst of energy and euphoria, but it can also produce headaches and palpitations, followed, a few hours later, by malaise and weakness (often from *hypoglycemia* [low blood sugar]). These symptoms occur from the surge of sugar pouring through the intestines, overwhelming capillary cells. It then enters the enterohepatic circulation, where it blindsides the capillary cells feeding the liver sinusoids. Liver cells are forced to ramp up metabolic processes to deal with the sugar surge. The pancreas is also stressed and throws out substantial amounts of insulin into the circulation to help the liver cells handle the surge. The large volume of sugar is processed in the liver quickly and converted into glycogen storage. A small amount is used for energy and protein synthesis, with the remainder packaged to fat cells, where it is stored as glycerol and eventually released into the circulation as fatty acids. The pace and volume of the sugar surge into the liver defines how much eventually goes to fat cells for storage.

With persistent and excessive surge of simple sugars into the liver, the capillary cells, followed by the liver hepatocytes, begin to lose their capacity to respond appropriately to the sugar blasts. This can result in "dumping" sugar directly onto liver hepatocytes. This barrage of sugar eventually exhausts the liver cells' capacity to effectively metabolize it, and they transform their metabolism and structure to become more like fat cells. This transformation increases insulin resistance, raises serum triglyceride levels, and diminishes the effectiveness of the liver cells to perform other processes. These changes can have the dangerous consequences of not only precipitating diabetes mellitus but also increasing blood LDL cholesterol and triglyceride levels. What follows is a spiral of vascular inflammation and capillary-cell dysfunction involving the entire arterial tree. These vascular inflammatory changes have been documented in numerous studies and are clearly demonstrated in a study by Stanhope and colleagues (see bibliography) on fructose corn syrup and its effects on glucose and lipids in young adults.

If this is not enough, persistent elevated blood sugar levels can act as free radicals. They can attach to proteins, without the benefit of an enzyme reaction, and damage them so that they can no longer function. This can occur in those eating diets that are high in refined sugars and/or in those who have diabetes. The process is called AGES (advanced glycation end products). Increased levels of AGES are thought to correlate with accelerated aging attributed to those who eat refined sugars and have diabetes. AGES disrupt all membrane surfaces of capillary and end-organ cells. In capillary cells, they block effective immune surveillance by preventing white blood cells access to the end organ. They decrease effective signaling and transport of nitric oxide into and out of the plasma and basement membranes. They increase membrane (plasma and basement) permeability, allowing entry of macromolecules that ordinarily would not have access into capillary-cell cytoplasm, and they increase ROS. All of these changes are proinflammatory and cripple capillary-cell function.

With persistent sugar surge and subsequent fat storage, the expansion of abdominal fat and girth occurs, and this has widely become known as a major risk factor for the metabolic syndrome, which becomes a perfect storm of vascular risk and subsequent vascular inflammation, diabetes, elevated lipids, hypertension, and obesity. With increasing capillary-cell dysfunction from inflammation, the function of the entire arterial tree withers, creating oxygen debt in energy-dependent organs such as the brain and heart. This is followed by the next wave of dysfunction involving the immune system, with corresponding reductions in capacity to fight infection. Autoimmune disease and cancer prevalence also increase.

Because of the effects sugar has on the body, it might seem that sugar substitutes are a good solution. But sugar substitutes are actually no better in limiting the consequences of increased sugar intake. Over the years, there have been a variety of false sugars that claim benefits of sugar-free eating while providing sweetened taste. The problem with sugar substitutes is that, like sugar itself, they confuse the brain's satiety center, as well as creating further addiction to and craving for sweets. Cravings for more food, particularly sweetened food, increases, and without appropriate feedback from the brain's satiety center about fullness, overeating (and not feeling or knowing it) becomes inevitable. It has become well known that those who drink diet colas actually gain more weight than those who drink the sugared varieties. The cravings for sugar and the desire for food increase with sugar substitutes.

Furthermore, there is no difference in adverse metabolic effects in sugar that is manufactured as compared to sugar that is raw (unprocessed) or natural sugar from sources such as honey, orange juice, or fruit juice. Sugar is sugar, no matter what the source or how it is processed. The risks increase commensurate with the volume ingested. Sugar intake perpetuates desire for more sugar.

In other words, sugar feeds an addiction that leads to serious vascular inflammation and then diabetes, obesity, and the metabolic syndrome. While natural fruit juices may have some vitamin benefit, the concentration of sugar from drinking them makes them risk adverse. The high-fructose corn syrup additive found in so many snack foods and desserts produces even more addiction because it is so sweet. The metabolic malignancy from all sugars cannot be overestimated, as all sugar leads to devastation of the arterial tree and capillary-cell function. The key to managing sugar's vascular inflammatory effects is limiting the quantity of simple sugars ingested and mixing small amounts of sugar intake with abundant complex carbohydrates, proteins, and fats.

Complex Carbohydrates

Complex carbohydrates provide the antidote to simple sugars and the malignant vascular inflammation they cause. Complex carbohydrates are found in most vegetables, ocean plankton, herbs, and the skins and pulp of fruit. Unlike simple sugars, complex carbohydrates can be used for energy purposes without "the urge to surge" that sugar causes.

By definition, complex carbohydrates are chemically more complex than sugars. Complex carbohydrates usually have many branches of carbon, hydrogen, and oxygen molecules, requiring multiple enzymes produced in the intestines and elsewhere to break them down to simpler forms. This results in a slower pace to the release of the smaller simple carbohydrates that can then trickle to the liver and integrate smoothly into the body's metabolic machinery. Think of vegetable fiber when visualizing complex carbohydrates.

Fresh vegetables produce the right mix of vitamins, minerals and antioxidants. The slower metabolism of complex carbohydrates produces a trickle of simple sugars to the liver. (see figure 9, in the appendix) This results in a steady processing and packaging of simple carbohydrates that can be used as energy to make proteins in the liver cells, or packaged as energy units (either glycogen or fatty acids) and mobilized to adipose tissue and other end organs in need of energy. It also eliminates blood sugar spikes and reduces LDL cholesterol and triglyceride production. Without these virulent proinflammatory molecules circulating in the blood, there is less stress on capillary cells throughout the vascular tree. That is, the ideal ratio of fatty acid to pyruvate (the glucose derivative) for energy production can be maintained, with less free- radical interference from LDL cholesterol, triglycerides, or other inflammatory residues.

In addition to optimizing the pace of metabolism, complex carbohydrates from fresh vegetables, herbs, and fruit include additional perks, with high concentrations of vitamins, minerals, antioxidants, and some protein. The antioxidants, which diminish in all cells with age, are vitally important in limiting free-radical exposure to capillary-endothelial-cell and end-organ intracellular function. Therefore, complex carbohydrates provide the correct pace of assimilating simple sugars, as well as antioxidant and mineral support that aging capillary cells need to surrogate end-organ function.

Eating a diet of vegetables, while also limiting simple-sugar intake, has many health benefits that extend beyond the capillary endothelium. Immediate clinical benefits involving all organ systems become obvious from the eyes to the brain, to the heart, kidneys, skeletal muscle, skin, and even the peripheral nerves. Clinical manifestations to this improvement include more energy, less pain, fewer infections, and lowered cancer risk.

When choosing vegetables to eat, with few exceptions, color becomes important. Stalks, leaves, and tubers that are darker in color generally have more essential vitamins, minerals, and antioxidants. For this purpose, purple, red, orange, and dark-green vegetables are better than pale-tan, or white ones. Fresh is always better than canned, frozen, dried, or packaged.

Fruit, in contrast to vegetables and herbs, has more simple- sugar content. Fruit has been eaten for thousands of years for various purposes, and it has also been used as a medicinal for prevention and treatment of infections. In the past hundred years, fruit has been eaten fresh, frozen, canned, dried, or processed. In the past sixty years, fruit has been canned, preserved, and fortified with numerous chemicals, engineered vitamins, and sugars. Additionally they have been genetically modified to increase the size and volume produced. Genetically modified fruit generally has more flesh volume, thinner skin covering it, fewer seeds, and more sugar (that is, it tastes sweeter). With large-scale worldwide production, which often includes genetically modified fruit as well as advancing chemical/refrigeration preservative techniques, fruit has become much more abundant, less expensive on a relative basis, and available year-round. Because of its abundance, coupled with advances that preserve shelf life, fruit has been successfully processed into pastries, cereals, yogurts, breads, candies, and desserts, including pies, cookies, and ice cream. To enhance sweetness, high-fructose corn syrup and other simple sugars, such as sorbitol and sugar alcohols, are also added.

Unfortunately, the genetic engineering of fruit for purposes of increasing size and harvest volume has had a downside, with net reductions in fiber and complex carbohydrate/simple sugar ratios. In other words, genetically engineered fruits have more sugar and less food value than their smaller natural counterparts. This can create sugar surges when ingested, which ultimately translate to higher blood sugars, LDL cholesterol, and triglycerides, as well as more vascular inflammation to all endothelia and capillary cells of the arterial tree. By genetically increasing the *mesocarp* (flesh) of the fruit and reducing the thickness of the exocarp (also known as *epicarp* [skin]), sugar volume from mesocarp increases, and the fiber, vitamin, and mineral benefit from the exocarp decreases. As the mesocarp-to-exocarp ratio increases, the nutritional benefit of fruit decreases. The effect of eating the larger genetically engineered fruit can result in more net sugar, and fewer vitamins, antioxidants, minerals, and fiber (complex carbohydrates). The vascular proinflammatory effects then follow. Genetically unmodified fruit is better, but knowing which fruit is modified and which is not cannot often be determined by simple inspection.

As with vegetables, darker-colored fruits usually harbor more vitamin, antioxidant, and mineral benefit. As a general rule, purple, orange, green, and red fruit can have more benefit than white, yellow, or pale fruit. Since the exocarp can be a great source of vitamins, minerals, fiber, and complex carbohydrates, fruit with higher exocarp-to-mesocarp ratios (smaller in diameter) should have more nutritional benefit. This would include most berries, figs, and grapes.

There are fruits, such as tomato and citrus, whose mesocarp contains a large volume of pulp. Like the epicarp, the pulp should not be discarded, as is contains fiber, complex carbohydrates, and other nutrients that help mitigate the sugar surge.

The seeds of most fruit should be avoided because of gastric upset and poisoning risks. However some seeds, like those from grapes, can have health benefits. Grape-seed extract has been used in naturopathic medicine to treat a variety of medical conditions. When in doubt, it is better to limit eating seeds from fruit.

In short, vegetables, herbs, and limited quantities of fruit (preferably not genetically modified) can limit vascular inflammation and produce health benefits. Together with abundant levels of complex carbohydrates, fiber, antioxidants, and some protein, fruit can serve as a cornerstone of capillary-cell health and the subsequent benefits that follow to end organs. In some cases, as in the bean group, fruit can also supply high-quality protein. In other cases, such as avocados, olives, nuts, and coconuts, fruit can supply oils which have vascular anti-inflammatory effects that further enhance capillary-cell function throughout the arterial tree. With genetically modified fruit, it would be appropriate to say, "Something gained is something lost."

Proteins and Monounsaturated Fats

Protein is the scaffolding support structure of all cells in the body; as such, it is an essential constituent in all diets. Protein comes from a variety of sources, but not all protein is created equal. Its value depends on the company it keeps, so to speak. Protein found in bacon, sausage, hotdogs, bratwurst, organ meats, bologna, salami, Spam, hamburger, and most red meat often contains high concentrations of saturated fat and is very vascular proinflammatory. In addition, these meats can have hormone additives, and are processed with preservatives and other chemicals that can contribute to capillary- cell stress at many different levels. When protein is associated with saturated fats, hormones, and preservatives, the table is set for vascular inflammation which can aggressively accelerate capillary cell decline.

Unlike simple sugars, for the most part, the calories consumed from fats and proteins do not trick the satiety center in the brain. By eating more fat and protein than sugar calories, dieting becomes easier, as the satiety center cannot be deceived in the way that it can be from sugar.

So what *does* constitute the best natural source of protein?

Bean and Nut Group

There are many sources of protein, but the clear choice is the bean and nut group.

Beans are not only a rich source of protein, but they are also high in antioxidants, complex carbohydrates (or fiber), calcium, and iron. Beans are best eaten fresh, but can also be stored or dried and packaged for a few months without losing too much of their nutritional value. Since purchasing fresh beans in some areas year-round can prove difficult, buying raw unprocessed beans, is an inexpensive way of obtaining high-quality protein, as well as a modicum of vitamins, minerals, and fiber, all with anti-inflammatory benefit to the capillary endothelium. Beans can easily be reconstituted in boiling water and used in a variety of ways. Mixing beans with fresh herbs, vinegar, and olive oil is tasty, and such ingredients produce value-added vascular anti-inflammatory health benefits to the arterial tree and capillary cells.

Raw beans should always be thoroughly washed and boiled for at least ten minutes prior to eating. Boiling beans does not cause excessive breakdown of proteins, and it eliminates possible poison risks, as chemicals in the uncooked bean may be converted to cyanide once digested.

In addition to supplying quality protein and antioxidants, beans also provide soluble fiber (fiber that can be metabolized to simple sugars, as opposed to insoluble fiber). Soluble carbohydrates are complex carbohydrates that can be metabolized to simple carbohydrates at a pace that the liver can use to make the right mix of energy units. Beans are not calorie dense in simple sugars and fat, they are also easily absorbed and digested, with their protein producing fewer allergy risks, as compared to eggs or nuts. Beans can, however, produce increased intestinal gas and abdominal pain. In spite of this, because of all the aggregate health benefits of the bean group, they can qualify as a super food.

Nuts are another excellent choice of protein for those that don't have allergic reactions to them. Like beans, they are composed of high-quality protein and contain higher concentrations of the vascular anti-inflammatory oils known as *omega-3 fatty acids.* Nuts also have higher concentrations of fiber and lower levels of simple sugars. Like beans, fresh, raw, unprocessed, and unsalted nuts also have high levels of antioxidants, as well as calcium, potassium, iron, and magnesium. Butternuts and walnuts have the highest concentration of the omega-3 fatty acids. The downside risk to nuts, in addition to fat calories, is that they can produce serious allergic reactions. Care must be taken to avoid this group when there is an allergic risk.

Allergy risk aside, a handful of mixed unsalted nuts daily can produce a quick and effective way to improve protein consumption with high-quality anti-inflammatory fats. There are two caveats that are important to remember. First, nuts do have a significant amount of fat in them, albeit the more vascular healthy omega-3 fatty acid. Nevertheless, calories do mount up when eating nuts. Consistently eating too many of them will cause weight gain and increase insulin resistance, in effect defeating their vascular anti- inflammatory effects. Second, nuts are usually packaged with salt and roasted to enhance flavor and lengthen shelf life. Too much salt may increase blood pressure and fluid retention, and if sustained, can lead to other vascular inflammatory residuals. Because of these issues, the nut-group serving size must be managed with intention, and if possible, purchased without added salt.

Seeds can also be a valuable source of protein and a quality snack food. Flaxseed and chia seeds have very high concentrations of omega-3 fatty acids (the good fats) as well as quality protein. Pumpkin and sunflower seeds are also plentiful and can be another useful source of protein. Like nuts, seeds are usually packaged with salt and therefore need to be eaten in smaller quantities when salt is added.

Seeds, like beans, can be used in a variety of contexts, including casseroles, salads, and dips, in combination with herbs, to produce a rich flavor and add nutritional value. When mixed with herbs, olive oil, avocado, and vinegar the emerging flavors negate the adage that "If it is good for you, it can't taste good."

Other Good Protein Sources

Vegetables are not always void of protein. Fresh or just lightly cooked asparagus, cauliflower, soy, spinach, broccoli, and quinoa offer small quantities of digestible protein. When coupled with fresh herbal dressings, seeds, beans, or nuts, concocting the right recipe for powerful antiaging, anti-inflammatory vascular benefits has begun.

Dairy and eggs are other sources of high-quality protein that, when used in moderation and in the right context, could have capillary anti-inflammatory benefit. Fats in the dairy and egg group generally lack the omega-3 fatty acids (unless fortified) and monounsaturated oils, and they can have more cholesterol. Although the quality of the protein is of high value and easily digestible, allergic reactions have been known to occur. In addition, many adults are lactose intolerant. (As mentioned, lactose, a disaccharide sugar found in milk and dairy products, can cause abdominal pain, bloating, and diarrhea.) On the other hand, cheese, yogurt, and eggs do not contain as much salt as roasted, salted nuts, and the fats in such dairy products, although often saturated, are not as vascular inflammatory as those in processed foods. Additionally, cheese and eggs have very little sugar and do not adversely affect insulin resistance, unless consumed in large quantities. Like the nut group, the cheese and egg group should only be eaten in modest quantities, as too many fat calories can produce weight gain, higher LDL cholesterol levels, insulin resistance, and obesity.

Fish like tuna, sardines, mackerel, and salmon are rich in omega-3 fatty acids, and are considered super foods for their anti- inflammatory effects to the capillary endothelium and the vascular tree. Unfortunately, these fish can accumulate mercury in their flesh and should be eaten in limited quantities; perhaps one pound a week or less. In addition, tuna and sardines are often packaged in aluminum cans which, along with preservative chemicals, can leech into the canned fish, creating the potential of additional toxicity if consumed in large quantities. In general, it's best to limit all canned food, and canned fish specifically, to one can per week or less, and eat fresh over canned fish whenever possible. Mercury, a trace metal that is found in wild fish, can accumulate in the body to produce a toxic-metal health risk. This becomes the primary reason to limit the quantity of fish consumed. It is best to be careful, as the world's seas become increasingly polluted with nuclear waste and river runoff from industrialization and population growth. Engineered and farm-fed salmon and other fish have their own set of risks, including pesticides that leach into the water where they are bred, and hidden additives or growth stimulants in their food to hasten maturity and increase size.

Skinless poultry provides a good source of protein, as compared to that of red meats, as it does not have the same quantity of inflammatory saturated fat, making skinless poultry less vascular inflammatory than red meat. If baked or broiled and eaten skinless, poultry can be an excellent source of high-quality protein without too much allergic risk. The downside of most packaged store- bought chicken is what could be hidden in the meat. Poultry is rarely fed on the open range in today's high-production farms. In addition to the chickens not seeing the light of day, the chicken feed may contain growth inducers (hormones) to increase their size more quickly. Unless the chicken is organically fed (no hormone or growth inducers) and free range (allowed to graze on open pasture), which is more expensive to purchase, it should be eaten in smaller quantities to limit these potential hidden toxicities.

In spite of government intervention, ensuring safe poultry and red meat can be difficult to gauge. Government agencies like the FDA have an enormous responsibility to ensure the public safety by monitoring methods of inducing artificial growth in livestock. Unfortunately, it sometimes takes decades to fully understand the adverse health implications of certain growth inducers to farm- raised fish, meat, and poultry.

Wild animal or bird meat—that is, meat coming from deer, rabbit, squirrel, antelope, buffalo, caribou, sheep, or pheasant—generally has less fat content. and therefore carries less vascular inflammatory risk to the endothelium of the arterial tree, as compared to farm- raised livestock. Besides having less fat content, the other advantage to the protein of these birds and animals is how they live and what they feed on. The natural feeding and grazing practices of wild animals and birds, providing their habitats are not polluted, result in a better mix of nutrients, making the meat less likely to have insecticides, hormones, or heavy-metal toxicity.

In summary, vegetable, bean, nut, and seed sources of protein offer superior health benefits to the vascular endothelium, as they are net vascular anti-inflammatory. Protein from fish that are high in omega-3 fatty acids is also beneficial, but quantity must be carefully monitored because of mercury poisoning and other exposures. Eggs, cheese, and other dairy products, when eaten modestly (four to six eggs and one-half pound of cheese per week) can also provide additional sources of high-quality protein while at the same time limiting sugar intake. Free-range poultry and wild animal meat, as compared to farm-raised livestock, although more expensive, have less total fat, less exposure to growth additives, and are a good source of high-quality protein. When these sources of protein are coupled with herbal accents and fresh vegetables of dark color, capillary endothelial-cell health is nurtured, end-organ health is facilitated, and antiaging benefits are accrued.

Conclusion

Lifestyle choices can make or break vascular inflammatory risk and capillary-cell health. When done in aggregate over time, the benefits can be substantial in terms of reducing vascular inflammation and improving end-organ health. The process can start with a modest daily exercise program and can gather momentum as the motivation to pursue other lifestyle changes increases. Making behavioral changes can be difficult, and there will be false starts and some failure. The point is that it is a process, with the most important tool being the awareness that behavioral choices are either pro- or anti- inflammatory to the vascular tree. That said, it is never too late to start making adjustments to improve capillary- and endothelial-cell health. With middle age and beyond, it can be anticipated that additional medicinal and supplement help will be required to haze aging and mitigate vascular inflammation.

The next chapter will explore different modalities that fine- tune further improvement in vascular health to "seal the deal" in managing vascular inflammatory risk.

8

Pharmaceuticals

Over the last seventy years, modern science has engineered many medications that have plant origins. Some have produced epic changes in the landscape of health care. Most of the important advances in medicines have, in some way and unbeknownst to the researcher, stabilized or improved capillary-endothelial-cell function. These interventions have either improved in some fashion capillary-cell free-radical profiles, metabolism, blood flow, and clotting pathology, or have enhanced capillary- cell immune function. Some, like antibiotics, immune suppressants, and chemotherapy, have facilitated important immune support to assist the vascular endothelium in combating situations that have gotten out of control, such as serious infections, autoimmune disease, and cancer.

In this section, we will not focus on urgent, out-of-control conditions that require antibiotics, immune suppressants, or chemotherapy, but, rather, on more subtle treatments that nurture the capillary cells, which then enhance vascular anti-inflammatory benefits. These treatments, because they are less invasive, can be viewed as less harsh, and they can facilitate both treatment and prevention of illness without the side effects of more invasive interventions. In the future, there will be several more classes of treatment developed that will focus on blocking or augmenting specific cellular receptors to preempt and treat disease. One thing is clear: for medicines to be effective to both treat and prevent disease, as well as limit aging, the science must go through the capillary cells to harness what is "best of breed" in the blood in order to create next-level benefits to the end organ.

When discussing prevention and treatment of inflammation and how it relates to endothelial-cell function, all medications and supplements used in treatment have potential indications, risks, benefits, and side effects. These must be weighed carefully in aggregate before use. At times, medications and some supplements can work better when combined with others to synergize their effect. As such, the integration of medications and supplements into a health plan should be treated with respect, used judiciously, and monitored closely by a health-care provider. Over time, dosing may change, while some treatments are started and others are stopped. These changes can be dependent on the health dynamics of a given individual, changes in science information, and/or a better understanding of risk and benefits. Given for the right reasons and at the right time, medications and supplements can be lifesaving and result in substantial benefit to the vascular endothelium.

In spite of all of the science behind them, dosing of medicines and supplements can be more of an art. Even in the most experienced hands, getting the right dose can be challenging when taking into consideration age, body habitus, genetics, other medications and supplements, and the functioning of the heart, liver, lungs, and kidneys. Taking too much medicine can produce toxicity and untoward side effects. Taking too little may produce negligible benefit (if any) in either prevention or treatment of disease.

With all of this in mind, let's embark on the journey to explore the benefits of optimizing endothelial-cell function through medicinals, and how this benefits the arterial tree, the capillary cells, and then the end organs they serve.

Aspirin

Aspirin has been used and prescribed for more than a hundred years to treat fever and pain. In the last thirty-six years, its role has expanded as a modifier to vascular inflammation. When taken at a daily dose of 81 milligrams (baby aspirin) to 325 milligrams (adult aspirin), the blood becomes "thin" and clots less easily.

The mechanism of daily aspirin intake involves preventing *platelets,* cells made in the bone marrow and found in the blood plasma, from adhering to endothelial-cell membranes in areas where they are damaged or inflamed. This blocks a cascade of inflammatory mediators, which makes the inflammation worse, eventually producing a *thrombosis* (clot) that occludes the blood vessel and cuts off circulation upstream. When blood stops flowing through the vessel, capillary and end-organ cells lose nutrient and oxygen support. For end organs and capillary cells that have high- energy requirements such as the brain or heart, quick death can occur to the affected cells. The lumen bore of the blood vessel affected, and its strategic location, will often determine the extent of end-organ damage from occlusion.

In some cases, a cluster of occlusions from smaller arteries can have the same net effect as an occlusion from a single larger- bored vessel. Therefore, as a clot forms, the capillary-cell function upstream from the clot and blood cutoff can deteriorate, leading to cascades of acute inflammatory breach, culminating in a chunk of end-organ death. This becomes a very serious matter, as a result of the accumulative effects of decreased blood flow and the subsequent progressive loss of end-organ function. At a critical point, end organs can only do so much with a limited blood supply, and then they fail.

In some cases, small-vessel occlusions are silent, in that they don't produce clinical symptoms. But these occlusions can aggregate and be just as lethal as one large-vessel occlusion. This can be seen in vascular dementia, where the aggregate accumulation of tiny subclinical strokes produces major deficits in cognition. For these reasons, it has become common practice to prescribe a dose of one baby aspirin (and is some cases more) to those over age fifty, in order to prevent the increased risk of vascular clots in both large and small arterial vessels.

If taken regularly over time, the benefits of aspirin can be substantial. All causes of vascular morbidity (complications from vascular clotting events) and mortality (death from vascular clotting events) are decreased by about one-third. This translates into fewer TIAs (transient ischemic strokes) to the brain, reduced episodes of angina (heart pain), and fewer heart attacks. Mitigating ministrokes (TIAs) and recurrent heart pain or heart attack results in the individual being able to live independently for a longer time, as such mitigation limits fatigue, shortness of breath, and decreased cognitive function.

Put in another way, by "thinning" the blood, aspirin limits inflammatory occlusive damage from preexisting large-vessel arterial vascular disease. By doing so, the capillary cells upstream are allowed to accommodate to reduced blood flow caused by the preexisting plaque, rather than die from blood-flow cutoff. End- organ function is subsequently preserved.

Taking a baby aspirin daily supports endothelial-cell health along the entire vascular tree; therefore, every end organ stands to benefit. A second important benefit of aspirin occurs directly in the smaller blood vessels. Preventing platelets from adhering to exposed inflammatory surfaces can limit the disruption of the highly active and permeable membranes that are pivotal to their function.

Additional proof of benefit can be seen in how aspirin affects capillary immune surveillance. Taking a baby aspirin over a period of years has recently been shown to reduce cancer's incidence. This would only make sense, as improving plasma and basement membrane permeability would also improve the capacity of the capillary cells to affect white blood cell and immune proteins trafficking from the blood to the end organ, which in turn would remove cancer cells. Maintaining selective membrane permeability is complex and involves input from the capillary-cell mitochondria. Aspirin assists in this function by mitigating adherence of platelets to free radicals on these membranes, thereby preventing the cascades of inflammation that follow. With improvement in membrane permeability, other immune-surveillance improvements involving infectious agents and particulates may also occur.

Aspirin has many FDA-approved indications, including the treatment of pain, fever, and arthritis, as well as the reduction of vascular risk of heart attack and stroke in those with preexisting vascular disease or at high risk for vascular-related events. Aspirin can cause bleeding in those who take other blood thinners, have peptic ulcer disease, low platelet counts, significant liver or kidney disease, and/or are being treated for cancer with chemotherapy. Therefore, aspirin must be used with caution and with the help of a health-care provider. With these attendant risks mitigated, and when taken on a regular basis, aspirin provides benchmark improvements in all causes of vascular inflammatory risk and is a cornerstone therapy for the management and prevention of vascular inflammatory disease. As such, it becomes a protector of capillary-cell function and a limiter of end-organ decline.

Statins

The statin group of medications, also known as *HMG-CoA reductase inhibitors,* have been prescribed for thirty years for the treatment of elevated blood LDL cholesterol (the highly vascular inflammatory cholesterol). The naturally occurring statin is found in red rice yeast, which has been used in Chinese medicine, possibly for centuries, for a variety of vascular and medically related purposes.

For quite some time it has been known that cholesterol and its constituent molecules are directly related to the processes of arteriosclerotic vascular disease (hardening and narrowing of the arteries), initiated from cholesterol-rich plaque formation. Since the initial indication for statin use in LDL cholesterol management, with the FDA approval of lovastatin in the 1980s, research has led to additional statins that can produce even more-aggressive lowering of LDL cholesterol, in order to further limit its potent vascular inflammatory effects on the vascular-tree endothelium.

As mentioned in the previous chapter, there are different types of cholesterols and inflammatory fats: HDL, LDL, and triglycerides are the primary culprits, and all three elements are managed as part of overall cholesterol management. Current guidelines call for statins to lower LDL cholesterol to less than 100 mg/dL in patients who have vascular risk (just about everyone over age fifty in Western culture), and less than 70 mg/dL in those who have proven vascular disease, such as heart coronary bypass surgery, carotid artery surgery/stent(s), vascular surgery/stent(s) in arteries to the legs, or coronary artery stent(s) in the heart. It is also recommended that statins be used in adult-onset diabetics. Getting patients to LDL goal has proved difficult for a variety of reasons, often associated with the muscle pain and weakness that can develop as a result of increasing doses of statin medications. Sometimes these side effects can be mitigated by switching to another statin or adding a supplement called *coenzyme* Q_{10} (CoQ_{10}).

Most recent guidelines support statin treatment for primary prevention of vascular disease when coupled with another vascular risk factor, such as hypertension. At the same time, there is less requirement for precise LDL cholesterol reductions, particularly if treatment goals cannot be met due to side effects. It turns out that even some treatment to reduce LDL cholesterol and vascular inflammation is better than none, even when the LDL cholesterol cannot be lowered aggressively. With newer LDL cholesterol–lowering medications on the horizon, it is not likely that anyone should be left behind in managing LDL cholesterol risk.

HDL (good) cholesterol management is more difficult, particularly for those with very low HDL cholesterol, which is considered to be another serious risk factor for vascular inflammation. High concentrations of the larger-particle HDL cholesterol provide endothelial cell support to decrease inflammation on capillary-cell membranes and intercellular apparatus. Most statin medications have little if any effect on HDL cholesterol levels, which can make low HDL cholesterol management even more frustrating. It is generally accepted that HDL cholesterol levels should optimally be 50 mg/dL or higher in order to mitigate vascular inflammatory risk. To raise HDL cholesterol levels significantly can require a combination of treatments, including regular aerobic exercise, certain statins or niacin, and small amounts of daily alcohol and garlic extracts. Implementing two to three of these strategies, with regular aerobic exercise as the cornerstone, can increase HDL cholesterol to acceptable levels. However, in terms of mitigating vascular inflammatory risk, raising HDL levels has not been shown to be as effective as lowering LDL levels.

Serum triglycerides, another vascular inflammatory fat, although generally not affected by statins, can often be decreased by multipronged strategies. These include reductions of sugar and saturated fat in the diet, weight reduction, treating thyroid hormone deficiency, regular exercise, taking omega-3 fish oils, and lowering HGBA1C (a blood marker indicative of diabetes control) levels in the blood to 6.5 or less. For additional benefit and to lower serum triglycerides to at least 150 mg/dL, niacin and oral fibrates (another group of blood-fat-lowering medications specific for triglyceride lowering) can be added. Combining treatments can serve the purpose of initiating discussions about primary prevention involving lifestyle changes that would advocate for improved vascular anti-inflammatory living. Using multiple medical strategies to lower serum fats always requires close supervision by a knowledgeable primary-care provider in order to assess for safety and risk of different treatment strategies. Care must be maintained in implementing these strategies, as they can become complex and increase risk for drug and supplement interactions. In the scheme of things, the best practice to prevent vascular inflammation would be to lower LDL cholesterol first, improve diabetes management if present, and then consider additional treatment for triglyceride lowering if necessary.

In the next several years, there will be further refinement in cholesterol management, as optimal levels of the different cholesterols become better understood. With the development of lovastatin and then several other more potent statins, the group as a whole, together with accompanying the research, has produced a seismic shift in the capacity to understand and control vascular inflammation. Because of this group and the positive clinical effects it has created, the landscape of vascular inflammatory reversal, the beneficial effects on capillary endothelial-cell health, and the potential to mitigate the aging process all have been realized.

The statin group of medications reduces LDL (bad) cholesterol through blocking its synthesis in the liver. Statins can be fat- or water-soluble. This is an important differentiation, as some statins, depending on their solubility, can produce side effects to the brain, eye, lungs, and/or skeletal muscle.

Simply put, statins reduce vascular inflammation and improve endothelial-cell function by decreasing the concentration of the small free-radical LDL particles at all levels of the arterial tree. By reducing this potent free radical of vascular inflammation, statins have been found to be a reliable intervention in stabilizing the complex functioning of endothelial-cell membranes. Below are several statin benefits to improved capillary-cell membrane function:

- Maintaining appropriate relationships between capillary cells and red blood cells, white blood cells, clotting factors, the immune system, blood proteins, and the complex signaling that capillary cells coordinate with end organs. Benefits could include reductions in cancer and infection risk. Research is trending to show decreased rates of several cancers when taking statins for several years.

- If LDL cholesterol is lowered to 70 mg/dL or less, and is coupled with other vascular anti-inflammatory interventions, some studies suggest that soft-plaque reversal and subsequent capillary-cell recovery can ultimately restore the function of end organs, including the heart and brain.

- Besides reducing stroke and heart attack occurrence, death rates from all causes have decreased, by conservative estimates, as much as 30 percent. Because of stroke and heart attack reduction, people are living not just longer but better, maintaining independence, performing activities of daily living, and requiring fewer invasive vascular interventions. Being productive and maintaining independence into advanced age is now a reachable goal, based on research pioneered by understanding the vascular anti-inflammatory benefits of such medicines as statins.

- Kidney function can improve on statin therapy. Serum creatinine levels stabilize, and can sometimes improve, indicating preservation of kidney function. These reductions in creatinine can often be associated with lower blood pressure.

- It is likely that with improved capillary and small-arteriole vascular membrane function from less free-radical LDL cholesterol, the net production and release of more nitric oxide occurs. This results in smooth-muscle relaxation in the walls of the arterial tree, dilation of their lumens, and reductions in the pressure flowing through them. The return of more-normal nitric oxide levels has an added benefit, seen clinically with reductions in blood pressure, that would then further result in a reductions in vascular events, such as heart attacks and strokes (and hence vascular dementia), as well as improved kidney, lung, and skeletal-muscle function.

- Leg skeletal muscles can demonstrate improved capacity to exercise.

- In the lungs, statins can decrease asthma and emphysema exacerbations, suggesting immune benefits to bronchial and alveolar capillary cells.

As mentioned, longer-term use of statins can have positive effects on reducing incidence of cancer. Preliminary evidence suggests the benefits of statins in reducing colon and prostate cancer. There has also been an association of statin use with reductions in malignant tumors of the esophagus, lung, and kidney. Taken together, there is accumulating evidence to suggest a statin benefit in preventing several types of cancers. It is likely that autoimmune diseases will see similar benefits from statins as well.

It is interesting to speculate how this beneficial effect may be developing. It is likely that capillary-cell immune-surveillance signaling has been stabilized through minimizing the inflammatory effects of free-radical LDL cholesterol molecules on capillary-cell membranes and intracellular organelles, thereby biasing outer membrane permeability toward more-normal functioning. This would result not only in improved nitric oxide transmission, but also in restoring the capacity of capillary cells to receive and send signals from multiple sources that would attract specific white blood cells to adhere to capillary membranes, and then seek and destroy abnormal tumor cells before they begin to multiply uncontrollably. It is also quite possible that statins facilitate additional surveillance mechanisms of immune enhancement that reside deep in the capillary-cell infrastructure, involving the functions of mitochondria and other organelles. Although these mechanisms are not well understood, it is likely that statins stabilize the function of capillary and end-organ cell membranes in any location where LDL cholesterol can attach and initiate inflammation.

When taken over a period of months to years, statins may also contribute to reductions in blood pressure, resulting in fewer pills needed for blood-pressure control. Since capillary-cell function improves throughout the vascular tree when taking statins, improvements can be expected in a host of chronic and progressive diseases—although these effects may be subtle and sometimes difficult to demonstrate clinically. Besides showing improvement in bronchial asthma, there are associations between taking statins and limiting the onset or progression of *Parkinson's disease,* a movement disorder involving increased resting tremor, generalized rigidity, and, often, association with dementia. There may also be benefits in reducing the progression of *multiple sclerosis* (MS), a chronic and progressive brain autoimmune disease. These relationships are preliminary but expected, based on the expanding role statins have in positively affecting capillary-cell membrane permeability. The seeds of hope have been planted for cause and effect in the relationship between preserving capillary-cell function and minimizing/preventing many different types of disease, including the prevalence of neurodegenerative diseases, which, along with the dementias, increase in frequency with the insidious progression of vascular inflammation.

Statins, like aspirin, can have nagging side effects that, in some cases, are serious. With aspirin, intestinal and stomach bleeding can be the most serious risk of long-term use. With statins, the most serious risk is the breakdown of skeletal muscle, called *rhabdomyolysis,* which can cause muscle pain and weakness that can lead to kidney failure. Concerns for this serious side effect must always be considered when patients complain of muscle pains while taking statins. Diagnosis is supported by withdrawal of the statin medication and checking for elevation of an enzyme in the blood called CPK (*creatine phosphokinase*). In less severe cases of muscle soreness without elevations of CPK, symptoms can be mitigated by either changing to another statin or adding CoQ10. When taken with a statin, CoQ_{10} can substantially reduce mild muscle achiness and fatigue.

In addition, alcohol intake should be limited, as combining a statin and alcohol may increase muscle pain and adversely affect liver function. Sugar intake should also be decreased, as there is a correlation of taking statins and increasing insulin resistance, which can lead to diabetes. This last recommendation is one I give to all patients over age fifty anyway, regardless of statin use, because of the substantial vascular inflammatory effects that simple sugars have on the arterial tree. Habitual sugar use should be addressed as early as possible in order to mitigate the addictive sugar dependency and it consequences of increasing both LDL cholesterol and blood sugars in midlife.

Statins have FDA-approved indications in preventing further vascular inflammatory disease progression involving several different disease states and end organs. Because of dose-related side effects that can include muscle pain and weakness, monitoring of symptoms, CPK, and liver function must occur on a regular basis. When taken consistently, statins produce major health benefits through mitigating vascular inflammation by optimizing endothelial-cell function throughout the arterial tree. Statins, aspirin, regular exercise, and reductions of dietary sugar and trans- and saturated fats, together, provide four of the proven cornerstones to manage vascular inflammatory risk and enhance endothelial-cell function. All vascular anti-inflammatory treatments should build on these cornerstones.

ACEs and ARBs

Angiotensin converting enzyme inhibitors (ACEs) and *angiotensin receptor blockers* (ARBs) are true laboratory success stories. These two groups of medications reduce blood levels of *angiotensin II,* a substance that causes smooth-muscle contraction and subsequent restriction of lumen diameter of all arterial vessels, which raises blood pressure, often to dangerous levels.

Angiotensin II is a naturally occurring molecule that requires integrated signaling from endothelial and epithelial cells in the kidney, liver, and lung. In the renin-angiotensin system, angiotensin regulates blood pressure, with its bias toward increasing it. Three end organs and their epithelial cells participate in a feedback loop that results in the production of angiotensin II. Endothelial cells facilitate angiotensin II production and circulation.

The angiotensin converting enzyme inhibitors (ACE) and angiotensin receptor blockers (ARB) were developed to block the production and vascular effects of angiotensin II, thereby reducing blood pressure, which then decreases the resistance the heart muscle contracts against. Doing this has repercussions that mitigate inflammatory influences which increased blood pressures produce on all other end organs, with particular reference to the kidney nephron. These ramifications involve reduced shear inflammation, increased nitric oxide levels, restored osmotic/oncotic pressure balances, as well as improved endothelial and capillary-cell membrane permeability—all by mechanisms completely different from statins or aspirin. This further potentiates the vascular anti-inflammatory effects of this group when added to aspirin and statins.

With aging and aggregate vascular inflammatory risk, the body produces too much angiotensin II, thereby elevating blood pressure. The elevations in blood pressure cause shear damage and subsequent narrowing of large arteries. Blood-flow volume can be subsequently reduced upstream through capillaries, which then adversely affects end-organ function. As has been discussed, when vascular inflammation reduces blood flow through large arteries, capillary cells can only go so far to mitigate these influences before end-organ function suffers. End-organ cells with high-oxygen/nutrient requirements, such as the brain, will suffer the most. Sustained vasoconstriction of blood flow from increased angiotensin II, with few exceptions, does not optimize endothelial function at any level.

These untimely events that lead to progressive arterial-tree vasoconstriction are exactly what the aging body does not need, as it puts in place mechanisms that further accelerate vascular inflammation and end-organ decline. Sustained elevations in angiotensin II, and its subsequent effects on blood pressure, can eventually lead to strokes, lethal heart arrhythmias, heart attacks, heart failure, kidney failure, and premature death.

The major pathology of sustained shear stress from sustained increases in angiotensin II concentrations is diffuse endothelial-cell-membrane thickening, followed by plaque development. Reductions in blood flow from large-vessel vascular disease set in motion the signals in the liver, lungs, and kidneys to increase angiotensin II even further, so that the process becomes self-perpetuating. At some level, without intervention, vascular inflammation accelerates, and end-organ catastrophe from capillary-cell failure is inevitable.

During the process of self-perpetuated increases in angiotensin II, the endothelia of smaller arteries and capillaries eventually recognize that facilitating angiotensin II production is not helping to solve blood-flow problems. They then evoke plan B, forming new capillaries through the production of VEGF (vasoactive endothelial growth factor) and other growth factors, in an effort to improve blood flow to end organs. This attempt has no lasting chance of success, as the larger arteries, because of membrane thickening and plaque development, cannot support the newly formed blood vessels with increased blood supply. At a critical point, capillary cells cannot compensate for progressive large-vessel narrowing downstream. As capillary-cell function slides, all of the added-on value and support they provide to the end organs slides as well. Reductions in immune surveillance contribute to more infections and cancer risk.

As an example, think of arterial blood flow as a river and vascular plaque as a dam, the flow of water upstream to where the dam was built is now obstructed. The reduced water flow behind the dam causes vegetation to dry up, impacting all the flora and fauna, and thereby changing the ecology. The same is true with large-vessel vascular plaque and its effects on capillary cells upstream to it. As blood supply decreases, the rich "ecological diversity" of end-organ function dries up, and aging dominos fall into place.

Enter the ACEs and ARBs. By blocking the expression of angiotensin II in those with preexisting large-vessel vascular disease and hypertension, they prevent the cascade that perpetuates higher blood pressures. When the cycle is broken, lower blood pressures result. Even though the angiotensin II cycle is broken, capillary cells must still adapt to fixed reductions in blood flow from large-vessel inflammatory narrowing downstream. This can be vexing in the brain, as nerve cells have a fixed demand for high levels of oxygen. The process of capillary-cell adaption to fixed reductions in blood flow from large-vessel plaque downstream is called *accommodation.*

Accommodation, by necessity, requires some down regulation in the capillary cells' ability to perform all of their integrative operations. This allows the capillary cells to perform at a reduced but still effective level.

Accommodation by capillary cells, from reduced blood flow to them, has been facilitated through the evolution of their mitochondria. Since about 90 percent of capillary-cell energy is produced anaerobically (does not require oxygen) in the cytoplasm, moderate reductions in blood flow, and subsequent reductions in oxygen delivery to the capillary cell, do not impact capillary membranes and intercellular function. Also, since the mitochondria are not required to make large shifts in energy production in order for capillary cells to function, they can facilitate effective feedback loops that control membrane and organelle function. If the mitochondria were required to make the most of the capillary cell's energy, not only would the cells' capacity to perform decrease with reductions in blood flow, but also the multiple feedback loops that mitochondria control would be lost as a result of wider fluctuations in energy output.

Instead, with modest oxygen and reduced blood volumes, capillary cells can still adjust and perform well. The impact of decreased oxygen from reduced blood flow is felt primarily in end organs of high-energy requirements, such as the brain, heart, and working skeletal muscle. Stabilizing the adverse effects of excessive angiotensin II limits spirals of increasing vascular inflammation caused by sustained blood-pressure elevations with subsequent reductions in blood flow and oxygen support to these oxygen-dependent end organs.

ARBs were developed in part due to the side-effect profile of ACEs, which often cause a dry hacking cough, and in a few cases, serious edema of the face and throat. Both classes of medication have similar net effects on the renin-angiotensin system in terms of controlling high blood pressure, even though they should not be used in combination, as their benefits are not additive.

Both classes of medication produce reductions in all causes of morbidity and mortality of cardiovascular events. Treatment with these medications can reduce vascular events by as much as 30 percent, with subsequent reduction in hospitalizations for heart attack or failure, kidney failure, or stroke. Additional improvements in kidney protection are seen when used in patients with diabetes mellitus. In this setting, capillary-cell function in the kidney glomerulus improves, and less protein is lost in the urine. In addition, using ARBs to treat hypertension can reduce vascular dementia. So far, long-term studies have not shown the same benefits to immune surveillance and cancer reduction as are seen in the statin group. The implication is that the ACE/ARB groups have only an indirect effect on capillary-cell function, with most benefits coming from larger-vessel-related lowering of blood pressure.

Is there any benefit to using low doses of ACEs or ARBs to prevent high blood pressure? This intriguing question is the beginning of a paradigm shift in addressing prevention of vascular inflammation before it establishes a foothold. This question and others like it represent next-level thinking in research to anticipate inflammatory risk before it becomes established.

ACEs and ARBs are not without risk or side effects, and should always be monitored with the help of a knowledgeable primary- care provider. Dosing adjustments can occur as blood pressure requirements change. Blood work should be done at regular intervals to check kidney function and electrolytes.

In summary, ACEs and ARBs can produce cascades of vascular benefit and are considered best in class for treatment of hypertension. In addition, they have several other FDA-approved indications to treat and prevent vascular inflammatory conditions. Their real value, however, may extend to a next level of vascular inflammatory prevention. Their mechanisms of action provide an understanding to the physiology of early vascular inflammatory changes, and the ways in which capillary and arteriole endothelial cells modify their functioning in response to these changes. The beneficial influences of these medications are felt throughout the vascular tree, in all capillary beds and end organs. They become the next cornerstone of medicinal hazing aging.

Beta-Blockers

For more than forty years, *beta-blockers* have been used to treat hypertension, angina (heart pain from oxygen deficit), heart attack, heart failure, and heart rhythm disturbances (such as atrial fibrillation). Hundreds of studies have been published documenting reductions of up to 35 percent or more in all causes of cardiovascular mortality when taking these medications for appropriate indications.

As the group name suggests, beta-blockers act by blocking beta-receptors (of which there are several types) to the effects of *epinephrine, norepinephrine,* and *dopamine.* These substances, which naturally occur in the body, increase the heart rate and the force of heart-muscle contraction, causing heart muscle to require much more oxygen in order to function. When there is preexisting coronary heart disease from plaque or heart valve damage, these substances can cause serious oxygen debt from insufficient blood flow to hardworking heart muscle. This oxygen debt can then produce chest pain, shortness of breath, and fatigue, which are associated with angina, heart failure, heart attack, and heart rhythm disturbances. The failing pump then cascades to affect the rest of the arterial tree.

The beta-receptors are found throughout the body, the vascular tree, and in most end organs, with higher concentrations in the heart. By blocking them, the net effect on heart muscle is to limit both the force and rate of contraction, which has the following benefits:

- It decreases heart muscle's oxygen requirements by reducing the heart's workload, which is known as "unloading" the heart.
- In those with preexisting coronary heart disease where there are fixed reductions in blood flow from coronary plaque, these

benefits from beta-blockers preserve viability of remaining heart muscle.

- These heart-muscle benefits also cascade to blocking beta-receptors elsewhere, as blood pressure decreases, which further reduces heart-muscle workload. Stroke risk diminishes, and kidney function is preserved.

- With further long-term reductions in blood pressure, shear stress decreases, resulting in less membrane thickening and plaque development in larger arteries of the vascular tree. This produces vascular inflammatory stability in those with preexisting disease, which then causes improvement in function of capillary cells by accommodation. End-organ function stabilizes throughout the body.

Newer beta-blockers are beta specific, in that they block only receptors found in the heart or arterial beds, sparing beta-receptors in other tissues. They can also increase nitric oxide production from capillary cells, which further improves capillary capacity to deliver oxygen to end organs. These influences produce net aggregate anti-inflammatory effects to capillary endothelial cells.

Endothelin (smooth-muscle constrictor) production is also decreased, which further limits arteriole smooth-muscle vasoconstriction. These effects beneficially reset the nitric oxide/ endothelin ratios in capillary beds, further improving blood flow in those with preexisting large-vessel membrane thickening and plaque development. These net benefits to capillary membrane function make the beta-blocker group beneficial in treatment and prevention of vascular inflammation. This translates to improved end-organ function and stalling of vascular inflammatory processes that influence and accelerate aging.

Some beta-blockers also decrease the release of renin, which, along with the ACEs/ARBs, becomes additive to reduce angiotensin II levels. It thus becomes synergistic with ACEs/ARBs to further lower blood pressure. Limiting vasoconstrictor bias can further stabilize capillary-cell function by allowing these cells to accommodate their changed relationships between blood and end organ in preexisting large-vessel plaque disease downstream.

Using ACEs/ARBs, newer beta-blockers, and statins in combination, along with aspirin, has additive effects in slowing or even reversing adverse vascular inflammatory effects, as they each have different contributing mechanisms of action. Developing a multipronged approach has merit in the war against vascular inflammation and aging consequences.

Beta-blockers should always be prescribed by, and have their doses titrated by, competent health-care providers experienced in their use. When used correctly, they can be life extending and lifesaving. It remains to be established what benefit there is to extending their use as a prevention treatment before vascular inflammation has produced disease. As with ACEs/ARBs, statins, and aspirin the capacity of beta-blockers to stabilize endothelial-cell function in an already compromised vascular condition has been well established.

There are side effects which are dependent on beta specificity and dose. In general, beta-blockers used in higher doses that block all beta-receptors have much higher side-effect risk. Using newer beta- blockers at carefully titrated doses mitigates most fatigue associated with this class. Dose reductions are common and dependent on age, liver and kidney function, as well as improvements caused by other vascular anti-inflammatory treatments. It is not uncommon to adjust the doses of beta-blockers several times in the course of a lifetime, and even to eliminate them, based on changes in heart rate, blood pressure, or side effects (such as fatigue).

Beta-blockers have multiple FDA-approved indications to treat and prevent vascular disease complications, including hypertension, coronary heart disease, myocardial infarction, and various heart rhythm disturbances. They consistently reduce all-cause mortality involving a variety of end organs. Because of affecting multiple vascular inflammatory mechanisms, beta-blockers collectively represent a powerful tool in combating the effects of vascular inflammation. Coupled with other modifiers of vascular inflammation, a holistic aggregate of vascular improvement occurs in the setting of preexisting vascular disease. As capillary cells accrue and accommodate these benefits, multiple end-organ function improves, and aging reverses. Health is restored, perhaps to levels not felt in decades.

Calcium Channel Blockers (CCBs)

Calcium channel blockers (CCBs) form another group of medications that has been prescribed for more than thirty years to treat high blood pressure and heart rhythm disturbances. These medications act directly on vascular smooth muscle by blocking the inflow of calcium ions through smooth-muscle cell membranes. By blocking calcium ion flux, smooth muscle relaxes, and the bore of a normal artery increases to accommodate more blood flow. This generally results in lower blood pressure. By doing this, the CCBs also "unload" heart muscle by decreasing the work (force of contraction times the heart rate) that is required for the heart to pump blood into the systemic arterial circulation. As such, when CCBs are used with or instead of a beta-blocker, and with an ACE/ ARB, their effects on reducing blood pressure are additive. Robust improvement in vascular mortality from CCBs is not as great as it is from ACEs/ARBs and beta-blockers.

As blood pressure comes under control by relaxing smooth muscle, capillary-cell function stabilizes, and, as happens with beta-blockers, this will evoke accommodation to the effects of large arterial vessel fixed narrowing from plaque or membrane thickening downstream. In addition, some CCBs also can hunt and reduce free radicals and their exposed electrons, preventing them from attaching to endothelial cell organelles and membranes. By acting as an antioxidant, CCBs limit the destructive effects of free radicals on the internal functioning of the capillary and other endothelial cells.

CCBs can also have beneficial effects on insulin resistance. Although poorly understood, CCBs cause both endothelial and end-organ cells to improve utilization of sugar (pyruvate) for making energy, even when there is an abundance of fatty-acid substrate. CCBs can also decrease blood pressure by a second mechanism involving increases in nitric oxide production. This relaxes the smooth-muscle cells that surround the endothelium of the arterial tree (except capillary cells) and decreases blood pressure by dilating the lumens of these vessels. All of these effects are attractive to aging dynamics, since advanced age and aggregate vascular inflammatory risk factors are associated with increases in free radicals, decreased nitric oxide levels, and increased insulin resistance/diabetes.

In spite of these additive benefits to capillary and end-organ cell function, CCBs have not shown the same benefits as ACEs/ARBs or beta-blockers in reducing all-cause mortality. It would seem that not all CCBs have the same benefits to limiting free radicals, increasing nitric oxide, and decreasing insulin resistance. In addition, older studies were done with short-acting CCBs. Medicines that stay in the bloodstream for just a few hours must be ingested three to four times a day at regular intervals in order to cause any benefit. Patient compliance is sharply diminished with this frequency of ingestion. With decreased patient compliance, the likely benefits in mortality that could be attributed to the medicine would be lost. Studies with long-acting CCBs that are ingested just once or twice a day have demonstrated improvement in mortality data. Yet, because of the lack of clarity, CCBs cannot be placed at the same pedestal level of vascular anti-inflammatory benefit as statins, beta-blockers, and ACEs/ARBs.

That said, the long-acting once-a-day CCB, nifedipine, appears to have a best-in-class combination of blood-pressure reduction, dose-related side-effect profile, and added-on vascular anti-inflammatory benefit. Like other prescription medications, CCBs may require frequent dose adjustments, both in initial treatment and subsequently during maintenance therapy, in order to achieve good blood-pressure control. Adjustments in dosage often need to be made to accommodate changes in liver, kidney, heart, and lung function that can occur with advanced age, changes in weight, or chronic illness. As such, they should only be prescribed and dose-titrated by a health-care provider knowledgeable about their use. Most people taking these medications develop annoying leg edema that often requires taking a diuretic or water pill, or using support hose to control the swelling.

CCBs offer an attractive alternative or addition to beta-blockers and ACEs/ARBs. Depending on the CCB, there are FDA-approved indications for treatment of hypertension, heart failure, and heart rhythm disturbances, while also limiting capillary and large-vessel inflammation. Additional clarification as to their effect on mortality is required before they are preeminently positioned in the hierarchy of hypertension treatment options. They can be considered for adjunctive and niche treatment, given other medical conditions. They can also be useful when there are intolerances to the ACE/ARB or beta-blocker groups. CCBs' cellular anti-inflammatory benefits are impressive, and further research is needed to clarify how these benefits translate to improved clinical outcomes. We have not yet heard the last word on clinical benefit from this intriguing group.

Conclusion

To summarize, the five different classes of medications discussed in this chapter offer several different mechanisms to lower vascular inflammatory risk. There are other groups of medicines that improve vascular inflammation by decreasing insulin resistance, such as metformin, that could also be included in the group of five. With the current group of treatments producing reductions in blood pressure, lowered LDL cholesterol, and blocked platelet stickiness, capillary-cell function has been accommodated in those with preexisting vascular inflammatory disease. This has produced pleasant secondary surprises involving less pain and fatigue, improved immune surveillance, and stabilized cognitive skills, allowing patients to stay relevant and independent for much longer periods of time.

Could the addition of supplements add further vascular anti-inflammatory clout? The answer is a qualified yes, but clinical evidence has been painfully slow in determining exactly what those benefits are and how the supplements achieve them. Given the current research models and how they are funded, proving prevention is much harder than treating disease.

With that said, the next chapter will separate out what is known about supplements and what needs more research.

9

Vitamins and Supplements

Vitamin supplements are often lab-created concentrations of certain vitamins, minerals, and herbs. Though benefits have been reported, there are many problems associated with vitamin supplements. Guidelines for their use are lacking. Research in the lab appears decades ahead of verifiable clinical benefits. Dosing can be problematic and is often a best guess. Interactions with other medicines or supplements are often not known or poorly clarified. Benefits, in combination with serious aliments like a cancer diagnosis, are not known. The quality of the supplement cannot be verified, and labeling is often inadequate. With so much headwind, care must be taken to err on the side of less may be better, so as to avoid unnecessary risks. By doing so, however, dosing may be inadequate to the point where there is no real clinical benefit. Therein is a summary of the current supplement dilemma. Intuitively, taking antioxidants and supplements makes good sense, particularly knowing that their levels diminish with advancing age and aggregate vascular inflammatory risks. How much? Of what kind? For what condition? For how long? All remain unanswered questions. Taking most supplements today requires a leap of faith, with a dose of pragmatism on the one hand and optimism about benefit on the other. Fundamental in this process is informed consent. That is, with the guidance of a trusted health-care provider, understanding known risks and benefits and developing informed consent is critical in helping patients make sound decisions about treatment.

Over the last seventy-five years, there have been hundreds of studies, mostly of poor quality, on all types of essential vitamins and minerals. The results of these studies have been mixed at best, often demonstrating no consensus as to benefit of treatment. The studies have been criticized on a variety of fronts. Often-cited flaws include using poorly absorbed, engineered tablets, and low or inadequate dosing. Other vascular risks to health, such as smoking, alcohol use, diabetes, or LDL cholesterols treatments, or other lifestyle choices, were often not controlled for, creating a bias toward no vitamin benefit. For a variety of reasons, these studies have provided fodder for controversy. Until there is improved intelligent design of vitamin and supplement studies, parties on both sides of the vitamin fence will have ample room to criticize.

In many cases, research on supplements is being done with mice or in other animals and is very preliminary. Extrapolating animal data to humans, although potentially exciting in providing hope of benefit, has limitations. The good news is that momentum is building toward translating basic laboratory research into clinical application. This process takes time but now has gradual involvement from many different levels of research.

Intuitively, supplements should be treated as medications and discussed as informed consent with a health-care provider. In some cases, certain supplements can overlap and may produce duplication of effect. In the absence of a clear indication, it may be better to choose lifestyle changes involving nutrition, regular exercise, sleep, and stress reduction. In still others, interactions with existing medications or problems with certain medical conditions preclude use. Supplements must be used with intelligent reflection based on thoughtful individual assessments of risks and benefits. Supplementing to augment vascular-tree capillary-cell, and subsequent end-organ health makes intuitive sense, but understanding the limitations of supplements in given individual contexts is equally important.

Most supplements highlighted here can be found in plants. When eaten fresh, and combined with regular exercise, consistent sleep, and stress mitigation, it may not be necessary to supplement with tablets or capsules until blood levels have proved the vitamin to be deficient. In others, preexisting vascular disease creates a greater sense of urgency to take supplements in order to avoid progressive vascular inflammation. With advancing age, levels in the blood of most vitamins diminish from either decreased absorption or production, in spite of adequate diets. Supplementing to improve deficiency states becomes more important in order to optimize capillary and end-organ cell function.

Niacin

Niacin is one of several B vitamins, which are essential for intracellular function. Niacin, also known as vitamin B3, has been known for more than fifty years to reduce serum lipids (fats) when taken in adequate doses. It is abundant, easy to engineer into tablet form, and cheap in comparison to most other lipid-lowering medications. It would appear on the surface to be the perfect treatment for lipid management, either alone or in combination with other lipid-lowering strategies.

Niacin affects LDL cholesterol, triglycerides, HDL cholesterol, lipoprotein (a), and other inflammatory cholesterols in ways that no other medication or supplement can duplicate. When coupled with a reduced-sugar and saturated/trans-fat diet, and taken at 2,000 milligrams (2 grams) per day, there is a predictable reduction of LDL (bad) cholesterol, increase in HDL (good) cholesterol, and reduction in triglycerides, of 25 percent or better for each. In addition, the sticky inflammatory cholesterol, lipoprotein (a), can be decreased by as much as 50 percent. When all of this is taken together, niacin offers the greatest advantage in across-the-board reductions in the inflammatory fats found in blood.

Taking niacin alone has been shown to confer benefits in many types of serious vascular-related conditions. These benefits are statistically reviewed in elegant fashion by Arora and colleagues (see bibliography). But when compared to statin therapies, niacin does not confer the same magnitude of improved clinical outcomes. This is bothersome since niacin, in contrast to statins, adjusts lipid levels in all the right directions. This has raised several questions involving the comparison of statins and niacin. The implications suggest that lowering LDL cholesterol is more important than improving blood levels of other lipid molecules, and that statins may have other benefits to cellular metabolism that have not yet been identified. In short, statins generally lower LDL cholesterol more effectively than niacin does, which on the surface, seems to be the most important parameter in lipid management.

Critics view these outcomes in one of two ways. First, the full benefit of niacin has had a negative bias in research comparing it to statins. When used alone, niacin confers substantial mortality benefit, but when added to a statin, it doesn't. It is possible that the statin treatment had already lowered LDL cholesterol sufficiently and adding niacin would not confer any additional benefit. We could further argue that patients should have been divided into other subcategories where niacin is known to be superior to statins, such as lowering triglycerides or lipoprotein (a). In these categories, adding niacin to a statin may confer additional benefit. It currently makes intuitive sense, but we still don't know. Investigations to date have failed to adequately evaluate patients with lipid issues that statins don't treat in order to determine if lowering lipoprotein (a), for example, confers additional vascular anti-inflammatory benefits. In other words, could niacin be more effective than a statin in niche treatment of certain lipid abnormalities?

Currently, niacin does not replace statins as the initial treatment for lipidemia, unless there is a compelling reason, such as intolerance or side effects to statins.

That said, niacin does offer benefit in reducing vascular inflammation and cardiovascular incidents. In doses of 2 grams per day, there is improvement in cardiovascular mortality of up to 25–30 percent, in patients with abnormal cholesterol profiles. The trials with niacin therapy have produced two important conclusions:

1. Niacin does reduce cardiovascular mortality but not as much as statins do, and it likely exerts its effects independent of raising HDL cholesterol.
2. Niacin should not be used with a statin unless there are compelling reasons, such as elevations in lipoprotein (a) associated with known coronary artery disease. The reasons for restricted use with a statin are based on increased risk for new adult-onset diabetes when the two are used together, and no additional improvement in cardiovascular outcomes.

The metabolism of niacin and its effect on cholesterol and triglycerides occur primarily in the liver and involve several enzymes. Niacin inhibits the mobilization of free fatty acids from fat cells. By doing this, the liver has less fatty acids substrate to make triglycerides and LDL cholesterol. In addition, a second mechanism may also affect enzymes in the liver that convert fatty acids to the precursor molecules which produce LDL-cholesterol and triglyceride molecules. Like statins, niacin can affect blood lipid levels through limiting cholesterol production in the liver; but unlike statins, niacin also affects several lipid producing pathways that involve adipose (fat) cells as well.

The risks of using niacin at therapeutic doses are similar to those of statins. Niacin should be used with care in those who drink alcohol, and sugar intake should be reduced because of the risk of acquiring diabetes when taking niacin. These behaviors are additive to preventing vascular inflammation and endothelial-cell damage, and should be adopted regardless of whether taking a statins or niacin. Patients with preexisting liver disease should be managed with reduced doses, and in some cases, depending on the cause and extent of liver disease, should not take niacin at all.

Side effects to niacin can be substantial and may include the following:

- sweating
- hot flashes

- dizziness
- rash
- lowered blood pressure
- generalized itching for one to four hours or more after taking niacin
- generalized muscle achiness (Also known as *myalgia,* muscle achiness is a common side effect of statins but may also occur with niacin at high doses. This is often worse in those with preexisting liver disease.)

Many of the above symptoms are mitigated by ingesting a baby aspirin at the same time as taking the niacin. Symptoms usually diminish after a few weeks of taking niacin regularly. Long-acting or sustained-release niacin produces fewer symptoms of itch and rash, but inflammation of the liver is more common. Muscle soreness can be more troublesome when taking niacin and requires checking blood liver enzymes, as well as the muscle enzymes (CPK), if there is persistent muscle soreness. In the absence of an elevated CPK, adding CoQ10 may reduce achy muscles.

To get the full benefit of lowering LDL cholesterol, 2 grams per day of niacin should be taken. Raising the HDL cholesterol, or lowering lipoprotein (a) by 25 percent, requires 1 gram of niacin per day. Most of the niacin research in recent years has been done with longer-acting niacin because it has fewer side effects. It is likely that there are no differences in lipid management regardless of which type of niacin used. Dosage is more important than type.

Additional research is required to determine the earliest age niacin or statins should be used to prevent vascular inflammation in those at increased risk. Research questions should evolve prevention protocols, as well as disease-specific interventions. Also, linking cellular anti-inflammatory mechanisms to clinical outcomes requires more work. Without this next level research, there will be continued debate about where niacin fits into the vascular anti-inflammatory treatment hierarchy.

Omega-3 Fatty Acids

All fatty acids are not created equal, and *omega-3 fatty acids* are at the top of the vascular anti-inflammatory ladder. They participate in a variety of roles that modulate inflammation. These long-chain fatty acids are not produced in human cells, and they decrease in concentration with advanced age; therefore, supplementing them becomes mandatory. Along with vitamin D and CoQ_{10}, omega-3 fatty acids have truly caught fire in the last ten years as a value- added supplement for vascular anti-inflammatory benefit.

Intended to lower serum triglycerides when taken in doses of 4 grams (4,000 mg) per day, the use of omega-3 fish oils at lower doses for other vascular anti-inflammatory benefits has exploded. Omega-3 oils have emerged, along with other monounsaturated oils—such as olive, avocado, and coconut—as preferred fats that reduce vascular inflammatory risks.

Omega-3 fatty acids can be divided into *long chain* (docosahexaenoic acid [DHA] and eicosapentaenoic acid [EPA]) and *short chain* (alpha-lipoic acid [ALA]). The shorter-chain ALA fatty acid can be made in the human body.

Docosahexaenoic Acid (DHA) and Eicosapentaenoic Acid (EPA)

The Mediterranean diet, along with its 30 percent reduction in all-cause cardiovascular mortality, features the intake of generous quantities of fish that have high concentrations of omega-3 oils, such as sardines, tuna, and salmon. Taking fish-oil capsules instead of eating fish has emerged as a healthy alternative, because of the expense and time involved in cooking fish, as well as the risk of increased mercury and other toxins that are found in wild, canned, and harvested salmon and tuna.

No matter how you ingest it, omega-3 fish oil contains the essential fatty acids EPA and DHA, which are precursors to *eicosanoids.* Because of the way in which they affect capillary-cell membranes, these fatty acids cause vascular anti-inflammatory benefits to accrue, resulting in improved immune surveillance. Observation and retrospective studies have shown subtle reductions in breast cancer when taking fish oil. Higher DHA levels suppress the development and progression of prostate cancer, but, paradoxically, higher EPA levels may have the opposite effect. Chronic arthritis pain improves as well with DHA omega-3 supplementing. This effect is potentiated when dietary inflammatory sugar intake is also reduced.

In addition to preliminary evidence for cancer prevention and arthritis support, improved heart health has been associated with omega-3 fatty acids. Still other research has demonstrated improvements in blood pressure, prevention of heart attack and heart rhythm disturbances, as well as reductions in depression, suicide, dementia, and autoimmune diseases, such as lupus (systemic lupus erythematosus) and Parkinson's disease, when taking fish oil. While these studies offer hope for improvement in common and serious medical conditions, the findings are still considered preliminary, albeit encouraging. Dosing, establishing optimal DHA-to-EPA ratios, and determining clinical indications for prevention and treatment are in very early trials and may take several more years to determine. With such a broad swath of clinical benefit, speculation would strongly suggest that there is a common pathway to these improvements. That pathway would suggest that improvement in endothelial and capillary-cell function is the primary driving instrument.

With research showing benefits in treatment and primary prevention, with few side effects, fish oil has become a supplement priority. Dosing of omega-3 oils for primary prevention of vascular inflammation remains empiric. In those with pre-existing coronary heart or vascular disease, several international societies and the American Heart Association have recommended supplementing omega-3 fish oil or eating two fish meals per week. The American Heart Association recommendations for fish-oil ingestion are summarized in an editorial by Kris-Etherton and colleagues (see bibiolgraphy). Taking larger quantities (greater than 2 grams daily) of fish oil, except for reducing high serum triglycerides, will remain speculative until these questions are answered.

In a given capillary cell, there is a signaling tug of war going on regarding whether to increase or decrease an inflammatory response. With age and aggregate vascular inflammatory risk factors, the bias is toward more vascular inflammatory response. This is made worse in the case of omega-3 oils, insofar as these levels decrease in capillary and end-organ cells with age, and often with other vascular inflammatory risk factors. When EPA and particularly DHA are more abundant in the capillary cell, chronic inflammation is suppressed. There is down-coding of inflammatory signaling by capillary cells, which results in less chronic inflammation, without suppressing the important response to acute inflammatory breach. With reductions in chronic inflammation, scarring of the end organ is diminished. Therefore, these long- chain omega-3 fatty acids suppress inflammation by suppressing and/or blocking inflammatory signals in cell membranes.

With aging and/or accumulations of vascular inflammatory risk factors, there are increased levels of inflammatory molecules and free radicals both inside and outside of the capillary endothelial cell and surrounding tissues. These molecules interfere with capillary-cell function, and also induce signaling of mediators that produce chronic inflammation leading to scar formation. This inflammatory process in the capillary cell is also known as *chronic oxidative stress.* Chronic oxidative stress not only increases capillary-cell dysfunction but also increases the risk for end-organ scarring and other immune-related conditions. This would include deterioration of immune surveillance, thereby raising the risk for infection, cancer, and autoimmune disease. Oxidative stress becomes a central factor to the declining capacity of capillary endothelial cell to function. Omega-3 fish oils reduce oxidative stress in capillary cells.

In contrast to the omega-3 oils (which include the short- chain fatty acid, alpha-lipoic acid [ALA]), the omega-6 oils can be proinflammatory. Their benefits may reside in the acute inflammatory response where there is serious trauma and/or particulate or infectious breach to an end organ. These oils, which include arachidonic acid, help facilitate an inflammatory response commensurate to isolate, contain, and then eliminate the foreign molecule. As such, these omega-6 fatty acids may have benefit in acute inflammatory responses. Their downside is that they may add to the chronic inflammatory response of so many end organs with advanced age. Therefore, they cannot be recommended as a supplement.

For purposes of suppressing chronic inflammation in capillary and all cells, it makes sense to supplement with omega-3 oils. Current recommended dosing is one to two capsules per day, depending on the concentrations of EPA and DHA in the fish-oil capsule. Fish-oil capsules are not regulated by the FDA, and there can be wide fluctuations in quality. Supplementing omega-3 fish oils should always be done with consultation of a trusted health-care provider.

Side effects from fish-oil capsules include nausea, burping, and a fishy odor from skin sweat. These side effects are often dose- related and can be minimized by reducing the dose, taking the fish-oil capsule with food, and/or changing the fish-oil capsule that is used. Sometimes, in patients with bleeding risk, such as those on blood thinners (including aspirin), as well as those who have low platelet counts, are on chemotherapy for cancer, have prostate cancer, or who have kidney or liver failure, will need to reduce the fish-oil dose or not take it at all.

There is little downside and much benefit to fish-oil supplementation in nurturing capillary-cell health. The omega-3 oils offer unique endothelial cell anti-inflammatory benefits that are not duplicated by other interventions. As such, they can be considered a cornerstone of anti-inflammatory antiaging treatment.

Alpha-Lipoic Acid (ALA)

As stated, *alpha-lipoic acid* (ALA) is a short-chain omega-3 fatty acid. It can be produced in the body, but it is also well absorbed as a nutrient in food. It is found in meats, spinach, broccoli, potatoes, yams, beets, carrots, and some other vegetables. A unique property of this fatty acid is its solubility, as it is both fat- and water-soluble. It therefore has the capability of penetrating most tissues and barriers, and then it can readily be used in the cell.

ALA has one important intracellular function: it rescues the mitochondria from the free radicals it produces, limiting the damage they cause to mitochondrial DNA and infrastructure. Reducing oxidative stress in capillary and end-organ cell mitochondria becomes ALA's primary purpose. As such, it functions as a vascular anti-inflammatory in a much different way than its long-chain omega-3 cousins, DHA and EPA, which optimize anti- inflammatory signaling at the cell membranes. ALA's scavenger function neutralizes exposed electrons of potentially toxic heavy metals. In addition, it forms a *scavenger free-radical triangle* with vitamins C and E to further enhance their antioxidant functions. The increased presence of ALA makes vitamins C and E more effective in their capacity to neutralize free-radical debris.

ALA levels decrease in concentration with age, stress, and chronic illness. For this reason, supplementing ALA to improve antioxidant intracellular function makes empiric sense. Yet research demonstrating the efficacy of supplemented ALA to improve clinical outcomes involving chronic illnesses of the elderly is limited. With no clear cause-and-effect benefit, there are still no FDA-approved indications for its use in preventing or treating any disease process.

Animal and some human studies worldwide have purported numerous benefits attributed to ALA supplementation:

- improvement in slowing or preventing Alzheimer's disease and dementia
- treatment/prevention of certain cancers, diabetes, and peripheral neuropathy
- prevention of cataracts
- prevention of kidney glomerular dysfunction in diabetics

As the number of clinical benefits of ALA supplementation upon multiple end organs gains traction, the inference increases regarding its effect on improving capillary-cell functioning.

Taking ALA as a supplement requires thoughtful integrative management with an experienced health-care provider. ALA may be positioned to improve vascular anti-inflammatory activity in targeted conditions associated with adult-onset diabetes and/or vascular dementia. It is best utilized as an antioxidant when coupled with vitamins C and E as well as N-acetyl-L-carnitine.

Dosing is completely empiric, as there are no approved indications or dosing standards. When used in diabetic neuropathy or vascular dementia, initial dosing of ALA can range from 200 to 600 mg per day and should be taken in combination with at least 500 mg of vitamin C, 400 IU of vitamin E, and 500 mg of N-acetyl-L-carnitine (the latter when used for dementia). With diabetic peripheral neuropathy, effectiveness of treatment can be measured by reduced numbness or burning in the feet or hands. Without targeting prevention or treatment of specific illnesses, ALA supplementing can be avoided in favor of eating beets, spinach, broccoli, and yams.

Attempts should be made to measure benefit from taking the supplement, such as improved cognition or less peripheral nerve pain. Without measuring benefit, and without well-designed research proving outcomes, taking this or other supplements can become expensive. In the elderly (those aged sixty-five or older), whose ALA and other antioxidant blood levels are almost universally low, enriching the diet with fresh vegetables and herbs becomes important to in order improve ALA and other antioxidant levels. Antioxidant studies in the elderly, where deficiency states are common and where the stakes of preventative health care are high, are desperately needed to measure clinical benefits in treatment and prevention of disease. To this end, we currently don't know if deficiency states in the aged population are related to changes in cell metabolism (decreased production of ALA), decreased absorption (malabsorption of ALA from the gut), or poor diet.

Side effects to ALA supplementation may include headache, muscle cramps, skin rashes, mild nausea, and possible vomiting; all these are dose-related. Like other antioxidant supplements, children and pregnant women should not take an ALA supplement. ALA can lower blood sugar and act as hypoglycemic agent, so diabetics must exercise caution when using it in the treatment of peripheral neuropathy. ALA may interfere with thyroid function, so thyroid hormone levels must be monitored. To date, ALA has not been linked to cancer growth, but in those with cancer, discussion about taking this supplement should occur with an oncologist. For those in cancer remission, taking ALA or other antioxidants should be determined on a case-by-case basis.

With the help of a collaborative and thoughtful clinician, use of ALA can reduce capillary and end-organ cell oxidative stress, thereby limiting vascular inflammatory consequences. Until more is known about ALA deficiency states and how they should be treated, improving ALA levels with vegetable-based eating, and using the supplement in selected clinical conditions where deficiency is likely, appears merited.

Vitamin D_3

Vitamin D supplementation has exploded over the last ten years, with the discovery that a preponderance of adults in Western culture over age fifty have vitamin D deficiency. One of the first studies to show the extent of adult vitamin D deficiency in Western culture was by Chapuy and colleagues and published in 1997 (see bibliography). Since then, several additional studies have confirmed these results highlighting an epidemic of vitamin D deficiency in Western culture which is made worse by combinations of advanced age, chronic illness, obesity, and the metabolic syndrome.

Most health-care providers are routinely ordering vitamin D levels on blood panels in patients over age fifty, because of the new awareness of deficiency states. What has become alarming is the epidemic of vitamin D deficiency that is tied to aggregate vascular inflammatory risks from advanced age, obesity, hypertension, diabetes, and metabolic syndrome. With the combination of limited UV sun exposure, changes in the skin architecture that reduce vitamin D production, and decreased vitamin D ingestion from the diet, blood levels of vitamin D decrease for multiple reasons, resulting in vascular inflammatory conditions and capillary-cell dysfunction.

Vitamin D blood levels tend to decline with age, with a decided majority of adults (as much as 75–100 percent, depending on the study and chronic illnesses) over age seventy being vitamin D deficient. Ninety percent of nonsupplemented vitamin D in the adult human comes from conversion of cholesterol substrates in the skin with the use of UV light. The consensus from experts is that that decreased production of vitamin D in the skin of older adults is secondary to spending less time in direct sunlight. While this may be true, aging reduces skin thickness. The change in skin architecture likely facilitates reductions in vitamin D production. In addition, sunscreen used to prevent sunburn, which increases with thin skin and advanced age, can block vitamin D production by as much as 98 percent.

With vitamin D deficiency, the best way to improve levels in those over age fifty is to take a supplement. The simple vitamin D_3 supplement is cheap and comes in a variety of doses, in easy-to-swallow soft-gel capsules. Once vitamin D_3 is ingested, the liver and kidneys work together to convert the inactive vitamin D3 to the active form of vitamin D, known as *1,25-dihydroxyvitamin D,* or *calcitriol.* If kidney or liver function is failing, which is more common with advanced age, this conversion does not occur, and then low vitamin D levels become refractory to the supplement. In these cases, using the much more expensive calcitriol may be required to increase stubbornly low vitamin D levels.

Vitamin D supplementation has shown impressive clinical benefit:

- Elderly women taking modest doses of vitamin D showed reductions in mortality, regardless of their underlying health. The mortality difference involved reductions in vascular events, such as stroke and heart attack, as well as cancer.

- In men and women, optimal vitamin D blood levels are associated with reductions in heart-attack and stroke mortality.
- In addition, improved vitamin D blood levels have been linked to better asthma control and lower incidence of pneumonia.
- Vitamin D supplementing could have benefit in preventing and treating multiple sclerosis.
- Fewer hospitalizations from fractures and fall risk in the elderly as a result of vitamin D supplementing to support optimal blood levels have been reported as well.
- There is evidence that vitamin D supplementation in pregnancy is associated with fewer complications to term pregnancy.

Once calcitriol (the active form of vitamin D) is produced, it percolates through the blood to capillary cells and then to all end-organ cells. Once inside the cell, it participates as a cofactor to support several chemical reactions, including those that involve binding to nuclear DNA receptors. Receptor binding is integral for optimal function of the nucleus, as vitamin D acts as a transcription factor that modulates the expression of genes involved in nuclear coding of all cells. This enables appropriate gene expression that codes for protein synthesis, as well as enabling the nucleus to receive and respond appropriately to signals. With diminished levels of vitamin D, there is more certainty to nuclear coding mistakes, independent of telomere shortening or free-radical cross- linkage of DNA chromosomes. Nuclear coding mistakes can result in terrible repercussions, causing up-coding of proinflammatory signaling.

In addition, with low vitamin D blood levels, levels and production of nitric oxide (a potent vasodilator) decrease in capillary cells, resulting in smooth-muscle vasoconstriction of arterioles and subsequent reductions in blood flow to the end organ. With persistent reductions in blood flow, proinflammatory signaling increases, and end-organ function can eventually become compromised. Vitamin D also participates in endothelial and end-organ cell glutathione production from the amino acid cysteine. *Glutathione* is a powerful all-purpose antioxidant that attaches to electrons of free radicals, thereby reducing them to become harmless, preventing them from adversely affecting membrane and organelle function in the cell. As vitamin D levels decline, glutathione levels decrease as well, which increases the risk of ROS and other free radicals in capillary and end-organ cells, where these molecules damage cell membranes and organelles.

Vitamin D also combines with parathyroid hormone and has been known for many years to affect bone metabolism and architecture through the regulation of calcium and phosphorus metabolism. There is much speculation as to just how vitamin D improves immune signaling in capillary cells to decrease end-organ inflammation. Empirically, since immune signaling requires capillary-cell coordination of signaling to and from white blood cells and plasma proteins, as well as end-organ cells, optimal vitamin D levels are required at several steps to support these complex feedback loops.

It goes without saying that accurate vitamin D dosing to correct blood levels, along with resistance exercise training, is most important to optimize bone health, prevent progressive osteoporosis (brittle bones), and maintain posture.

Dosing of vitamin D_3 requires careful monitoring of blood levels. Using the more expensive calcitriol may be required in those with malabsorption and/or liver or kidney disease. Too much vitamin D can be as bad as too little. Maintaining vitamin D blood levels between 35to 55 nanograms per milliliter appears to be safe and to confer all the advantages of vitamin D supplementation—without any disadvantages.

High vitamin D levels from taking too much supplement can be toxic and can increase risks for muscle and joint pain, as well as potentially increase risk for certain cancers. Clearly, vitamin D has an optimal therapeutic window, and blood levels need to be monitored to assure correct dosing.

Vitamin D supplementation offers a powerful tool in maintaining capillary cell and subsequent end-organ cell function by supporting processes that affect nuclear, antioxidant, and immune function.

Unlike other supplements, research has identified cause- and-effect relationships between deficiency states and capillary-cell/end-organ dysfunction. There is substantial support for vitamin D supplementation based on blood levels, which should cause widespread use to support both capillary and end-organ cell health. Vitamin D supplementation, particularly in those over age fifty, becomes another cornerstone treatment for primary prevention of age-related inflammatory processes tied to capillary-cell health and end-organ function.

Coenzyme Q10 (Co-Q10)

Co-Q_{10}, or *ubiquinone,* is an oil-/fat-soluble molecule (like ALA) essential to intracellular mitochondrial energy production. The mitochondria are the organelles in all cells (including capillary cells) that make energy using oxygen; as such, mitochondria are often called the *cell's aerobic respirator.* Cells that are dependent on making more energy from mitochondria—such as the heart, brain, and skeletal muscle—have the highest CoQ_{10} concentrations. In addition to directly participating in energy production, CoQ_{10} (again, like ALA) is also a free-radical scavenger. This becomes important when aerobic energy production increases, as ROS can also increase, and CoQ_{10} can keep these free radicals from causing damage by reducing them (making free radicals electron neutral so that they will not have an affinity to attach to proteins or membranes).

The function of CoQ_{10} in the mitochondria involved in the processes of making energy is unique. For this reason, CoQ_{10} levels, which decrease with advanced age and with statin medications, can become a rate-limiting cofactor in energy production. That is, as CoQ_{10} levels decrease, energy production in the mitochondria falls. Since 95 percent of all the energy produced in the brain, heart, and skeletal-muscle cells can come from mitochondria, the presence of abundant levels of CoQ_{10} in these cells becomes critical to maintain energy production, whether or not pyruvate, fatty-acid, and oxygen supplies remain optimal to support their function.

CoQ_{10} has the capacity to both receive and donate electrons. Donating electrons becomes important in energy production; receiving them becomes critical in neutralizing dangerous free radicals, which reduces oxidative stress on both capillary and end-organ mitochondria. By accepting electrons, CoQ_{10} can regenerate active (reduced) vitamin E, another powerful antioxidant vitamin. When in the reduced (active) form, vitamin E can return to reducing free radicals. This cooperative antioxidant effort between CoQ_{10} and vitamin E allows for different free radicals to be preferentially reduced, as well as preventing free-radical chain reactions, where neutralizing one free radical then causes an equally toxic one. The combination of being an energy cofactor and a flexible free-radical scavenger makes CoQ_{10} a powerful molecule, integral to energy production and inflammation mitigation inside and outside of capillary and end-organ cells.

Those taking statin medications should also supplement with CoQ_{10}, particularly those who feel weakness or muscle pain. CoQ_{10} is produced in the body as part of a multistep process that involves the enzyme HMG-CoA reductase. *HMG-CoA reductase* is the enzyme that all statin medications block in the liver to reduce the production of LDL cholesterol. Because statins are so effective in blocking this enzyme, they can also block CoQ_{10} production and create deficiency states that can decrease CoQ_{10} levels by up to 40 percent in all cells. Since CoQ_{10} levels decrease with statin use, advanced age, and/ or the presence of multiple vascular inflammatory risk factors, it would make sense to empirically supplement with CoQ_{10} in these settings.

CoQ_{10} can add additional benefit to statin therapy by acting as an LDL-cholesterol free-radical scavenger. In spite of statin therapy's LDL cholesterol lowering, some LDL cholesterol still circulates, thereby causing vascular inflammation. CoQ_{10}, by attaching to the exposed LDL electron (Ox-LDL, which is highly inflammatory), reduces the LDL particle and neutralizes the electron, making the LDL molecule incapable of attaching to capillary and end-organ cell membranes.

CoQ_{10} therefore stops inflammatory LDL cholesterol in its tracks; as such, it can be an important additive to statin therapy.

CoQ_{10} has also been shown to limit the frequency and duration of migraine headaches. This was demonstrated in a well-controlled study by Rozen and colleagues (see bibliography) that showed modest daily CoQ10 administration could prevent migraine headaches. Other preliminary research has shown CoQ_{10} to have benefit in preserving heart-muscle contractility after cardiac arrest.

CoQ_{10} supplementing can lower blood pressure, with reductions of as much as 17 mm/Hg of systolic pressure being reported. Regular CoQ_{10} intake can improve aerobic-exercise capacity by 10 to 20 percent, and it can also stabilize heart rate and rhythm in patients taking statins. Unfortunately, dosing of CoQ_{10} is empiric, as there is no firm guidance for use in disease prevention or aerobic-exercise capacity

In the natural world, CoQ_{10} can be found in modest quantities in most meats and fish. It can also be found in olive and avocado oils, as well as in most nuts, grape seeds, parsley, and other herbs. Supplementing with CoQ_{10} can be expensive and currently is not covered by insurance. Doses of between 100 to 300 milligrams per day, taken with meals, are safe and should not cost more than twenty-five dollars for a three-month supply, if purchased in larger quantities at big-box stores. Most people who take the supplement subjectively report more energy and less muscle ache/ fatigue with exercise. Exercise performance improves with CoQ_{10} supplementing those who take statins and/or have a history of heart failure. There are few if any side effects of the supplement when taken at these doses.

In spite of improvements in intracellular function and clinical outcomes in higher-risk patients, the FDA has not approved CoQ_{10} supplementation for any specific medical condition. In spite of the FDA snub, CoQ_{10} supplementation offers unique benefits to energy production and free-radical protection, while further limiting LDL-cholesterol free-radical influences. As with other antioxidants, both production and blood levels decline with advanced age, chronic illness, statin use, and/or the presence of multiple vascular risk factors. For this reason, taking CoQ_{10} becomes an essential piece to improve clinical outcomes, optimize health, and crack the aging barrier.

B Complex Vitamins

B complex vitamins are essential water-soluble vitamins. Each member of the B complex is different and have specific functions. The B complex is a set of eight vitamins:

- B_1 (thiamine)
- B_2 (riboflavin)
- B_3 (niacin)
- B_5 (pantothenic acid)
- B_6 (pyridoxine)
- B_7 (biotin)
- B_9 (folic acid)
- B_{12} (cobalamin)

These vitamins participate as cofactors in multiple capillary and end-organ intracellular processes; as such, they are essential to normal functioning of all cells throughout the body. As with CoQ_{10} and vitamin D, with advanced age, all B vitamin levels more or less diminish in the blood, as well as in capillary and end-organ cells. Because they are essential, and because levels are reduced in many patients with advanced age, supplementing them to improve blood levels should improve the functioning of all the capillary and end-organ intracellular processes that involve these vitamins.

It has been hard to prove benefits in primary prevention or disease treatment with B vitamins. There may be reasons for this apparent lack of success. First, study design often does not control other inflammatory mediators or modifiers. Controlling for diabetes, smoking, and LDL cholesterol, as well as other vascular inflammatory mediators, become important as they may override and block any benefit the B vitamins may provide. Second, patient noncompliance, as well as variable quality of the B vitamin preparations used, can skew outcomes toward no benefit. Varying levels of each vitamin being dosed in a given study can also limit effectiveness. It could also be possible that the amount of B vitamin ingested in these pills is too low to demonstrate clinical effect. Sometimes patients are too sick or far advanced to receive preventative benefit from B vitamins. For a variety of reasons, flaws in study design may collectively influence outcomes toward a no-benefit bias. This is particularly true with the diverse group of vitamins in the B complex, with each serving cellular metabolism in different ways.

The best argument for supplementing B vitamins is only empiric and is based on declining blood levels of B vitamins with advanced age or chronic disease. By maintaining adequate levels of the B vitamin cofactors, empirically, capillary and end-organ cells can function better, as compared to their function in deficiency states. Wound healing, skin health, cholesterol management, lowering homocysteine levels, preventing pregnancy complications, and limiting alcohol withdrawal symptoms are some of the benefits of these vitamins, so, supplementing the B vitamins for therapeutic reasons can be very important. Except for those allergic to niacin (evidenced by flushing and itching when taken in high doses), B vitamins are well tolerated and inexpensive; they lack side effects when taken in modest quantities and do not create toxicity from excessive absorption. Thus, they can be a useful supplement to facilitate efficient intracellular functioning at several different levels of metabolism.

Supplementing B vitamins where it is known that deficiency states are likely could further improve the benefits to other vitamins and cofactors, such as vitamin D, CoQ_{10}, and other antioxidants.

This is because many of the same intracellular functions that involve them also involve the B vitamins. Studies showing benefit of B vitamins to other supplements have yet to be demonstrated, but research has confirmed benefit of specific B vitamins in at least four important clinical outcomes:

1. In cholesterol management, in those patients with combinations of low HDL cholesterol (less than 35 mg/dL), high triglycerides and elevated lipoprotein (a), taking niacin (vitamin B_3)at 1 to 2 grams per day, as discussed previously, produces measurable improvement in all causes of mortality by reducing vascular inflammation caused from these abnormal lipid levels. (Also as previously discussed, those who have or develop an allergy to niacin cannot follow this protocol.)

2. In those drinking even modest amounts of alcohol, taking B vitamins (particularly thiamine [B_1] and folic acid [B_9]) can limit muscle, peripheral-nerve, and brain side effects, and also support treatment of the more serious alcohol withdrawal syndrome.

3. B_{12} deficiency is increasingly being recognized and linked to anemia as well as capillary and brain-cell dysfunction. A consequence of B12 deficiency is *macrocytosis* (enlarged red blood cells). These larger red cells, which pick up and carry oxygen to capillaries for delivery to end organs, can easily get lodged in capillaries and fragment because of their increased size. This makes them much less effective in oxygen delivery. Taking B_{12} (500 to 1,000 micrograms per day), particularly when B_{12} levels are low, can help restore red blood cell levels and reduce their size, thereby limiting fragmentation and improving oxygen delivery to capillaries and end organs. When it comes to oxygen delivery in vulnerable end organs, such as the brain and heart, approaching improvement at every angle can help.

4. In pregnancy, the fetus and placenta require a rich source of vitamins to support their rapid growth. Taking B vitamins has been shown to improve pregnancy outcomes and limit complications of malnutrition.

B complex vitamins come in many over-the-counter preparations. They are inexpensive and can be found in most pharmacies and vitamin stores. B vitamin preparation should typically contain 50 to 100 milligrams of thiamine (B_1), riboflavin (B_2), niacin (B_3), pyridoxine (B_6), and pantothenic acid (B_5). They can also contain 100 to 250 micrograms of cobalamin (B_{12}), 400 micrograms of folic acid (B_9), and 50 to 100 micrograms of biotin (B7). Higher concentrations can be obtained when purchasing each B vitamin individually. There are few if any side effects when taking these vitamins at recommended doses (except for niacin, as previously discussed). Overdosing is unlikely, as toxicity has not been described with higher blood levels.

B complex vitamins provide an inexpensive way of maintaining important cofactors to a variety of chemical processes involving multiple membranes and organelles in order to support capillary and then end-organ cell function. Since levels of these vitamins decline with age, taking them on a daily basis can serve as insurance for prevention of cellular dysfunction. In specific clinical situations, taking individual B vitamins at much larger doses is warranted. Taking higher doses of B vitamins should always be done in consultation with a skilled health-care provider. Although B complex vitamins taken as a supplement have no FDA-approved indications, when taken regularly in deficiency states (such as occur in the malnourished and the elderly), supplementation could improve capillary-cell function and help mitigate vascular inflammatory influences.

Resveratrol

Resveratrol, a molecule found in red wine, as well as in fruits, flowers, roots (Japanese knotweed), seeds, and bark, has been found to have anti-inflammatory vascular benefit. Because it is a naturally occurring substance, resveratrol is found ubiquitously in a variety of natural plant-based settings. It holds enormous promise as a vascular anti-inflammatory treatment. Resveratrol can target multiple different mechanisms to inhibit vascular inflammation at the capillary-cell level. Since resveratrol is not produced in humans, it must be ingested or supplemented to achieve blood levels. Baur and associates, in two excellent reviews (see bibliography), summarize various human trials and aggregate resveratrol benefits, which are summarized below.

Resveratrol has the following benefits:

- Research at the cellular level has shown that resveratrol may affect several metabolic intracellular pathways in capillary and end-organ cells, resulting in net up-coding of an anticoagulation benefit (increased blood thinning to limit clotting and thrombosis). It does this by affecting platelet adhesiveness (stickiness).

- Resveratrol facilitates capillary-cell immune support to result in antifungal, anticancer, and antimutagenic effects. (*Antimutagenic effects* refer to the prevention of DNA cross-linkage, which leads to the protection of nuclear DNA from free radicals.)

- In capillary cells, resveratrol's anti-inflammatory effects are primarily related to inhibition of the aggregation of platelets (cells that contribute to clotting). Resveratrol also stimulates nitric oxide production. (Nitric oxide relaxes the smooth muscle around endothelial cells.)

- Resveratrol reduces LDL and superoxide free radicals; therefore, it is an antioxidant and lowers oxidative stress.

- Resveratrol may improve insulin resistance by increasing sugar (pyruvate) utilization for energy production in capillary and end-organ mitochondria.

Research directly implicating resveratrol as having cause-and-effect benefit in clinical outcomes involving vascular inflammatory conditions in humans has been difficult to demonstrate. However, in research published by Marambaud and associates (see bibliography) in mice, resveratrol has been found to reduce amyloid plaque formation in brains, suggesting a vascular benefit tied to improved capillary-cell/blood-brain-barrier function and subsequent improvements in brain-cell function. This resveratrol effect supports the hypothesis of the cause-and-effect relationships between vascular inflammation, decreased cerebral blood flow, increased insulin resistance, and subsequent increases in amyloid plaque production on atrophied brain cells, to decreases in capillary- cell support and function. This implies that the amyloid plaque buildup associated with dementia is an effect of deficient brain-cell oxygen/nutrient support rather than the cause of dementia. The finger of vascular inflammatory cause and effect points directly at reduced large-vessel vascular blood flow to the brain, often associated with increasing insulin resistance and aggregate vascular inflammatory risk, producing untoward effects to capillary cells at the blood-brain barrier, as the root cause of brain-cell atrophy and amyloid plaque development. Utilizing strategies to limit large- vessel obstructive plaque and accommodate capillary-cell function at the blood-brain barrier, such as reducing insulin resistance with resveratrol, then becomes a primary target for prevention and treatment of dementia.

Another improvement from resveratrol found in mice includes decreases in arthritis. Other studies have demonstrated improved treatment of viral infections, as well as increases in sperm production and testosterone levels.

In spite of benefits found in mice, resveratrol does not have any FDA-approved indications for human use. Dosing and interactions with other supplements are also poorly understood. For these reasons, taking this supplement should always be discussed with a trusted health-care provider. Resveratrol supplements should not be taken by those under age forty or by pregnant women. Taking resveratrol in daily doses of 50 to 100 milligrams per day in those over age fifty appears to be safe, but there have been no long-term studies demonstrating safety.

Well-controlled research in humans, with an eye toward primary prevention, should yield definitive answers about where and how resveratrol fits in to limit vascular inflammation and aging progression. The table has been set in animal studies to suggest that this molecule holds enormous promise in mitigating vascular inflammation.

N-Acetyl Cysteine (NAC)

N-acetyl cysteine (NAC) is a well-known molecule that has been used in medical practice for years to prevent kidney failure when using contrast dyes for imaging studies, as well as in management of lung conditions, including bronchiectasis, emphysema, fibrosis, and pneumonia. It has also been used to save lives by preventing irreversible liver damage in cases of Tylenol (acetaminophen) overdose. Other lesser-known clinical benefits include the adjunctive treatment of bipolar disorder and symptomatic polycystic ovary syndrome (PCOS). Trending practice patterns worldwide indicate the potential for expanded usage of NAC in the treatment of other medical conditions. Support for NAC use as a preventative vascular anti-inflammatory supplement has shown limited benefit, in spite of expanding antioxidant attributes.

Cysteine (without the N-acetyl group from NAC), is converted in most cells to *glutathione,* a potent antioxidant that binds to exposed free-radical electrons in all cells. Glutathione is a potent all-purpose antioxidant. Binding to toxic free radicals, it stabilizes intracellular function by decreasing oxidative stress.

When taken by mouth, cysteine is not well absorbed. However, with the addition of the N-acetyl group, virtually all of the resulting NAC is easily absorbed and rapidly enters the bloodstream. In cells, NAC can be easily converted to cysteine and then to glutathione. Cysteine is found naturally in poultry, yogurt, egg yolks, red peppers, garlic (including chives), onions, broccoli, oats, and brussels sprouts. There is some absorption of cysteine from these sources, but enhanced absorption requires converting cysteine to NAC.

Although NAC can benefit capillary endothelium and end-organ cells in a variety of ways, its central mechanism of action is to increase intracellular glutathione. Reducing oxidative stress with optimal levels of glutathione improves capillary-cell organelle and membrane function, limits DNA cross-linkage, and optimizes mitochondrial energy production. This maintenance of capillary- cell infrastructure from toxic influences improves the cells' signaling, coordinating, and integrative functions to and from the blood and end organ. This translates to maintaining the specific interests of the end organ, as well as optimizing immune support to protect against infections, autoimmune complexes, and cancer cells. When effective, acute inflammatory responses are comprehensive and appropriately robust, and chronic inflammatory conditions are limited. In effect, glutathione activity reduces excessive chronic vascular proinflammatory influences, thereby optimizing endothelial and capillary-cell health to create seamless end-organ functioning.

With age, levels of glutathione decrease in the blood and all cells. Combinations of advanced age, poor sleep, processed foods, stress, lack of exercise, chronic illness, and aggregate vascular inflammatory risks contribute to decreased glutathione levels. In spite of glutathione deficiency with age and chronic illness, there are currently no FDA-approved indications for NAC supplementation. With that understanding, there are concerns about higher levels of glutathione reducing certain types of free radicals that may actually be necessary in feedback loops to promote some levels of protective inflammation. Finally, there are concerns that abnormal cells, such as cancer cells, may use increased glutathione levels for their own purpose, to minimize free-radical exposure that could have influences on their capacity to replicate and spread.

Because of the NAC/glutathione connection, and the fact that glutathione can become deficient in the elderly or those with chronic illnesses, the argument of supplementing NAC can be made in selected clinical venues. When taken as an antioxidant, dosing should be from 600 to 1,500 milligrams daily and should be managed with a trusted health-care provider. There are few if any side effects at these doses, but little is known about side effects when taking the supplement over a long period of time.

Research in mice has shown that a dose about twenty times higher than what would be given in humans caused pulmonary hypertension. Implied is a serious adverse side effect from NAC, but only at doses considered toxic to humans. Medications and supplements work best in a therapeutic window. That is, there is an optimal dose that is both safe and effective. With most supplements, not only are indications for use vague, but also the therapeutic window for optimal dosing has not been established. Dosing for many supplements becomes a best guess, based on limited research, clinical application, and experience.

Side effects that have been reported include mild nausea, diarrhea, and postnasal drip (all of these are dose-related). In addition to endothelial and capillary-cell support, NAC has been found to have benefit in patients with pulmonary disease from combinations of bronchiectasis, chronic bronchitis, asthma, and COPD (emphysema), as NAC couples antioxidant properties with mucolytic benefits.

Supplementing a powerful antioxidant, such as NAC, for best clinical practice makes sense when tied to chronic lung conditions. When considering any supplement, making a conscious effort to acquire antioxidants through fresh vegetables and herbs should always come first. Future research on NAC should clarify dosing and long-term benefits to prevention and treatment applications.

N-Acetyl-L-Carnitine (ALC)

N-acetyl-L-carnitine (ALC) is manufactured from L-carnitine by adding the N-acetyl group. This process occurs in human cells as L-carnitine becomes ALC, and ALC can convert back to L-carnitine. L-carnitine is an amino acid that is found in abundance in meat and is easily absorbed from the intestines. In most cells, L-carnitine is acetylated to make ALC. In contrast to L-carnitine, ALC is not found in high concentrations in meat and must either be supplemented or converted from L-carnitine in human cells. ALC, in contrast to L-carnitine, crosses the blood-brain barrier to enter the cerebrospinal fluid where it can affect brain-cell metabolism.

ALC serves two important functions to capillary cells and end organs. First, it can facilitate transport of fatty acids into the mitochondrial matrix to become the preferred substrate to make energy. This can be very important in organs requiring very high energy demands, such as the skeletal muscle and heart. When endurance is required in high-energy situations, glucose to pyruvate for energy production becomes exhausted. ALC facilitates the mitochondria to use fatty acids for energy, thus enabling skeletal muscle and heart muscle to work harder for longer periods of time. By doing so, ALC facilitates consumption of calories and may promote weight loss associated with exercise.

While capillary cells do not produce most of their energy from mitochondria, thereby minimizing ALC's effect on utilizing fatty acids for energy, they do facilitate the use of fatty acids by heart and skeletal muscle by responding to energy-dependent signals and increasing fatty-acid transport across their membranes. The presentation of fatty acid in usable form to heart and skeletal muscle is fundamental to successful end-organ function in sustained hardworking conditions. Utilizing fatty acids instead of pyruvate in mitochondrial metabolism produces a different ROS exhaust, and in some cases more of it. This translates into different ROS-driven feedback loops in the mitochondrial matrix and capillary and end-organ cell membranes and organelles.

In the brain, ALC has a different effect. Since brain cells do not use fatty acids for energy, the unique benefits of ALC come from a different function. ALC easily crosses the blood-brain barrier, and from there it can be used as a precursor in the production of acetylcholine. *Acetylcholine* is an important neurotransmitter that is tied to cognitive function. In patients with dementia, acetylcholine levels are decreased in the brain. Using treatments to increase acetylcholine, with either supplements or other types of medications, while not addressing the root cause of dementia, can still produce improvements in cognitive function. This improvement, although beneficial, is often temporary, unless vascular inflammatory risks to the capillary cells of the blood-brain barrier are addressed.

Even before dementia is recognized (and it is often diagnosed too late or when already far advanced), with advanced age, acetylcholine levels, as well as other neurotransmitters in the brain, are reduced. Supplementing acetylcholine with ALC, while also paying attention to mitigating vascular inflammatory risks, can be a very effective two-step process in limiting cognitive decline.

There are currently no FDA-approved indications for ALC supplementation. Flaws in study design, control of vascular inflammatory risk factors, as well as dosing questions have contributed to inconsistent clinical outcomes. Support for supplementing ALC is based on primarily anecdotal human case studies and animal studies. Because of diminished levels of acetylcholine in the brains of the elderly, to support cognition, empiric supplementing with ALC can make sense.

ALC side effects can include mild nausea, restlessness, and a fishy odor to sweat. Thyroid function should be checked at least yearly when taking this supplement. In addition, blood-thinning medications may need adjustment. Without FDA-approved guidelines for ALC use, dosing requires a discussion about risks and benefits with a trusted health-care provider. Measuring a clinical response, such as an improvement in cognitive metrics, should always occur in order to determine supplement effectiveness after regular intake for a period of time. ALC dosing can range from 500 to 2,000 milligrams per day, with side effects increasing with higher doses. Since the elderly are usually more sensitive to side effects, but could be a prime target group for treatment with ALC, extra caution is advised when initiating treatment and measuring intended clinical outcomes.

ALC offers one more tool to improve end-organ performance, with at least two mechanisms of action. With its ability to cross the blood-brain barrier and shed its acetyl group to increase acetylcholine, it confers additional benefit to senescent brain cells. Facilitating fatty-acid utilization in skeletal and heart muscle improves endurance, is facilitated by capillary cells to these end-organ cells, and can improve endurance to increase the total number of calories expended with exercise. While holding promise as a useful supplement, additional research is required to enable understanding of therapeutic dosing and indications, and to quantify effectiveness.

Vitamins C and E

Vitamin C and *vitamin E* are potent antioxidants to all cells. With the short-chain omega-3 alpha-lipoic acid (ALA), they form an interwoven antioxidant triangle in capillary and most end-organ cells. Together, they set the stage for each other to detoxify unstable free radicals in the capillary and other end-organ cells. By doing so, in aggregate, they reduce oxidative stress to cell membranes and organelles.

Vitamin E, also known *alpha tocopherol,* is actually part of a large family of tocopherols. Other tocopherols in the family of vitamin E, such as delta and gamma tocopherol, found in numerous plant species, could provide even more antioxidant benefit than alpha tocopherol. In those that do not have regular access to fresh spinach, kiwi, tomatoes, broccoli, almonds, fish, or mango, or who are of advanced age, malnourished or with chronic illness, deficiency of vitamin E is common. In these settings, taking a vitamin E supplement could be prudent.

There are currently no FDA-approved indications for vitamin E supplementation. There are few if any known side effects when taking alpha tocopherol at 400 to 800 IU daily. In a recently published double-blind trial as part of a Veterans Administration cooperative published in *JAMA,* Dysken and colleagues (see bibliography) demonstrated that taking a vitamin E supplement at higher doses (2000 IU) improved cognition in those with serious dementia. This would suggest that the vitamin E antioxidant plays a critical role in limiting intracellular capillary cell and nerve oxidative stress in preexisting dementia.

When supplementing vitamin E, my preference is to also use vitamin C with vitamin E, as they both support each other in reducing oxidative stress. Some research has tied vitamin E to adverse heart-disease outcomes, but there is still no consensus about this. When taking vitamin E, as with any supplement or medication, assessing overall risk and benefit is prudent and requires a discussion with a trusted health-care provider.

Vitamin C also reduces toxic ROS produced by mitochondria exhaust, such as the *superoxides* and *peroxynitrite*. These inflammatory free radicals can do substantial harm to cell membranes and organelles, including the capacity to damage mitochondrial and nuclear DNA. Taking too much vitamin C, however, can also cause harm, as the *ascorbate* (oxidized vitamin C) formed from neutralizing the superoxide electron can act as a free radical, attach to metal ions (such as copper), and subsequently make the oxidized metal a toxic free radical. This is where ALA can step in and neutralize the heavy metal before it is oxidized by ascorbate. Thus, these three antioxidants—ALA, vitamin C, vitamin E—work together to prevent the chain reaction of free radicals that accelerate oxidative stress and subsequent damage to cell membranes and organelles.

Like vitamin E, vitamin C is best obtained from whole food, primarily fresh citrus fruit and vegetables. Also like vitamin E, levels decline with advanced age, malnutrition, chronic illness, and aggregate vascular inflammatory risks. In these settings, supplementing with a 500-milligram tablet of vitamin C daily is safe for most adults.

Vitamins C and E (and ALA) have important antioxidant roles in capillary and end-organ cells, as they act together to neutralize toxic intracellular free radicals. These vitamins are found in abundance in a diet rich in vegetables and nuts, as well as some fish and fruit. Supplementing them to improve insufficient blood levels may be required in specific situations. Caution about supplementing these or any other vitamins is always advised in those with active cancer, and a discussion with an oncologist is recommended before using any supplement while undergoing treatment. Reducing oxidative stress in senescent capillary cells to improve/accommodate their function, and subsequently passing on the benefits of improved function to end-organ cells, could have far-reaching outcomes that could modulate improved immune surveillance and feedback loops, limiting inflammatory signaling and aging dynamics.

Garlic Extracts

Garlic is a naturally occurring antioxidant herb that can be procured as a clove or tubular green chive. It can be harvested fresh, packaged (preserved) as a sprinkle, or condensed into a capsule or tablet. The garlic chive is similar to the onion chive, but it has unique flavor and antioxidant/soluble-fiber content. Both forms of garlic are valuable antioxidants.

The fresh garlic chive (which is my personal preference) is a hearty, water-resistant, thin, tubular green leaf that grows abundantly and is resistant to most insects, rodents, and animals. It can easily be cut and used as a fresh, flavorful additive to many food dishes, providing a rich depth to the taste of food. Garlic, parsley, tarragon, and chervil comprise the classic quartet of French fine herbs.

Although garlic bulbs have about as many benefits as garlic chives, the chives have superior soluble-fiber benefits (2.5 grams of fiber per 100 grams of leaf). The chive also has high concentrations of thiosulfinite, which converts to allicin when the leaves are cut or cooked lightly. *Allicin* is another inhibitor of *HMG-CoA reductase,* which is the same enzyme that statins inhibit in the liver to lower LDL cholesterol (as discussed previously).

Allicin also has antibacterial, antifungal, and antiviral properties, as well as having effects on nitric oxide, increasing its levels to dilate arteriole and small-vessel vascular lumens from smooth-muscle relaxation, subsequently lowering blood pressure. It can also affect blood clotting, producing a weak inhibition of platelet aggregation; therefore, is additive in supporting efforts to make the blood clot less (thin the blood) by preventing vascular events such as stroke and heart attack in those with preexisting vascular inflammatory disease. It can even help augment factors that clean up clots that have already formed, thereby reducing the clot scar.

Garlic chives also have high concentrations of lutein, vitamin A, and zeaxanthin, which, together can help support vision and reduce risk of macular degeneration. Other vitamins and minerals found in garlic chives include vitamin K, B vitamins, vitamin C, copper, zinc, manganese, and calcium. All of these constituents found in aggregate from garlic chives support capillary-cell health, producing a net anti-inflammatory effect. These effects cascade to improve a seamless coordination of benefits between blood and end organ.

Garlic chives have up to 85 percent more food value when freshly cut and used immediately in food preparation. They do not require a lot of space to grow and require only light watering. They are relatively cold resistant, as they can withstand temperatures to twenty-five degrees Fahrenheit. They can grow more than an inch daily, given ideal conditions. With just a small amount of attention, the chives will increase in volume as they subpopulate open spaces in the garden. Once cut, the tubular green shoots grow back quickly. In their growing season, chives can be cut from the same shoot, up to two to three times per week. This results in a very practical, hardy, and reliable source of herb, requiring only a small space to grow but offering potent antioxidant benefits.

There are no FDA-approved indications for garlic in the treatment or prevention of any disease, nor are there any firm recommendations about dosing garlic products. When used in cooking or to dress up a salad, garlic in any form enhances flavor, and it can also provide an abundance of health benefits. In the case of chives, these benefits also include a high concentration of soluble fiber, as previously indicated. Allicin supports capillary cell anti-inflammatory activity and immune surveillance (which involves effects on white blood cells and immune proteins), and it limits blood clotting, while improving blood flow to the capillary cells. With aggregate vascular anti-inflammatory benefits and the relative ease of growing it, garlic can be classified a super food. When used consistently, it prevents capillary-cell dysfunction and therefore correlates with reducing aging dynamics. Fresh garlic unlocks the key to capillary-cell performance at several levels, improving end-organ function and becoming a cornerstone of antiaging and vascular anti-inflammatory treatment.

Magnesium

Magnesium has been used for decades in various preparations, with FDA approval in clinical medicine to treat constipation and seizures, reduce acid indigestion, and prevent heart arrhythmias. In addition, the mineral has been used to treat arthritis symptoms, muscle leg cramps, and osteoporosis.

Magnesium participates as a cofactor in more than three hundred intracellular chemical processes which involve membrane function. As such, along with calcium, potassium, and sodium ions, it facilitates the management of capillary and end-organ cells' electromechanical membrane gradients. The maintenance of these gradients is specific to each membrane in the cell and is critical to cell function. After mitochondria make ATP, it is often coupled with magnesium and then transported out to the cell's cytoplasm, where ATP can then be utilized by membranes and organelles. Research has shown that optimal magnesium levels in the blood can stabilize capillary and end-organ cell membrane function, reduce inflammatory markers in the blood (interleukin 1 and 6), and facilitate increased synthesis of nitric oxide. Optimal magnesium levels may also reduce clotting activity and promote vascular neogenesis (new blood vessel growth), when appropriately needed, by increasing VEGF (vascular endothelial growth factor). Clinical outcomes attributed to magnesium include improvements in cardiovascular mortality, particularly in those with coronary artery disease, heart rhythm disturbances, and hypertension.

With advancing age, magnesium levels in the blood can trend lower, necessitating the need to supplement. Careful use of magnesium is necessary, as reduced kidney and liver function, also common in the elderly, can actually increase serum magnesium levels, making universal supplementation of this mineral dangerous. For these reasons, magnesium blood levels must always be obtained prior to supplementing, and a discussion of magnesium supplementation should take place with a trusted health-care provider.

Magnesium, in addition to its abundance in vegetables, nuts, and beans, can be found in small quantities in calcium supplements and multivitamin preparations. In my opinion, it should be used as a stand-alone supplement. Magnesium levels should be checked on a regular basis in order to adjust dose and limit potential toxicity. Safe dosing for most adults is 300 to 400 milligrams per day, but could range from 200 to 1,600 milligrams per day, or more, depending on blood levels, underlying heart conditions, level of deficiency, and refractoriness to treatment.

When used appropriately, magnesium can support membrane electromechanical function of capillary and end-organ cells. Secondary benefits involve optimizing nuclear coding, as a participant to the mechanics of immune surveillance, and bolstering nitric oxide levels. These net vascular anti-inflammatory effects translate to improvements in end-organ function that include bone, nerve, skeletal and heart muscle cells, as well as benefits to the gastrointestinal system. Supplementing magnesium, when deficient, can be viewed as a preventative tool to reduce serious heart rhythm disturbances that often trigger falls in the elderly, which are often tied to fractures of long bones. With measurable benefits to capillary and end-organ cell function, magnesium supplementation, when appropriate, offers value in limiting serious adverse consequences in the capacity to function independently with advanced age.

The Herb Group

> "Let food be thy medicine and medicine thy food"
> (Hippocrates, 431 BC)

The *herb group* includes *basil, cilantro, dill, ginger, oregano, parsley, peppermint, rosemary, sage, tarragon, thyme,* and *turmeric.* For the most part, all of these herbs can be grown fresh, require only a small space for planting, and can be picked and used year-round, provided they are sheltered in the winter. When carefully tended, they can act as perennials.

All of these herbs share common characteristics and have been used over the centuries for different purposes. They all have few calories and almost no sugar, but are packed with significant amounts of plant fiber and a variety of vitamins and minerals associated with antioxidant benefits. Yanishlieva, Pokorny, and colleagues (see bibliography) have recently reviewed antioxidant benefits of this group, as well as several other herbs, with preliminary research from around the world, collaborating the virtues of these superfoods. From this and similar reviews, anticipated reductions in vascular inflammatory oxidative stress should improve capillary- cell function and result in more effective end organ function, even when preexisting vascular disease is present.

All of the aforementioned herbs can be extrapolated to have the following beneficial qualities

- promote vascular anti-inflammatory benefits
- affect capillary-cell function to facilitate the integration of anticlotting, immune surveillance, smooth-muscle relaxation, filtering, barrier and pump support
- increase oxygen and nutrient flow to and from the blood and the end organ
- limit the inflammatory effects of dangerous free radicals, and their antioxidant benefits stabilize organelle and membrane function in both capillary and end-organ cells
- correlate to many clinical health benefits, including lowering LDL cholesterol/triglycerides and blood pressure, reducing the risk of heart attack, stroke, and dementia, reducing pain syndromes, decreasing cancer and infection risk, and slowing the decline of ADLS (activities of daily living) with advanced age

Herbs in this group have diversified uses. They can be used in salads or salad dressings, as part of dips for snacks, in baking, or to supplement a stir-fry. Using a variety of herbs on a daily basis can produce substantial soluble fiber, and a rich, diversified blend of vitamins and minerals that provide antioxidant benefits while improving the taste of food. Using the fresh herb is critical to optimal nutritional support, with processed and dried extracts and capsules losing up to 80 percent of their nutrient value. Harvesting fresh is an extra step, versus a few shakes from a store-bought product, but the improved content quality and taste are worth it. In those who choose not to embark on the culinary trail, these herbs can be taken as supplements in the form of capsules and tablets. My bias, when it comes to using herbs, is to use them fresh to enhance the vitamin, mineral, and fiber content, and also to improve cooking flavors.

None of these herbs have FDA-approved indications for disease prevention or treatment, nor have any dosing recommendations been given. With the new era of preventative health care, the science and health benefits of fresh-vegetable and -herb cuisine will expand. That said, the herb group offers a win-win from the culinary, antioxidant, metabolic, and soluble-fiber points of view. In the meantime, we don't have to wait years, or even decades, for these results to begin using these herbal plant based resources to enhance food flavor and vascular endothelial-cell/end-organ health. When coupled with a comprehensive program of mitigating vascular inflammatory risks, hazing aging then kicks in full throttle.

Berberine

Berberine is a relatively unheralded molecule found in a variety of plants. It can be identified by its deep-yellow color. Like other powerful antioxidants, it has been used for centuries for many different health problems. Research has tied berberine to reductions in blood LDL cholesterol and the toxic superoxide free radical, as well as to reducing insulin resistance by improving pyruvate (glucose) utilization in all cells. It has also been shown to have anti- cancer benefits and to reduce dementia risk. Aggregate benefits have been reviewed and summarized in a journal article by Sun and Chen, and in a second article from Shen and colleagues, which can be found in the bibliography. By extrapolation from these results and reviews, berberine produces benefits to capillary cells that are net vascular anti-inflammatory. With berberine's intracellular metabolic benefits, the aging, proinflammatory influences of insulin resistance and the metabolic syndrome are mitigated, on the one hand, which may lessen oxidative stress and improve immune surveillance, leading to reduced infections and cancer on the other.

Berberine does not have an FDA-approved indication, and like many other vitamin or mineral supplements, should not be used in young adults or children. It can interact with other medications, and as such, should be used with caution, in those taking complex medicine treatments. When used as a supplement, with proper dosing, side effects are uncommon, are dose-related, and include nausea and mild abdominal pain. Dosing can range from 500 to 1,500 milligrams per day, but there are no firm guidelines for its use, long-term benefit, or safety.

Berberine, when coupled with diet, exercise, and other aggregate anti-inflammatory behavior, can assist in reversing some of the adverse effects of the metabolic syndrome and improve immune surveillance. It should always be used in conjunction with behavior modification and improved lifestyle choices. Since aging is directly associated with increasing insulin resistance (reduced capacity to utilize glucose/pyruvate for energy), berberine could provide assistance in mitigating this relentless progression seen with advancing age. As science unlocks connections between intracellular metabolic pathways and improvements in preventative health care, natural plant-based molecules like berberine will make sense as a gentle and resilient treatment to mitigate inflammatory influences.

Grape Seed Extract (GSE)

Grape seed extract (GSE) from the grape seeds of red wine contains high quantities of substances that have powerful antioxidant activity, with preliminary research showing beneficial effects involving multiple end organs. These attributes suggest vascular anti- inflammatory activity involving the arterial tree and capillary cell.

At the capillary endothelial cell level, grape seed extract can have the following benefits:

- relaxing vascular smooth muscle (increasing nitric oxide levels)
- reducing platelet aggregation (clotting) and blunting chronic immune inflammatory responses (reduced response to cause aggregation of white blood cells and other inflammatory constituents) that contribute to symptomatic chronic illness
- causing blood pressures to trend lower (associated with increases in nitric oxide levels)
- improving immune surveillance of foreign/infectious invaders and cancer cells, as a result of more-effective capillary-cell function

The above net multiple benefits to capillary-cell functioning would also spill over to improvement in heart and brain health associated with less vascular inflammation and improved or stable blood flows.

Research on GSE has often been anecdotal, with clinical work involving small studies that have not been well controlled. An interesting question involves whether GSE has more vascular anti-inflammatory value than the sum of its individual parts. Nature, and the processes of natural selection, may have the upper hand when it comes to the aggregate best mix of molecules to create the most health benefits. That is, the molecular context of antioxidants found in whole fruits and vegetables have value-added benefits associated with context, as compared to molecules isolated from the vegetable and utilized separately. The whole food would thus have more benefit than the sum of its parts. This revelation has credence with GSE, which, in addition to containing significant quantities of the known antioxidants vitamins C and E, also contains other antioxidants that are additive to vascular anti-inflammatory activity.

As with other supplements, GSE holds great promise, but with no FDA indications and a paucity of guidelines about dosing, GSE must be used carefully. There are few if any side effects with GSE, but when used as a supplement, there may be interactions with other medicines, and for this reason supplementation should be discussed with a trusted health-care provider. Included in this discussion should be some advice about indication, dosage, side effects, and interactions. As with other supplements, the decision to use GSE should be a mutual agreement between patient and health-care provider.

Another phytonutrient, *pycnogenol,* derived from French maritime pine bark extract in southwestern France, has similar net antioxidant, vascular anti-inflammatory effects as GSE, and can be considered as a suitable alternative to the antioxidant flavonoids found in GSE. One potential difference in favor of pycnogenol involves improvement in high blood pressure. Pycnogenol's capacity to increase nitric oxide concentrations throughout the vascular endothelium produces relaxation of vascular smooth- muscle cells and can reduce high blood pressures.

With increasing complexity of supplement and medication use, concerns about interactions and duplication of effect become real and should be avoided whenever possible. The lesson that should be learned about supplementing is that sometimes less is more. An abundance of fresh, preferably home-grown vegetables and herbs is the preferred, natural method of obtaining the rich sources of antioxidants, vitamins, complex carbohydrates, and soluble fiber, as opposed to taking multiple supplement capsules. This is true even with advanced age and known deficiency states.

Unfortunately neither GSE nor pycnogenol can be obtained from a vegetable/herb garden, which means they must be used as supplements. GSE, which can be taken as a capsule in doses of 50 to

100 milligrams per day, has few side effects (nausea, headache, and itchiness) at these doses. Pycnogenol dosing for most adults is in the range of 100 to 200 milligrams per day. These supplements should be avoided until age fifty or older, when noticeable loss of antioxidants becomes evident. GSE can affect platelet aggregation and will augment the effect of blood thinners, such as aspirin or Coumadin. Pycnogenol may have additive effects with other blood- pressure medicines and can increase symptoms of dizziness or light-headedness. Safety is always foremost in taking these and other supplements, as they can interact with standard treatments for common medical problems. Informed consent with a trusted health-care provider about risks and benefits is always best practice. When used wisely, they both can confer health benefits and, in the case of pycnogenol, when taken consistently, may result in reduced doses of standard blood-pressure medications.

Probiotics and Silymarin

Probiotics and *silymarin* are associated with restoring ailing capillary, intestinal, and liver cell function. Used alone or in combination, they are helpful for supporting the capillary endothelia of many organs.

Probiotics, used either in prevention or treatment of digestive disorders, contain helpful (or "friendly" bacteria), such as lactobacillus, that support intestinal epithelial and capillary endothelial cells in the absorption of nutrients and minerals.

Probiotics can be very helpful in situations where there has been an overgrowth of unwanted bacteria or yeast that affect absorption and cause subsequent diarrhea and abdominal pain. These symptoms and bacterial pathology become particularly relevant in antibiotic-associated diarrhea. In separate research papers by Gunzer, Meddings, and colleagues (see bibliography) probiotic bacteria, when used in the right clinical context, have benefits in restoring proper absorption of nutrients and reducing intestinal epithelial cell membrane permeability. This translates to improvement in the intestinal epithelial cell-capillary cell absorption axis which subsequently reduces the many potential causes of *"leaky gut" syndrome.*

With improvements in permeability and nutrient absorption to the intestinal epithelial cell membrane, probiotics then facilitate improvement in capillary-cell immune surveillance, which creates a beneficial feedback loop to the intestinal epithelium to limit unwanted inflammation. The net effects reduce bleeding, abdominal pain, diarrhea, and malabsorption. Since there are no absolute contraindications for their use, probiotics can be considered a safe supplement in preventing and treating intestinal abdominal pain and diarrhea, or as an "add-on" treatment in more serious intestinal disorders. All probiotics are not created equal, and a discussion with a knowledgeable health-care provider is merited before starting this supplement.

Silymarin is a blend of seven plant molecules found in milk thistle. Silymarin provides benefit as an anti-inflammatory to capillary and liver cells after prolonged exposures to toxic substances like alcohol. Silymarin may block further toxicity of the foreign substance to protect remaining liver tissue as well as stimulate the production of VEGF to result in new capillary and liver cells. In addition, silymarin may augment support capillary-cell/Kupffer-cell immune surveillance to liver cells by enhancing the recognition and removal of abnormal precancer or cancer cells. While these effects to liver cells are encouraging in the laboratory, translating these benefits from the laboratory to improved human clinical outcomes involving liver inflammation has proved difficult. It is clear that when patients present with acute and severe liver disease (end-stage cirrhosis) or severe intestinal inflammatory disease associated with bleeding or hemorrhage, there is no health benefit when taking probiotics or silymarin in these settings until the severity of symptoms has been stabilized.

There are no FDA-approved indications for probiotics or silymarin. Current dosing for probiotics varies, but they are usually taken as a capsule or packet (powder then dissolved in liquid) one to three times daily. Probiotics are generally safe, with few side effects, but as previously mentioned, consultation with a trusted health- care provider should be obtained prior to initiation of treatment. In some cases, ingesting other medicines or treatments at least one hour away from most probiotics may be required.

Doses of silymarin range from 200 to 400 milligrams per day and can be used for treatment of mild to moderate liver inflammation associated with excess alcohol or other toxin ingestion. Silymarin is generally considered safe and should be used in conjunction with removal of offending toxicities to the liver, such as alcohol, IV drug use, or overuse/abuse of acetaminophen (Tylenol) providing there is no risk of imminent liver failure.

Both probiotics and silymarin can offer prevention and treatment benefits to intestinal and liver dysfunction, as well as producing favorable attributes to corresponding capillary cells to these end organs. Solid long-term clinical benefit from laboratory observations has proved elusive, requiring more work to determine dosing, clinical indications, and therapeutic windows, as well as measured responses to treatment. Because of their limited downside risk, thoughtful use of these supplements can prove useful to potentially affect improvement in specific clinical applications.

Conclusion

The use of supplements, particularly when coupled with traditional allopathic medicines, can be challenging. Questions about how much and for what clinical benefit must be addressed in the context of a given patient. For this, the FDA offers no specific guidelines. Dietary supplements, unlike approved medications, are not required to undergo clinical/laboratory vigor in order to be marketed. As such, they cannot be marketed for any specific disease state; rather, their marketing can only state that they may be used to "support" certain organs. Because of these limitations, indications, dosing, and other important clinical parameters for their use are lacking. Thus, by definition, classification as a supplement makes clinical measurement of benefit difficult to prove, as proof is not required in order to market. Because of this, questions surface regarding clinical efficacy.

In spite of these uncertainties, laboratory benefits at the cellular level for these antioxidant supplements have been shown in countless studies. These studies have produced one irrefutable point: By promoting anti-inflammatory activity of the arterial tree and capillary cells, the subsequent benefits to their health are passed on to include the end organs they serve. These benefits further limit collateral damage to end organs caused from adverse genetic and environmental influences.

Although still speculative, specific antioxidant supplements provide value in promoting vascular anti-inflammatory wellness. Some antioxidants are preferred in certain clinical situations. However, by nature of their ability to affect improvement in capillary cells, clinical benefits to one end organ should extend to all end organs. What these antioxidant supplements have in common is their capacity to improve capillary-cell function, leading to improvements in immune surveillance, clotting and blood-flow dynamics, as well as a host of other vascular anti-inflammatory attributes to end organs.

Due diligence must be maintained in assessing these benefits. For a variety of reasons, research of most antioxidants has been slow to connect improved capillary and end-organ cellular benefits to clinical outcomes. This may change as more-precise clinical models are developed to more accurately address known cellular benefits. Further research may also humble us to recognize that benefit at the cellular level may not transfer to clinical benefit, no matter how hard we try to find it. This would suggest that there are other variables at work that are either unknown or misunderstood.

The most significant error in supplementing antioxidants could be excessive supplementing. That is, supplements may contain small amounts of vitamins or minerals that are also found in other supplements. This needs to be fettered out, as getting too much of a vitamin can produce no benefit, and in some cases, can result in harm. I typically see this in patients taking separate vitamin supplements for their eyes, bones, prostate, and other organs, in addition to a multivitamin tablet. Each may have duplication of B vitamins, and of vitamins E, A, and C, as well as some minerals. In other situations, supplementing for one vitamin without also supplementing another (i.e., vitamins C and E, and ALA) could produce more cellular oxidative stress from free-radical chain reactions, since these vitamins are often codependent to each other for their antioxidant effects. In another example, taking statins to reduce LDL cholesterol may also produce deficiency of intracellular CoQ_{10}, which can increase fatigue and muscle pain. Taking CoQ_{10}

with a statin often eliminates these symptoms. (We've explored the foregoing examples in deeper detail throughout this chapter.) Sometimes, taking antioxidants for purposes of improving health can have other adverse consequences. Taking any of these vitamin supplements in the presence of preexisting cancer may cause the cancer to grow. For this reason, treating oncologists should be involved with patients about what should and should not be taken during cancer treatment. Connecting all of the dots for antioxidant supplementation must be based on a case-by-case basis where a "one size that fits all" approach will result in unpleasant surprises.

That said, which supplements should be used to improve arterial-tree, capillary-cell, and end-organ health? In addition to such medications as aspirin, statins, ACEs/ARBs, and beta-blockers, when clinically indicated, I have found that adding B complex vitamins, omega-3 oil, vitamin D, magnesium (being careful to measure blood levels first), and probiotics as supplements has little downside risk and much upside potential. These supplements take on added significance in the elderly, malnourished, or those with chronic illnesses, as they are often deficient in these clinical settings. Adding CoQ_{10} with statin use, to limit muscle fatigue and cramping, creates a group of six supplements that offer consistent endothelial cell benefit and can be safely integrated into most medicine programs.

Adding additional supplements then becomes a case-by-case situation, based on specific underlying conditions and focused disease prevention. For example, those prone to memory loss or early dementia could benefit from taking antioxidant vitamins E and C, along with alpha-lipoic acid (ALA) and N-acetyl-L-carnitine (ALC). In those with chronic bronchitis, asthma, or COPD, adding N-acetyl cysteine to traditional medicines can cause further improvement in cough, expectoration, and shortness of breath. Coupled with intentional lifestyle changes involving improved sleep, stress management, regular exercise, and healthy diet, medication and antioxidant supplements can form a foundation to optimally support the capillary and small-vessel endothelia, which then reduces the pace of disease relapses, inflammation, and aging.

Conclusion

The Foundation for Preventative Health and Age Reversal

When I became a physician, I took the Hippocratic oath, which, to put it simply, states that I should do no harm while treating a patient to the best of my ability. During more than thirty-six years of medical practice, I have learned that there is both art and science in patient care. Listening to what the patient is really saying is the most important instrument a health-care provider has. Often what is said is layered, requiring intuition to translate, and cannot necessarily be taken at face value. Context of care, assessing the nuance around the complaint, becomes important to identify meaningful diagnosis and treatment. In these assessments and corresponding treatments, I have observed repeated patterns of ugly aging progression. In spite of thoughtful interventions, changing the course of aging was frustrating and often futile. Not to mention that the outcomes of so many of these progressive end-stage conditions, such as dementia, were emotionally draining to patient, family members, and even me.

My own nearly fatal experience with denial, involving a blocked artery in my heart, helped seal my awareness of just how important vascular risk is to health. What became evident is that most of us willingly let life chew us up. We don't allow ourselves a chance to wrap our arms around the destructive processes happening to us and get control of them before they hopelessly consume us. Our nature, when it comes to health, is to be reactive.

When I was in medical school, we were constantly reminded of snake-oil treatments and the long history of medical quackery that changed with the evolution of investigating benefits of treatment in terms of the scientific method. With that understanding, it became easy to dismiss any treatments that did not conform to the rigor of the scientific method's proof. Medicinals passed from generation to generation in some cultures were rejected outright on the basis of not meeting scientific method standards.

This medical ethnocentrism has slowly eroded over the last four decades, as many so-called primitive treatments have been shown to confer clinical benefits. At the same time, many big pharma products, using the scientific method to gain FDA approval for treatment, have exhibited surprising toxicity, and in some cases, not provided the clinical benefit or safety intended. The repeated misadventures of big pharma have caused many to start questioning the validity of this process and look for alternative, more natural treatments. An emerging field of preventative health care is gaining momentum, with emphasis on healthy lifestyle choices involving food, exercise, sleep, stress reduction, and natural supplements.

Coinciding with this renaissance is the understanding that patients cannot be put in a box and assigned treatments based on accumulative big-data metrics. Adjustments in care should be made depending on individual context, which takes longer than a five- to ten-minute office visit. Clarifying prevention strategies takes time. A physician cannot be rushed if listening to the patient, observing how he or she responds to questions, doing a thoughtful, focused examination, ordering blood work and other tests, and providing education and treatment strategies with appropriate follow-up. Furthermore, rushing these processes will result in lost opportunity for quality intervention.

Prevention strategies are enhanced with an understanding of cause and effect from capillary-cell dysfunction to end-organ decline.

Linking these changes to the processes involving chronic illnesses and aging spearheads a unified approach to prevention. The awareness of vascular inflammation—what it is, what it does, and how it does it—serves to deepen clinical wisdom for the health- care provider and provide insight into the patient. Interventions that optimize arterial-tree and capillary-cell health also improve end-organ function. They make the patient feel better, and they feed on themselves for further improvement. As the dividends of prevention accrue, there is quiet resolution of vascular risk. Pain decreases, urgent and emergent care diminish, and quality of life improves. Arterial-tree and capillary cell treatment brings the sum of its parts together in order to integrate a treatment plan for both specific illnesses and the patient as a whole. This establishes an effective approach to chronic illnesses and aging, with an easy-to- understand, inside-out basis, rather than treatment of an array of age-related chronic illnesses that appear complex, unrelated, and disjointed.

The arterial tree, which completes its business to end organs at the capillary level, forms a complex integrative network of sophisticated signaling and coordination of responses to and from the blood, other endothelial cells, and all end organs, as well as the specific end organ served. These connections make endothelial cells "all for one and one for all," in terms of the maintenance of human homeostasis. The extent to which the entire vascular endothelium fails is the same extent to which homeostasis fails and end organs decline. End organs are not isolated, and the cause and effect of disease in one also leads to cause and effect in regard to all the other end organs with similar vascular inflammatory processes.

How fast an end organ fails is often predetermined by genetics, and even more often by environmental influences that cannot be adequately compensated by the capillary cells optimizing their immune or metabolic support. Inherent in these processes to mitigate persistent end-organ stressors are capillary-cell adaption and accommodation. At some point, given enough end-organ dysfunction, capillary-cell support will fail. When this occurs, end-organ dysfunction leading to death can spiral quickly.

There are three major conclusions that can be drawn from the study of the arterial tree and capillary cells.

First, capillary cells are dynamic, adaptable, and accommodative. Along with all endothelia, capillary-cell function and morphology change based on their location in the arterial tree and the specific needs of the end organ they serve. In large-bored arterial vessels the endothelia function primarily as flexible pipes moving blood through the arterial tree. The volume of blood flowing through them is regulated by their smooth-muscle tone, responding to substances that constrict or dilate the thick vascular smooth-muscle bed that surrounds the endothelial cell. On the other hand, the much-smaller-bored capillary cells at the far end of the vascular tree, without any smooth muscle encircling them, have evolved to serve as an efficient conduit between blood and end organ. As such, they have developed unique signaling and morphology in order to manage blood flow, essential nutrients, and clotting mechanisms, as well as mediating immune surveillance to optimize end-organ function. These functions involving capillary cells are in stark contrast to what was previously believed. Just twenty-five to thirty years ago, capillary cells were viewed as passive instruments, where passive diffusion across their membranes to and from the blood and end organ summed up their function. From passive instrument to orchestral conductor, they have essentially unlocked the secret to how end organs thrive.

When it comes to brain and heart function, capillary cells have no margin for error, as even slight reductions in blood supply and subsequent reductions in nutrient/oxygen support can produce influences that reduce optimal end-organ function. This often begins downstream in large-bore arteries where endothelial-cell membranes become thickened and soft plaque forms on their basement membranes. This beachhead of inflammation can become chronic and progressive, often producing ischemic symptoms when artery narrowing reaches a critical level. (Ischemic symptoms refer to stroke/TIA in the brain, and angina/heart attack in the heart.) The inflammatory progression, and subsequent suffocation of endothelial- and capillary-cell functional capacity, is caused by vascular inflammatory influences. The partial list includes elevated blood levels of LDL cholesterol, triglycerides, and sugar, as well as hypertension, stress, insomnia, and toxicity from alcohol, drugs, tobacco, and highly processed sugary food.

Furthermore, the narrowing of larger-bored arteries inevitably produces slippage of capillary-cell function upstream. At some point, as blood volume diminishes to a critical level, the capillary cells can no longer support end-organ function. When this occurs, end-organ cells become vulnerable to dysfunction, as atrophy, infection, and/or cancer increase, and normal tissue is often replaced by scar tissue. Therefore, end-organ cells decline from the inside out (inflammatory causes from blood), from the outside in (environmental exposures or genetic damage to end-organ cells), or as a result of both causes. In any case, the decline occurs from the diminished capacity of the capillary cell to adapt and accommodate its metabolism, morphology, and immune support in order to fill the voids that it is presented with, either from the blood or end organ.

Second, capillary cells manage a highly complex array of immune signals to and from the blood in order to limit infection, cancer, and autoimmune influences. Immune surveillance, because of its codependency on blood and end-organ signals, becomes an excellent barometer of capillary endothelial-cell health. The extent to which the tools of managing appropriate immune responses are maintained is the same extent to which capillary cells are optimally functioning in terms of meeting the needs of the end organ. Therefore, as the function of the capillary cell is facilitated, so also is the health of immune surveillance to the end organ to limit cancer, infection, autoimmune disease, and foreign particulates. Mitigating vascular inflammatory risks facilitates capillary immune function.

Third, with aging, most vitamin and antioxidant levels decrease in the entire vascular endothelium, all capillary cells, and, subsequently, all end-organ cells. These reductions predispose capillary and end-organ cells to more susceptibility to free radicals, and, thereby, to greater damage to their DNA, organelles, and membranes. Therefore, adding back important vitamins and minerals that have become deficient becomes necessary in order to sustain capillary-cell function, which is critical to support end-organ function.

Thus, we can see that taking care of capillary-cell health becomes priority one. Let me summarize the process of hazing aging in twelve key points. To assault the influences of aging requires a thorough prescription of lifestyle, and in some cases, medicinal and supplement support. Not paying attention to some inflammatory issues will negate benefit to mitigating others. In other words, you must go "all in" to make a substantial difference in prevention outcomes. We all slip up on occasion, and this is to be expected. It is also recognized that change is a process that requires patience. Being overly critical of yourself or others usually produces more harm than good. Behavioral modification is learned, takes time to master, and is individualized. There will be failure; it is just important to make adjustments and move on. Don't be too hard on yourself.

The twelve key points listed below will provide clarity of purpose and motivation to make the necessary behavior/lifestyle changes.

1. The origin of most acquired chronic adverse health outcomes is vascular and inflammatory, and thereby affects the endothelial cells that line the entire arterial tree.

2. The endothelial cell has evolved at the capillary level as a highly integrative cell that has adopted specific morphologies and functions, depending on the end organ served. No matter where they are and what epithelial end-organ cells they are connected with, the capillary cells mediate complex signaling that connects blood constituents to efficient end-organ function.

3. All capillary cells signal to and from the blood and end-organ mediators that influence effective immune function, clotting

mechanisms, regulation of blood flow, and exchange of oxygen, minerals, and nutrients.

4. Maintaining the health of the arterial tree and capillary cells becomes a central and dominant theme in preventative health care and hazing aging. Vascular anti-inflammatory benefits to capillary cells include maintenance of membrane and organelle function, limiting DNA damage, and maintaining feedback loops for integration of information from these cells to and from the blood and end organs.

5. Daily continuous movement (exercise) for at least thirty minutes becomes the single most important cornerstone for supporting endothelial-cell health. Exercise provides impetus to adapt other anti-inflammatory behaviors. Time spent in exercise should be divided into roughly two-thirds aerobic (continuous movement) and one-third anaerobic (intermittent movement, such as lifting weights). Exercise should have built-in flexibility to accommodate changes in environment and/or personal limitations. Aerobic exercise has a direct benefit to endothelial-cell health, whereas anaerobic exercise primarily supports the body's infrastructure (skeletal muscle, ligaments, tendons, and bones).

6. The capacity (intensity and duration of exercise) can be measured through exercise stress testing, using protocols that estimated MET. The extent to which the MET decreases from expected levels at age twenty-five (peak performance) can be used as an approximate gauge for aging (with some built-in assumptions). For example, if the MET has declined by 25 percent from expected peak performance (again, usually at age twenty-five), the body in aggregate has aged by that amount.

7. Other behavioral interventions complement exercise and improve arterial-tree and capillary-cell function. This list

includes eating whole unprocessed food, drinking plenty of water, and sharply limiting sugars and trans fats. In addition, treating elevated blood sugars, lipids, and blood pressures is important. Eliminating tobacco and drugs, restricting alcohol, and maintaining a BMI (body mass index) of 18 to 26 are important goals. Stress reduction, purposeful sleep, and balanced social and spiritual interactions facilitate an anti-inflammatory lifestyle. Finally, taking medications and supplements for specific indications may also be warranted. With advancing age, there is increased insulin resistance and predilection for diabetes, which is very vascular proinflammatory. For this reason, everyone, particularly those over age fifty, should eat as if they were diabetic, sharply limiting simple sugars. Most antioxidants also decrease with age, as do hormones (such as the thyroid hormone). Use of supplements and hormone-replacement medication can be helpful. On the other hand, long-term use of estrogens and testosterone may have vascular proinflammatory effects.

8. Genetics and adverse environmental influences can and should be mitigated as much as possible by vascular anti-inflammatory living.

9. Noninvasive ultrasound and imaging techniques can be very useful in evaluating large-vessel membrane thickening and plaque development. More-elegant testing for screening purposes is generally not necessary or cost- effective, unless special imaging is required on a one-time basis. CT imaging has accumulative radiation drawbacks and should only be used when other techniques cannot provide enough information or invasive interventions are being contemplated. Exercise stress testing, with or without an echocardiogram, is often all that is necessary to safely evaluate heart structure and function, enabling the formulation of a safe exercise prescription. All

of these tests produce indirect measurement of capillary-cell function. Noninvasive and direct measurements of capillary-cell function may be just around the corner and will be a welcome advance in deciphering effectiveness of vascular anti-inflammatory prevention outcomes.

10. Improving endothelial-cell function provides the opportunity to improve all end-organ function and to slow, or even halt, the aging process to all end organs. As such, treatment and prevention strategies to the arterial tree and capillary cell produce a holistic effect on all end-organ function.

11. Much more research is required on capillary and other endothelial cells in order to assess benefits of specific interventions on nuclear telomeres, mitochondria, other organelles, and cell membranes. What becomes critical is linking science at the cellular level to clinical applications of prevention. This requires a fresh approach in research protocols, meaning protocols that will ask questions about disease prevention rather than disease treatment.

12. Even with the paucity of cause-and-effect research linking the capillary cell to clinical outcomes, there is enough information to begin a transformation to hazing aging. Since implementing vascular anti-inflammatory strategies are additive, it is anticipated that with consistent application, most people could add years if not decades of independent and productive living.

As discussed throughout this book, the earlier vascular anti-inflammatory living is implemented, the easier it is to prevent the aggregate of heart, brain, and other end-organ dysfunction that becomes prevalent in midlife. Adopting early strategies to manage weight, sleep, and stress pays dividends later, as these strategies will serve as a foundation for prevention that can be implemented for life's duration. When life gets hectic, it's far easier to incorporate positive behaviors that are already part of our daily routine.

In addition, the cost of managing emerging chronic medical problems gets very expensive and time consuming. With emergency-room visits, imaging interventions, hospitalizations, and some cancer chemotherapy costing more than $100,000 per day, it is easy to see an impending economic crisis in health care. In addition, lost work time and permanent disability increase, which causes job-related inefficiencies and increased business costs. These spirals of cost simply cannot be sustained, requiring a paradigm shift in how we view health. Taking ownership of vascular health risks, accepting responsibility for our behaviors, and adopting vascular prevention techniques will go a long way to limit the costly, out-of-control spirals of health-care expenditures.

It is never too late in life to effect change in mitigating arterial- tree and capillary-cell damage from vascular inflammatory risk. Even in advanced medical conditions, intentional anti-inflammatory behaviors can have beneficial effects to mitigate disease progression.

Driving the renaissance of understanding arterial-tree, capillary-cell, and then end-organ function is the emergence of understanding the basic science of these cells. These advances have provided a greater awareness of how and what the capillary cell does to bridge the blood to the needs of the end organ served. Central to this understanding is recognizing just how active the capillary cell is in supporting the end organ. Forty years ago, this complex integration to end-organ function would not have been imaginable.

For optimal functioning of the capillary cell, three essential criteria must be met:

1. The integrity of the nuclear and mitochondrial DNA in the cell must be protected against cross-linkage in order to prevent errors in coding, signaling, and protein synthesis.
2. The fatty acid/pyruvate (glucose) ratios for energy substrate must be optimal in order to facilitate feedback loops that involve all membranes and organelles.

3. Oxidative stress from all oxidative processes in the cell must be mitigated properly in order to prevent excessive and toxic free-radical exposures that damage DNA, membranes, and organelles.

To combat toxic ROS, the emergence of antioxidants as an essential factor in capillary-cell health has occurred. With aging, antioxidant levels decrease in all cells and increase exposure to the toxicity of free radicals. Mitigating them with antioxidant support is critical to limiting the damage they cause to membranes and DNA, which subsequently disrupts cellular function.

Diet has emerged as a fundamental to arterial-tree and capillary-cell health. The benefits of fresh, unmodified, organic whole food grown from the ground are substantial. The chemical arrangements in whole food provide the right context for obtaining the necessary mix of antioxidants, protein, complex carbohydrates, and fatty acids to support arterial-tree and capillary-cell function. Eating whole food has greater nutritional benefit than eating processed or genetically engineered food.

With this in mind, developing a garden of vegetables, herbs, and fruit should make its way back into mainstream living. Developing a garden patch becomes both a pragmatic and intentional move to better health. Becoming familiar with simple food-preserving techniques also becomes important in storing extra fruit and vegetables from the garden for future use.

We have a choice when it comes to how we age. For the first time, science has provided a basic foundation for understanding interventions that can mitigate the aging mechanisms that can be tied to vascular inflammation. We make choices of exposure that either inflame the endothelia and accelerate aging, or, alternatively, that optimize their function and limit inflammatory influences. In short, limiting inflammatory influences to capillary cells becomes the cornerstone of hazing aging.

Glossary

acetylcholine: A chemical neurotransmitter that decreases in brain tissue with advanced age and is associated with dementia.

adenosine diphosphate (ADP): The precursor to ATP, which, when phosphorylated in processes that utilize primarily glucose/ pyruvate and fatty acids, with or without oxygen, is converted to ATP. The ATP/ ADP ratio in the cell's cytoplasm becomes a very sensitive feedback loop, causing mitochondria to make more ATP.

adenosine triphosphate (ATP): The primary energy unit of the endothelial cell and all cells of the human organism. It is produced from adenosine diphosphate (ADP) in the cytoplasm via anaerobic metabolism (without oxygen) by glycolysis, and in the mitochondria via aerobic metabolism using the Krebs cycle and electron-transport chain.

advanced age: For our purposes, this is defined as greater than seventy-five years of age; it is used interchangeably with the word *elderly*.

advanced glycation end products (AGES): These are usually proteins, but occasionally fats, to which glucose attaches as a free radical, damaging the protein and limiting its effectiveness to function. This attachment is completed without an enzyme facilitator. The result is a buildup of dysfunctional proteins, which has been associated with capillary-cell dysfunction and high- glycemic-index foods, such as bread.

aging: Clinically defined as a result of progressive arterial- tree and capillary-cell decline from combinations of acquired genetic aberrations and the accumulation of aggregate vascular inflammatory risks. Inherent in this discussion is progressive damage to nuclear and mitochondrial DNA, which causes functional decline of the nucleus and mitochondria to code, make energy, and control feedback loops to other organelles and the end organ. When coupled with increases in inflammatory free radicals, reductions in antioxidants (increased oxidative stress), as well as increased membrane thickening and plaque formation in larger arteries, the table is set for aging consequences. Aging affects all aspects of capillary function, with its greatest impact on immune surveillance.

allopathic medicine: Also known as *modern medicine,* involves the use of taking a thorough history and performing a physical examination, coupled with laboratory and imaging studies, to arrive at a diagnosis and treatment of disease caused by symptoms. Critics of allopathic medicine point toward too much connection of treatments with big pharmaceutical company products/drugs, disintegration of the doctor-patient relationship, increased cost of delivery, fragmentation of care, and lack of emphasis on preventative health care.

alpha-lipoic acid (ALA): A short chain omega-3 fatty acid that has a diversified anti-inflammatory effect on capillary and end-organ cells.

alveoli: The specialized epithelial cells of the lung that couple with capillary cells which function in gas exchange of oxygen and carbon dioxide.

aneurysm: A balloon-like sac that occurs in large arteries from combinations of shear stress and free-radical and inflammatory debris in the walls of these arteries, causing them to thin and dilate. As the walls thin, the aneurysm gets larger, becomes more sack- like, and is prone to leak blood into the artery walls, eventually rupturing and causing sudden death.

angina pectoris: A symptom, usually chest pressure or pain, that originates from heart muscle lacking adequate oxygen to support a given workload (force of contraction times the heart rate).

angiogenesis: The process where new blood vessels are formed through the stimulation of VEGF (vascular endothelial growth factor). The process of making new blood vessels to assist end organs to function better is controlled by signaling of capillary cells to and from the blood and end organ.

angiotensin II: A potent vasoconstrictor that causes smooth muscles in all arteries except capillaries to contract, making their lumens smaller and increasing blood pressure.

angiotensin converting enzyme inhibitors (ACEs): A group of engineered medications that block the production of angiotensin II, thereby relaxing artery smooth muscles, increasing their lumen diameter and decreasing blood pressure.

angiotensin receptor blockers (ARBs): Another group of medications that decrease the hypertensive effects of angiotensin II by blocking the receptor sites that are used by angiotensin II to cause smooth muscle in arterial walls to constrict.

anions: Negatively charged minerals that are attracted to the positively charged cations. An anion example would be chloride or phosphate. Sodium chloride (table salt) is a common combination. (Compare with *cations*.)

antioxidants: Substances/molecules (often vitamins) that can attach to free radicals and limit their toxicity to cell membranes and organelles.

apnea: Occurs during sleep and is associated with excessive snoring and daytime drowsiness. The breathing patterns during sleep become irregular, or stop all together, resulting in reduced oxygen levels and altered sleep physiology. (Also see **obstructive sleep apnea.**)

arrhythmia: A comprehensive term used to describe a heart rhythm that is something other than normal sinus rhythm. Arrhythmias imply dysfunction of the heart's electrical system and can cause a variety of symptoms, from thumping in the chest, palpitations, dizziness, or even loss of consciousness. Some arrhythmias are benign and are more of an annoyance, whereas others can be very dangerous and lead to stroke or sudden death. No matter if benign or dangerous, arrhythmias need to be fettered out and treated if they cause serious symptoms.

arteriosclerosis/atherosclerosis: Also called *hardening and narrowing of the arteries,* this is a chronic and progressive disease that correlates with vascular inflammatory risk factors and advanced age. The process begins with arterial-membrane thickening and progresses to the development of soft plaque, often at bifurcation or branching of arteries, and eventually becomes calcified to what is known as *hard plaque.* Once plaque matures to obstruct 70 percent or more of the arterial lumen, symptoms to end organs upstream from the plaque occur, and capillary function to these end organs becomes stressed. Symptoms are most common in end organs that are very energy and oxygen sensitive, such as the heart or brain.

basement membrane: The membrane of the capillary cell that is on the end-organ side of the cell. The basement membrane's morphology can vary substantially between different end organs and is used to define the relationship of the capillary cell to the end-organ cell. It can be a cohesive tight barrier, or fenestrated, full of pores of varying size, or even large spaces (as in the liver) where there is no membrane.

berberine: A substance found in many plants and roots. It has a bright-yellow color and has been used for medicinal purposes for over three hundred years. Most recently, it has been found to be useful in treating insulin resistance, the metabolic syndrome, as well as in cancer treatment and prevention. It may also have benefit in improving heart-muscle performance. As with any natural substance used for treatment of serious medical problems, it should be used with care, discussed with a health-care professional, and, at least initially, used as an adjunct to traditional treatments.

beta-blockers: A group of medications that block various beta- receptors throughout the body. *Beta-receptors* are involved in many different body functions, but one group effects heart rate and vascular smooth muscle. When blocked by this group of medications, combinations of reductions in heart rate and blood pressure occur, thereby producing a very effective way to "unload the heart," or cause the heart to beat requiring less energy. Beta- blockers therefore decrease all types of heart-related complications, including angina, heart failure, heart attack, and heart rhythm disturbances. They also effectively reduce blood pressure, and when used correctly, can be a foundation to effective vascular anti- inflammatory treatment.

blood-brain barrier: A critical barrier of protection for brain and spinal-cord nerve cells, composed of capillary cells, pericytes, and astrocyte epithelial cells. The capillary cells and their membranes and gap functions participate in actively transporting molecules to and from the blood and the brain-cell bath (cerebrospinal fluid). These processes require more energy than what capillary cells use in managing other end-organ function elsewhere. Breakdown of this barrier and leakage into the cerebrospinal fluid of blood constituents not appropriate for brain cells can lead to brain dysfunction.

body mass index (BMI): A number, based on height, weight, age, and sex, that estimates body-fat percentage. BMI has increased over the last forty years in Western culture. BMI of 36 or higher is considered to be the definition of morbid obesity and is tied to increases in diabetes and the metabolic syndrome.

calcitriol: The active form of vitamin D.

calcium channel blockers (CCBs): A diversified group of medications that block calcium reuptake in vascular smooth muscle in arterial walls, resulting in relaxation of smooth muscle, subsequent increases in lumen diameter, and then reductions in blood pressure. Some CCBs also reduce heart rate and can be used, when beta blockers are contraindicated or produce side effects, to treat angina and heart rhythm disturbances. Unlike beta-blockers, CCBs proven benefits to cardiovascular mortality have been more difficult to demonstrate.

carbohydrates: Substances that contain carbon, hydrogen, and oxygen and are used to produce and store energy. Simple carbohydrates are called mono- or disaccharides. When elevated in the bloodstream as the monosaccharide glucose, they produce metabolic consequences that are very vascular proinflammatory to the arterial tree and capillary cells. High glucose levels are linked to diabetes and elevated LDL cholesterol and triglycerides. In contrast to simple carbohydrates, complex carbohydrates, which consist of complex and branched chains of carbon molecules, are considered vascular anti-inflammatory; they have the opposite effect on diabetes, LDL cholesterol, and triglyceride blood levels.

carotid imaging/ultrasound: A noninvasive tool used to evaluate the lumens of the carotid and vertebral arteries for obstructive plaque and membrane thickening. Since these vessels supply the brain with blood, they can be used as an indicator of brain blood supply, a barometer for systemic vascular inflammation, and as prevention for stroke in those with preexisting obstructive carotid plaque. They can be used serially to measure changes in these arteries, as they pose no radiation risk from dye.

cations: Positively charged minerals often involved in membrane functioning; they include sodium, potassium, calcium, and magnesium. (Compare with *anions*.)

cerebral atrophy: Also called *shrinkage of the brain*, it is linked to loss of brain volume, net reduction in arterial blood flow to the brain, and loss of cognition.

cerebrospinal fluid (CSF): The unique fluid bath that is made by specialized capillary cells called the *choroid plexus* and supported by the remainder of the capillary network to the brain, known as the *blood-brain barrier*. The clear colorless bath provides brain cells with optimal combinations of electrolyte, nutrient, oxygen, and immune support. Maintaining the CSF requires capillary cells to be part of a blood-brain barrier unit that blocks and pumps out many blood constituents that the brain cells do not want.

chronic obstructive pulmonary disease (COPD): Progressive scarring of the lungs, usually from sustained particulate exposure, such as smoking cigarettes. Over time, these particulates overwhelm the lung's immune system, producing permanent scarring and reducing the ability to take a deep breath, which thereby decreases oxygen/carbon dioxide exchange. The degree of obstruction or restriction is often measured by a screening pulmonary function test, which can both diagnose and guide therapy. Chronic exposures to toxic particulates also increase the risk of pulmonary fibrosis, lung cancer, chronic bronchitis, and asthma.

chronic oxidative stress: A term used to describe the net accumulation of factors (free radicals) that impact the functioning of cells, including capillary cells. The term implies conditions that persistently increase free radicals, either due to increases in free-radical exposure or reductions in antioxidants to neutralize (reduce) them. (Also see **oxidative stress.**)

cirrhosis: A disease of the liver occurring from sustained exposure (usually over a period of twenty or more years) to toxic substances (alcohol) or viruses (hepatitis B or C) that infect the liver. The result replaces normal liver tissue with scar tissue. Liver capacity to function is substantially diminished. With removal of the offending toxin, and/ or treatment of the offending virus, normal liver tissue can sometimes regenerate.

coenzyme Q_{10} (CoQ_{10})/ubiquinone: Can be described as a cofactor integral to the production of energy in all cells. It also serves as an antioxidant and can be used to lessen muscle fatigue and pain in those taking statins or niacin for LDL cholesterol reduction.

collateral circulation: Most often used in reference to heart-muscle or brain circulation recovery, this implies adjacent circulation of blood from other blood vessels that would supply blood to end organs that have been otherwise compromised by a vascular occlusion or plaque.

computerized tomography (CT) scan: An imaging tool used to evaluate in two, and sometimes three, dimensions the internal structures of the body. Used to diagnose and treat serious illness, CT scans emit radiation, and as such, can produce harm to the immune system if done excessively over the course of a lifetime.

congestive heart failure: Occurs when heart muscle beats ineffectively to move blood either to the central circulation or the lung. It can be caused from leaking valves, fluid buildup around the heart, or poorly contracting heart muscle. Treatment often requires a variety of interventions that restores the capacity of the heart muscle to contract more effectively to move blood forward.

continuous positive airway pressure (CPAP): A treatment for obstructive sleep apnea. It usually involves a breathing mask that is applied at night during sleep in order to prevent abnormal breathing patterns and hypoxia.

coronary arteries: Originate just above the aortic valve annulus, and supply blood and oxygen to heart muscle and its infrastructure. When narrowed or obstructed by plaque, blood flow diminishes and oxygen deficit occurs, resulting in compromise of heart-muscle function and leading to a variety of serious heart conditions.

creatine phosphokinase (CPK): A muscle enzyme that is found normally in the blood. When levels increase, it can signal serious muscle pathology known as *rhabdomyolysis,* which can adversely affect kidney function. A serious side effect to statin treatment is the development of elevated CPK levels in the blood, which increase muscle pain and fatigue and effect kidney function.

creatinine: A molecule found in the blood and used as a proxy in assessing kidney function. Higher blood levels correlate with reduced kidney function.

cross-linkage: An inflammatory process caused by free radicals and associated with damaged DNA and altered coding capacity of nuclear or mitochondrial DNA. Protein synthesis, energy production, and signaling function of the cell are altered. Cross-linkage increases with age and is associated with increased free-radical concentrations, decreased antioxidant levels, and shrinkage of the telomere cap that protects the nuclear chromosomal DNA.

cysteine: An amino acid that is a precursor to *glutathione,* a potent all-purpose antioxidant.

cytokines: Small proteins that can be pro- or anti-inflammatory. They are ubiquitous to blood plasma, as well as to capillary and end-organ cells. They can assist in managing inflammation by being used for signaling purposes to attract or inhibit white blood cells and other plasma proteins.

diabetes mellitus: A disease that describes elevations of fasting blood sugars (above 125 mg/dL) and correlates with elevations in hemoglobin A1C (HbA1C). Diabetes can be juvenile-onset (type 1), which is caused by reduced insulin levels, or adult-onset (type 2), caused by lack of response of cells to use insulin in processes that metabolize glucose (sugars). Therefore, adult-onset diabetes is a disease of progressive increasing insulin resistance of cells to utilize glucose.

disaccharide: A simple carbohydrate that is composed of combining two monosaccharide molecules. For example, glucose and fructose are monosaccharides which, when combined, form sucrose (table sugar), a disaccharide.

docosahexaenoic acid (DHA): A long-chain essential omega-3 fatty acid that has numerous vascular anti-inflammatory benefits.

echocardiogram: Also known as a *2-D echo of the heart,* this is a noninvasive test/ultrasound that evaluates the anatomy and contractility of the heart. It can also be used in connection with exercise stress testing in order to improve accuracy in detecting serious coronary artery disease. The 2-D echo of the heart has become standard practice in screening for structural heart abnormalities.

eicosanoids: Are derived from both omega-3 and omega-6 long-chain fatty acids and can have numerous beneficial effects on vascular inflammation, immunity, and membrane function.

eicosapentaenoic Acid (EPA): A long-chain essential omega-3 fatty acid that, along with DHA, supports capillary and end-organ cell health and is considered vascular anti-inflammatory.

end organs: All the organs in the body that capillary cells connect with to support human life. Examples include skin, heart, brain, lung, kidney, and liver.

endothelial cells: These are the cells that line the lumens of the entire vascular tree. At the capillary level, they develop a specialized function in association with epithelial cells from specific end organs. For example, in the kidney, the capillary endothelial cells associate with kidney epithelial cells to form the glomerulus, which functions as part of a nephron in order to make urine.

endothelial membrane: Is the part of the endothelial cell that forms a barrier between the blood and the cytoplasm and organelles of the endothelial cell. (The endothelial membrane is also referred to as the *plasma membrane.*)

endothelin: A molecule produced by capillary cells that causes vasoconstriction of the smooth muscle surrounding the small arterioles and larger arteries, thereby narrowing their lumens, which reduces blood flow and potentially proinflammatory effects to capillary-cell and end-organ function. With advanced age and aggregate vascular inflammatory risk, endothelin levels increase.

endothelium (see **vascular endothelium**)

enterohepatic circulation: A network of blood vessels that picks up packaged nutrients from the intestines and sends them to the liver for processing and manufacturing.

epidemiology: The science of studying disease patterns in different cultures and populations. The results can be used to produce public-health initiatives.

epithelial cells: The cells that have evolved their form and function to become specific end-organ tissue. They have unique and specific interactions in capillary endothelial cells in each end organ.

epithelium: A term that encompasses all the epithelial cells of all the end organs in the human organism.

exocarp: The skin or outside protective layer of fruit. Is also known as epicarp.

fats: Molecules composed of fatty acids and glycerol. Fats that are saturated or trans fat are vascular proinflammatory. Other fats that are monounsaturated, or are composed of omega-3 fatty acids, are anti-inflammatory to the arterial tree and capillary cells.

fatty acids: Fat molecules that are often reduced from glycerol or triglycerides. Fatty acids can be long chain or short chain, and proinflammatory or anti-inflammatory to the arterial tree and capillary cells. Proinflammatory fatty acids are linked to insulin resistance, diabetes, and the metabolic syndrome.

fenestrated openings: Also referred to as *pores,* are the anatomic description of primarily the basement membrane of the capillary cell. Pores allow for more rapid filtering and/or movement of substrates to and from the blood, through the capillary cell, and then to and from the end organ. Most capillary cell basement membranes of the intestinal tract, kidney, and liver have pores of varying size.

free radicals: Potentially dangerous molecules that are both inside and outside of all cells, including capillary cells. Free radicals can be toxic (as in toxic ROS [reactive oxygen species]), which increases damage to cell infrastructure and membranes. Toxic free radicals are vascular proinflammatory. Other ROS can serve in feedback loops between organelles and membranes, and as such, can serve as a communication link. As cells age, they produce more toxic ROS and have fewer mechanisms available to eliminate them.

gap junction: This is the space between cells. Gap junctions can be loose or tight. Depending on their location, they can participate in barrier protection or active transport of molecules/nutrients from the blood to the end organ.

glomerulus: The specialized filtering unit of a nephron in the kidney, made up of capillary cells and podocyte epithelial cells that filter blood plasma to make urine.

glucose: A simple monosaccharide used in all cells to make energy. It is converted to pyruvate both in the cytoplasm and mitochondria. In the mitochondria, it is further reduced to acetyl coenzyme A (CoA), where it then enters the Krebs cycle to facilitate the production of reduced NAD and FAD for purposes of making even more energy through the electron-transport chain. Glucose/ pyruvate competes with fatty acids in mitochondria to make acetyl Co A. Too much fatty-acid substrate increases insulin resistance.

glutathione: A potent all-purpose antioxidant whose levels generally decrease with advanced age, aggregate vascular inflammatory risk, chronic illness, and increased oxidative stress to adversely affect capillary-cell and then end-organ function.

glycation: Usually describes the combination of a simple sugar (glucose) to a protein, without the benefit of an enzyme. This process can cause malfunction of the protein and therefore makes glucose act like a free radical.

: Used to describe the sugar concentration in diets. Diets with a high have more sugar in them and are considered much more vascular inflammatory.

glycogen: The form of how the liver stores carbohydrate.

grape seed extract (GSE): A process that creates a tablet or capsule of compressed grape seeds. Depending on the grape, a variety of polyphenol, antioxidant vitamins and minerals, including resveratrol, can be derived.

HbA1C/HGBA1C: A sensitive blood marker in assessing diabetes or management of diabetes. Generally, levels above 7 imply diabetic management that requires further treatment. High HbA1C levels imply diabetic management that is inadequate and is very vascular proinflammatory.

high-density lipoprotein (HDL cholesterol): This "good" cholesterol is considered vascular anti-inflammatory. It is composed of small and large particles, with the larger ones being more effective. With aging, HDL levels decrease, and this is correlated with less activity.

highly sensitive C-reactive protein (HSCRP): A marker in the blood used to assess vascular inflammation. The higher the number, the more inflammation of the vascular tree.

HMG-CoA reductase inhibitors: Naturally occurring and engineered molecules that block LDL cholesterol production in the liver. (Also see **statins.**)

holistic medicine: A philosophy of treatment in medicine emphasizing interventions that improve the entire human organism. As modern medicine has become more specialized and isolated, holism has found increased interest in finding treatments that improve emotional, spiritual, and physical well-being. The antithesis to holistic medicine is to treat a symptom without identifying the cause.

homeostasis: A comprehensive and integrative term summarizing how all the end organs work together to optimize total body function. Implied in the term is the integrative function of capillary cells throughout the arterial tree in effectively managing the needs of specific end organs for the benefit of the whole human. "One for all and all for one" best describes this unique symbiotic relationship of capillary cells, the vascular tree, and the end organs they serve.

homocysteine: A substance in the blood which, when elevated, is associated with increased vascular inflammation; it can be refractory to most conventional treatments.

hydrostatic pressure: The pressure on the endothelial plasma membrane caused by the force of blood being pushed through the lumen of the blood vessel. With hypertension, the hydrostatic force is increased. With large-vessel obstructive plaque, the hydrostatic pressure upstream behind the obstruction is decreased. Hydrostatic and osmotic pressures, together, produce influences that affect capillary-cell diffusion and active transport across their plasma membranes.

hypertension: Defined as blood pressures taken by an arm cuff of greater than 130/85 mm/Hg. Blood pressure is treated with medications when pressures consistently exceed 140/90 mm/Hg. Hypertension increases shear-force inflammation in large arteries and is considered very vascular inflammatory.

hypoglycemia: Described as when blood sugars fall below 70 mg/ dL. Hypoglycemia is often associated with weakness and headache; it can be made worse with overtreatment of diabetes, or by eating either too little food or too much simple sugar.

hypoxia: Defined as a reduction in blood oxygen levels to less than 90 percent oxygen saturation of hemoglobin. Hypoxia can be caused from heart or lung conditions, as well as vascular narrowing from arteriosclerosis of large vessels that reduces blood flow to end organs, thereby effecting capillary cell and end-organ function.

immune system: This is composed of a variety of inflammatory cells and molecules that fight infection and cancer and eliminate foreign particulates. Immune system surveillance is regulated by capillary cells. Depending on capillary-cell dysfunction, genetics, and environmental exposures, the immune system can under- or overachieve, resulting in serious infection, cancer, autoimmune disease, and/or too much scar tissue.

insulin resistance: Reduced effectiveness to metabolize simple sugars. Factors involved include advanced age, stress, lack of sleep, lipid disorders, hypothyroidism, depression, obesity, immobility, and genetics. Insulin resistance is considered highly vascular proinflammatory. Insulin resistance is a precursor to type 2 (adult-onset) diabetes. Insulin resistance can be prevented, in large part, by changing diet, doing regular exercise, and losing weight.

interleukins: Immune plasma proteins that mediate inflammation, and can either inhibit or stimulate an inflammatory response. Some, such as interleukin 6, can do both. Vascular proinflammatory conditions have increased levels of interleukin 6 in the affected tissues.

Krebs cycle: A process in the mitochondrial matrix of all cells that takes acetyl CoA and reduces it to water and carbon dioxide, yielding ATP and several molecules of reduced NAD and FAD (NADH, FADH), which then can be used by the electron-transport chain of the inner membrane to make even more ATP.

Kupffer cells: Specialized white blood cells in liver sinusoids. Kupffer cells support immune surveillance of capillary cells as they process blood plasma to liver hepatocytes. The Kupffer cells specialize in identifying foreign debris, bacteria, and viruses, removing them before they inflame the liver cells.

"leaky gut" syndrome: A condition where the intestinal epithelium does not package correctly, subsequently allowing larger molecules, such as proteins, and longer-chain fatty acids to be absorbed without being broken down into smaller constituents. The cause of this epithelial cell dysfunction is thought to be either related to abnormal intestinal bacteria, internal derangement of the epithelium cell, or capillary-endothelial-cell dysfunction that adversely affects intestinal epithelial cell function.

lipidemia: A generic term implying elevated blood lipids (fats), including LDL cholesterol and triglycerides.

lipoprotein (a): A subtype of LDL cholesterol that is vascular proinflammatory. Lipoprotein (a) is refractory to most lipid-lowering treatments, except high doses of niacin.

low-density lipoprotein (LDL cholesterol): The "bad" cholesterol that is vascular inflammatory. When oxidized as a small particle (Ox-LDL), it is very inflammatory to vascular membranes and endothelial cell infrastructure. Small LDL particles often begin the processes of large-vessel plaque development and arteriosclerotic vascular disease (hardening of the arteries).

lumen: The space in arteries and veins. It can increase or decrease, based on preexisting vascular plaque, membrane thickening, or effects of various molecules on vascular smooth muscle.

macrocytosis: A process often tied to B_{12} deficiency or alcoholism, it involves the enlargement of red blood cells. A larger red blood cell is clumsy as it traverses the small capillary lumen and is also prone to fragmentation.

macrophage: A specialized type of white blood cell. Also known as *scavenger cells,* they swallow debris, bacteria, abnormal proteins, and viruses and remove them from where they do not belong.

magnetic resonance imaging (MRI) scan: A sensitive imaging tool used to diagnose and treat disease. MRI is considered more sensitive than CT scan imaging, the expense of which, coupled with the use of dyes that can affect kidney function, limits usage to specific conditions. MRIs can be very helpful in evaluating neurodegenerative brain disease but not so much in establishing primary-care prevention strategies.

medication tolerance: A process that occurs over time, whereby taking a medication at a given dose produces less desired effect. When the dose is adjusted, side-effect risk increases.

mesocarp: The flesh of fruit.

MET: Also referred to as the *metabolic equivalent,* this is a quantifying tool for expressing energy utilization at rest or during exercise, expressed in kilocalories/kilogram/hour. One MET is equal to the amount of energy utilized at rest. Using exercise stress testing protocols, the maximum MET based on the level of exercise performed can be estimated. This allows for the MET variance (the difference between the estimated measured MET from stress testing and what would be expected at age twenty-five, or at peak performance) to be used as an approximate gauge to determine aging, with certain assumptions. For example a MET variance of 50 percent from what would be expected for maximal exercise at age twenty-five would reflect a 50 percent increase in aging of the vascular system; this would be expressed as an aging index of 2X.

metabolic syndrome: A perfect storm of vascular inflammation involving combinations of obesity, high blood pressure, high LDL cholesterol, and diabetes mellitus.

mitochondria: The primary energy-producing organelles in the endothelial cells and all end-organ cells. They require oxygen and have evolved extensive feedback loops, involving ADP/ATP ratios, calcium, nitric oxide, and ROS, that control membrane and organelle functioning. In capillary cells, mitochondria are responsible for 10 to 15 percent of energy production, whereas the anaerobic glycolysis cycle in the cytoplasm yields 85 to 90 percent of the capillary cell's energy needs.

monosaccharide: The simplest form of sugar. Examples of monosaccharides include glucose and fructose.

monounsaturated fats: Are considered vascular anti-inflammatory oils, as they are not sticky to vascular membranes and tend to not become trans fats when subjected to heating for purposes of cooking. Examples include extra virgin olive and avocado oils.

morbidity: A term used to define medical complications associated with a disease or treatment of disease. For example, morbidity of congestive heart failure could be fatigue, breathlessness, or atrial fibrillation. A comorbidity of diabetes could be peripheral nerve pain, blurred vision, or erectile dysfunction.

morphology: Describes cellular or gross anatomy. Morphology of cells is linked to how they function. For example, in the kidney, the glomerular epithelial cells have developed foot-like projections, known as *pods,* to increase surface area exposure to the glomerular endothelial cells so that they can filter more blood plasma to make urine.

mortality: Another word for *death,* it is often used to discuss a cause or effect of death, and is quantified as a mortality rate.

myalgia: A term that describes skeletal muscle pain.

myocardial infarction (MI): Irreversible injury to heart muscle caused by lack of oxygen supplied by coronary arteries. A large myocardial infarction can cause congestive heart failure, heart rhythm disturbances, and sudden cardiac death.

N-acetyl cysteine (NAC): Cysteine with an added acetyl group that improves intestinal absorption of cysteine. NAC can be converted to glutathione in all cells, a potent antioxidant.

N-acetyl-L-carnitine (ALC): A molecule that facilitates fatty-acid transport to make energy in skeletal muscle during periods of sustained demand (exercise); it is also used in the brain to increase acetylcholine levels. These levels decrease in the brains of the elderly and are tied to reduced cognition.

nephron: The unit that makes urine in the kidney. It is composed of a glomerulus (the filter of capillary cells and podocytes) as well as a network of collecting epithelial cells that serve to further concentrate or dilute the urine before it is emptied into the renal pelvis.

nitric oxide (NO): A molecule produced and controlled by capillary and small-artery endothelial cells, it causes relaxation of smooth muscle and increases lumen diameter, promoting more blood flow through the vessel. The production and maintenance of adequate levels of nitric oxide is considered vascular anti-inflammatory. With advanced age and aggregate vascular inflammatory risks, levels of nitric oxide decrease.

nucleus: In endothelial and all cells in the human organism, this is the organelle that contains the DNA to mastermind the blueprint of cellular function. Damage to DNA from free-radical cross-linkage and telomere shortening alters nuclear coding and reduces the capacity of the cell to function normally. This has serious repercussions to capillary and end organ-cell funciton.

obstructive sleep apnea: Refers to altered breathing patterns during sleep, associated with snoring and obesity, which can result in dangerous reductions in blood oxygen, as well as heart rhythm disturbances, heart attacks, strokes, and sudden death. During the day it is associated with excessive daytime drowsiness, accidents, and poor focus/concentration. It is treated with weight reduction, pressure masks, and dental appliances. The elderly have a higher incidence of undiagnosed sleep apnea as well as other sleep disturbances that are associated with vascular inflammatory risks and dementia. (Also see **apnea.**)

occlusion: Describes the processes linked to vascular plaque and sealed by thrombosis (platelet adhesion), or clot, whereby blood flow is completely cut off upstream, producing major stress to capillary and end-organ cells and often leading to death of end-organ cells and loss of function.

oncotic pressure: The effect that protein in the blood plasma has on pulling extravascular fluid from tissues back into the systemic circulation. (Also see **osmotic pressure.**)

organelles: Subunits suspended in the cytoplasm of endothelial and all cells in the human organism. Organelles have specific functions and respond to elaborate feedback loops. Two examples of important organelles are the nucleus and mitochondria.

osmotic pressure: A suction-pressure gradient usually caused by higher concentrations of proteins on one side of a membrane as compared to the other. Without active transport processes in place, the membrane bias is to allow dispersion of molecules to result in an isodense (neutral) molecular relationship on both of its sides. To maintain an osmotic gradient, membranes require energy to pump molecules back in order to prevent them from seeking equilibrium. When the osmotic pressure gradient involves protein or albumin, it is also known as *oncotic pressure.* Both osmotic and hydrostatic pressures in blood exert influences on capillary cells that can affect how they interact with the end organ. (Also see **oncotic pressure.**)

oxidative stress: Is defined as the inflammatory effect of toxic free radicals (ROS) on cellular membranes and organelles. Persistent oxidative stress (also called *chronic oxidative stress*) implies damage to nuclear and mitochondrial DNA and disruption of cell membranes rendering endothelial cells of the arterial tree, capillary cells, and then end-organ cells dysfunctional. With advanced age or aggregate vascular inflammatory risk oxidative stress increases. (Also see **chronic oxidative stress.**)

oxidized low-density lipoprotein (Ox-LDL): A highly inflammatory LDL particle with exposed electrons that easily attaches to and inflames membranes to start spirals of inflammation. When LDL particles are reduced by antioxidants, they become harmless in terms of causing inflammation, as their electrons have been covered.

pericytes: Cells that assist the capillary cell with immune support. Found adjacent to capillary and astrocyte cells of the blood-brain barrier, they provide additional barrier and immune-surveillance support in order to limit molecules' access to the cerebrospinal fluid.

peroxynitrite/superoxide: Inflammatory free radicals that can produce oxidative stress and intracellular membrane and organelle damage in endothelial and capillary cells, as well as end-organ cells. These free radicals usually leak from the mitochondrial matrix, increasing in levels as a result of advanced age and/or aggregate vascular inflammatory risks.

platelets: Small cells made in the bone marrow which can aggregate and cause blood to clot. They can be very dangerous in preexisting vascular plaque, and their effects are blocked by aspirin.

podocytes: Specialized epithelial cells composing the kidney glomerulus. Along with capillary cells, these cells filter blood plasma to make urine.

probiotics: Bacteria and some yeast that can nurture intestinal epithelial and capillary-cell function to assist in the absorption and packaging of nutrient.

prostacyclin: A naturally occurring vasodilator (relaxes smooth muscle, much like nitric oxide) and inhibitor of platelet aggregation.

protein: Constituent in the diet and in blood that contains amino acids and is considered essential for life.

pycnogenol: A substance found in a specific type of pine bark. It can have many different beneficial effects but can assist in lowering blood pressure by increasing nitric oxide levels.

pyruvate: The molecule made from reducing glucose. It can then be utilized to make energy.

reactive oxygen species (ROS): Oxidized potentially inflammatory free radicals that are formed inside cells, including the endothelial and capillary cell. ROS can contribute to oxidative stress and intracellular damage, or act as messengers in feedback loops to membranes and organelles. ROS increase with age and are mitigated (reduced) by antioxidants, which decrease with age. Increased ROS, coupled with nuclear telomere shortening as a result of advanced age, is considered a major risk factor to DNA damage and the nuclear/ mitochondrial coding mistakes that lead to cellular dysfunction.

renin-angiotensin system (RAS): Feedback loops from lung, liver, and kidney epithelia. When activated, RAS produces a net increase in blood pressure from large-artery vasoconstriction. RAS can be vascular inflammatory. With aging, there is a bias toward increased activation of RAS, producing higher blood pressures, with concomitant increases in large-vessel vascular inflammation from increased shear stress.

resveratrol: A unique molecule found predominantly in red wine that has numerous antioxidant and vascular anti-inflammatory properties that support capillary-cell function to all end organs.

rhabdomyolysis: A process involving painful muscle injury, which results in leakage of muscle enzymes into the blood. This leakage can damage the kidneys. Rhabdomyolysis can be a serious side effect to statins or high-dose niacin therapy. It can usually be reversed by discontinuing the medication and implementing supportive measures.

shear stress: A vascular inflammatory process associated with hypertension and aggregate vascular inflammatory risk. Shear stress occurs when a large-bored vessel divides into two smaller-bored vessels. The increase in velocity of blood flow through the smaller bore increases pressure on endothelial-cell membranes and leads to membrane inflammation, made worse from higher blood pressures and other vascular inflammatory risks.

silymarin: A molecule that has benefit in supporting capillary and hepatocyte-cell function to liver sinusoids.

sleep hygiene/efficiency: These terms are used to qualify and quantify sleep. *Sleep hygiene* involves behaviors that increase or decrease sleep quality, including sleep timing and place, food, alcohol, caffeine, drugs, stress, frequency of bathroom trips, and other influences that interfere with sleep intentions. *Sleep efficiency* involves the quality of sleep and is measured by awakenings/ arousals, apnea, total sleep time, and the percentage of time spent in the deeper levels of sleep. Both sleep hygiene and efficiency decrease with age and are correlated with dementia.

statins: Medications and supplements that lower LDL cholesterol. Also called *HMG-CoA reductase inhibitors,* statins have been used for centuries in Chinese medicine as red rice yeast. Statins can be divided into water- and fat-soluble, and are very effective in lowering the vascular inflammatory LDL cholesterol. Statins lower vascular inflammatory risk and many of the comorbidities of vascular disease. They are a powerful tool and a cornerstone medicine in fighting vascular disease and stabilizing endothelial and capillary-cell function. Because of this improvement, statins may influence capillary-cell immune surveillance and cause lower rates of cancer. When taking statins, supplementing with CoQ_{10} can reduce muscle pains. Because of a possible link to diabetes, all patients taking a statin should be on a sugar-restricted diet.

stress testing: A valuable tool for determining an exercise prescription, diagnosing coronary artery disease, and establishing a maximum exercise MET. Stress testing can be coupled with echocardiography or nuclear imaging to improve sensitivity in diagnosing coronary artery disease.

therapeutic window: The ideal blood level and dosage range of a medicinal or supplement, resulting in maximum clinical benefit with the fewest side effects. Some treatments have a narrow therapeutic window, which means the dose and blood level must be monitored carefully to get the best clinical result.

thrombosis: Also known as *clot formation,* implies the likelihood of vascular occlusion and cutoff of blood supply upstream to capillary and end-organ cells.

tissue plasminogen activator (T-PA): A potent anticlotting protein that is naturally made in the body and controlled by capillary-cell signaling. It is also commercially available as a potent clot-busting medicine used to improve outcomes in acute ischemic stroke and acute myocardial infarction.

tocopherols: The family of vitamin E compounds.

triglycerides: Fat molecules which, when elevated in the blood, are vascular inflammatory. The levels of triglycerides are increased in a variety of conditions, including obesity, alcoholism, pancreatitis, hepatitis, hypothyroidism, insulin resistance and diabetes mellitus, and inherited lipid disorders. Lowering serum triglycerides often requires a multipronged approach addressing liver, pancreas, and thyroid issues, as well as treatment of diabetes.

ultrasound scan: Noninvasive test that provides 2-D and 3-D imaging of arteries and end organs. It is considered a very safe and effective way of getting information about structures inside the human body.

vascular endothelium: All of the endothelial cells that line the lumen of the entire arterial and venous tree throughout the body, including the capillaries.

vasoactive endothelial growth factor (VEGF): A substance secreted primarily by capillary cells to produce new blood vessels in situations where the end organ needs more oxygen and nutrients.

vasoconstriction: The process whereby smooth muscle that surrounds the endothelium of larger arteries contracts, thereby reducing the lumen (or diameter of the blood vessel), usually resulting in higher blood pressures. When sustained, increases in shear forces produce vascular inflammation, membrane thickening, and plaque formation, often in arteries that bifurcate, where resistance is highest. (A *vasoconstrictor* is an agent of vasoconstriction.)

vasodilation: The opposite of vasoconstriction. (A *vasodilator* is an agent of vasodilation.)

vasoregulation: A process controlled by endothelial/capillary cells and involving the net signaling of influences that constrict or relax smooth muscle. Managing smooth muscle has the effect of increasing or decreasing blood flow through capillaries and the end organ.

VO_2 Max: The measured amount of oxygen utilized with maximum exercise. It is the gold-standard measurement for evaluating exercise performance. A proxy to measured VO_2 Max is the estimated MET.

Von Willebrand factor: A clotting factor which, when present in blood or tissue, promotes thrombosis.

Bibliography

Absi, M., J. I. Bruce, and D. T. Ward. "The inhibitory effect of simvastatin and aspirin on histamine responsiveness in human vascular endothelial cells." *Am J Physiol* 306 (7): C679–86.

Adams, O., and U. Laufs. "Antioxidative effects of statins." *Arch Toxicol* 82 (12): 885–92.

Agosti, V., S. Graziano, and L. Artiaco. "Biological mechanisms of stroke prevention by physical activity in type 2 diabetes." *Acta Neurol Scand* 119 (4): 213–23.

Ahima, R. S., and D. A. Antwi, "Brain regulation of appetite and satiety," *Endocrinology and Metabolism Clinics of North America* 2008, 37 (4):811-823.

Akar, J. G., W. Jeske, and D. J. Wilber. "Acute onset human atrial fibrillation is associated with local cardiac platelet activation and endothelial dysfunction." *J Am Coll Cardiol* 51 (18): 1790–93.

Albrecht, E. W., C. A. Stegeman, P. Heeringa, R. H. Henning, and H. van Goor. "Protective role of endothelial nitric oxide synthetase." *J Pathol* 199 (1): 8–17.

Aldini, G., M. Carini, A. Piccoli, G. Rossoni, and R. M. Facino. "Procyanidins from grape seeds protect endothelial cells from peroxynitrite damage and enhance endothelium-dependent relaxation in human artery: new evidence for cardio protection." *Life Sci* 73 (22): 2883–98.

Asosingh, K., G. Cheng, W. Xu, B. M. Savasky, M. A. Aronica, X. Li, and S. C. Erzurum. "Nascent endothelium initiates Th2 polarization of asthma." *J Immunol* 190 (7): 3458–65.

Atkins, K. B., I. J. Lodhi, L. L. Hurley, and D. B. Hinshaw. "N-acetylcysteine and endothelial cell injury by sulfur mustard." *J Appl Toxicol* 20 (suppl. 1): s125–28.

Bachschmid, M. M., S. Schildknecht, R. Matsui, R. Zee, D. Haeussler, R. A. Cohen, D. Pimental, and B. V. Loo. "Vascular aging: chronic oxidative stress and impairment of redox-signaling consequences of vascular homeostasis and disease." *Ann Med* 45 (1): 17–36.

Bajari, T. M., W. Winnicki, E. T. Gensberger, S. I. Scharrer, K. Regele, K. Aumayr, C. Kopecky, B. M. Gmeiner, M. Hermann, R. Zeillinger, and G. Sengolge. "Known players, new interplay in atherogenesis: chronic shear stress and carbamylated LDL induce and modulate expression of atherogenic LR11 in human coronary artery endothelium." *Thromb Haemost* 111 (20): 323–32.

Bakris, G. L. "Pharmacological augmentation of endothelium derived nitric oxide synthesis." *J Manag Care Pharm* 13 (5 suppl.): S9–12.

Bauer, J. A. and D. A. Sinclair, "Therapeutic potential of resveratrol: the in vivo evidence," *Nature Reviews Drug Discovery, 2006 (5):493-506.*

Bazzoni, G., O. Martinez-Estrada, and E. Dejana. "Molecular structure and functional role of vascular tight junctions." *Trends Cardiovasc Med* 9 (6): 147–52.

Behrendt, D., and P. Ganz. "Endothelial function, from vascular biology to clinical applications." *Am L Cardiol* 90 (10C): 40L–48L.
Bendsen, N. T., S. Stender, P. B. Szecsi, S. B. Pedersen, S. Basu, L. I. Hellgren, J. W. Newman, T. M. Larsen, S. B. Haugaard, and A. Astrup. "Effect of industrially produced trans fats on markers of systemic inflammation: evidence from a randomized trial in women." *J Lipid Res* 52 (10): 1821–28.

Berk, M., L. S. Williams, F. N. Jacka, A. O'Neil, J. A. Pasco, S. Moylan, N. B. Allen, A. L. Stuart, A. C. Hayley, M. L. Byrne, and M. Maes. "So depression is an inflammatory disease, but where does the inflammation come from?" *BMC Medicine* 11, no 1 (200): 1–16.

Bian K., M. F. Doursout, and F. Murad. "Vascular system: role of nitric oxide in cardiovascular diseases." *J Clin Hypertens (Greenwich)* 10 (4): 304–10.

Bijl, M. "Endothelial activation, endothelial dysfunction and premature atherosclerosis in systemic autoimmune diseases." *Neth J Med* 61 (9): 273–77.

Blum, A., and R. Shamburek. "The pleiotropic effects of statins on endothelial function, vascular inflammation, immunomodulation and thrombogenesis." *Atherosclerosis* 203 (2): 325–30.

Bolduc, V., N. Thorin-Trescases, and E. Thorin. "Endothelium-dependent control of cerebrovascular functions through age: exercise for healthy cerebrovascular aging." *Am J Physiol Heart Circ Physiol* 305 (5): h620–33.

Brodskaia, T. A., V. A. Nevzorova, B. I. Gel'ter, and E. V. Motkina. "Endothelial dysfunction and respiratory diseases." *Ter Arkh* 79 (3): 76–84.

Brutsaert, D. L. "Cardiac endothelial myocardial signaling: its role in cardiac growth, contractile performance, and rhythmicity." *Physiol Rev* 83 (1): 59–115.

Brutsaert, D. L., and K. Verh. "The indispensable role of cardiac endothelium in the structure and function of the heart." *Acad Geneeskd Belg* 65 (2): 75–116.

Buddi, R., B. Lin, S. R. Atilano, N. C. Zorapapel, M. C. Kenney, and D. J. Brown. "Evidence of oxidative stress in human corneal diseases." *Histochem Cytochem* 50 (3): 341–51.

Buscemi, S., L. Cosentino, G. Rosafio, M. Morgana, A. Mattina, D. Sprini, and S. Verga. "Effects of hypocaloric diets with different es on endothelial function and glycemic variability in overweight and in obese adult patients at increased cardiovascular risk." *Rini GB Clin Nutr* 32 (3): 346–52.

Calo, L. A., E. Pagnin, P. A. Davis, A. Semplicini, R. Nicolai, M. Calvani, and A. C. Pessina. "Antioxidant effect of L-carnitine and its short chain esters: relevance for the protection from oxidative stress related cardiovascular damage." *Int J Cardiol* 107 (1): 54–60.

Carman, A. J., P. A. Dacks, R. F. Lane, D. W. Shineman, and H. M. Fillit, "Current evidence for the use of coffee and caffeine to prevent age related cognitive decline and Alzheimer's disease," *The J of Nutrition, Health & Aging*, 2014, 18 (4): 383-392.

Carmina, E., F. Orio, S. Palomba, R. A. Longo, T. Cascella, A. Colao, G. Lombardi, G. B. Rini, and R. A. Lobo, "Endothelial dysfunction in PCOS: role of obesity and adipose hormones," *The American J of Medicine*, 2006, 119 (4): 356.e1–356.e6.

Carreiro-Lewandowski, E. "Update on selected markers used in risk assessment for vascular disease." *Clinical Lab Sci* 17 (1): 43–49.

Chan, A. C. "Vitamin E and atherosclerosis." *J Nutr* 128 (10): 1593–96.
Chapuy, M,-C., P Preziosi, M. Maamer, S. Amaud, P. Galan, S. Hercberg and P. J. Meunier, "Prevalence of vitamin D insufficiency in an adult normal population," *Osteoporosis International* 1997, 7 (5): 439-443.

Chen, Y. H., M. Chang, and B. L. Davidson. "Molecular signatures of disease brain endothelia provide new sites for CNS directed enzyme therapy." *Nat Med* 15 (10): 1215–18.

Choi, E. Y., S. Santoso, and T. Chavakis. "Mechanisms of neutrophil transendothelial migration." *Front Biosci* (landmark ed.) 14: 1596–1605.

Cines, D. P., E. S. Pollak, C. A. Buck, J. Loscalzo, G. A. Zimmerman, R. D. McEver, J. S. Pober, T. M. Wick, B. A. Konkle, B. S. Schwartz, E. S. Barnathan, K. R. McCrae, B. A. Hug, A. M. Schmidt, and D. M. Stern. "Endothelial cells in physiology and in the pathophysiology of vascular disorders." *Blood* 91: 3527–61.

Coin, A., E. Perissinotto, M. Najjar, A. Girardi, E. M. Inelman, G. Enzie, E. Manzato, and G. Sergi, "Does religiosity protect against cognitive decline in Alzheimer's dementia," *Current Alzheimer Research*, 2010, 7 (5): 445-452.

Conway, D. E., and M. A. Schwartz. "Flow-dependent cellular mechanotransduction in atherosclerosis." *J Cell Sci* 126 (pt. 22): 5101–09.

Courtois, A., C. Prouillac, I. Baudrimont, C. Ohayon-Courtes, V. Freud-Michael, M. Dubois, M. Lisbonne-Autissier, R. Marthan, J. P. Savineau, and R. Muller. "Characterization of the components of urban particulate matter mediating impairment of nitric oxide dependent relaxation in intrapulmonary arteries." *J Appl Toxicol* 34 (6): 667–74.

Cromer, W. E., J. M. Mathis, D. N. Granger, G. V. Chaitanya, and J. S. Alexander. "Role of the endothelium in inflammatory bowel diseases." *World J Gastroenterol* 17 (5): 578–93.

Dalaklioglu, S., J. Golbasi, and C. Ogutman. "Comparative effects of preoperative angiotensin converting enzyme inhibitor, statin, and beta-blocker treatment on human internal mammary artery reactivity in patients with coronary artery disease: a pilot study." *Open Cardiov Med J* 7 (2013): 69–75.

D'Alessio, P. "Aging and the endothelium." *Gerontol* 39 (2): 165–71. D'Alessio, P. "Endothelium as a therapeutic target." *Investig Drugs* 2 (12): 1720–24.

De Beer, V. J., D. Merkus, S. B. Bender, D. L. Tharp, D. K. Bowles, D. J. Duncker, and M. H. Laughlin. "Familial hypercholesterolemia impairs exercise-induced systemic vasodilation due to reduced NO bioavailability." *J Appl Physiol* 115 (12): 1767–76.

Deer, R. R., and C. L. Heaps. "Exercise training enhances multiple mechanisms of relaxation in coronary arteries from ischemic hearts." *Am J Physiol Heart Circ Physiol* 305 (9): h1321–31.

Del Bo, C., A. S. Kristo, A. Z. Kalea, S. Ciappellano, P. Rios, M. Porrini, and D. Klimis-Zacas. "The temporal effect of a wild blueberry (Vaccinium angustifolium) enriched diet on vasomotor tone in the Sprague Dawley rat." *Nutr Metab Cardiovasc Dis* 22 (2): 127–32.

Delles, C., G. Michelson, L. Harazny, S. Oehmer, K. F. Hilgers, and R. E. Schmieder. "Impaired endothelial function of the retinal vasculature in hypertensive patients." *Stroke* 35 (6): 1289–93.

Demmer, R. T., and M. Desvarleau, "Periodontal infections and cardiovascular disease," *Jada* 2006, 137 (10s): 14s–20s.

De Silva, T. M., and F. M. Faraci. "Effects of angiotensin II on the cerebral circulation: the role of oxidative stress." *Front Physiol* 3: 00484.

Dhein, S., A. Kabat, A. Olbrich, P. Rosen, H. Schroder, and F. W. Mohr. "Effect of chronic treatment with vitamin E on endothelial dysfunction in a type 1 in vivo diabetes mellitus model and in vitro." *J Pharmacol Exp Ther* 305 (1): 114–22.

Dimasi, D., W. Y. Sun, and C. S. Bonder. "Neutrophil interactions with the vascular endothelium." *Int Immunopharmacol* 17 (4): 1167–75.

Ding, L., T. L. Saunders, G. Enikolopov, and S. J. Morrison. "Endothelial and perivascular cells maintain haematopoietic stem cells." *Nature* 481 (7382): 457–62.

Dobarro, D., M. C. Gomez-Rubin, A. Sanchez-Recalde, R. Moreno, G. Galeote, S. Jimenez-Valero, L. Calvo, E. Lopez, de Sa, and L. L. Lopez-Sendon. "Current pharmacologic approach to restore endothelial dysfunction." *Cardiovsc Hematol Agents Med Chem* 7(3): 212–22.

Dong, C., and X. X. Lei. "Biomechanics of cell rolling: shear flow, cell surface adhesion and cell deformability." *J Biomech* 33 (1): 35–41.

Dos Reis-Neto, E. T., A. E. da Sila, C. M. Monteiro, L. M. Camargo, and E. I. Sato. "Supervised physical exercise improves endothelial function in patients with systemic lupus erythematosus." *Rheumatology (Oxford)* 52 (12): 2187–95.

Duggal, J. K., M. Singh, N. Attri, P. Singh, N. Ahmed, S. Pahwa, J. Molnar, S. Singh, S. Khosla and R. Arora, "Effect of niacin therapy on cardiovascular outcomes in patients with coronary artery disease," *J Cardiovasc Pharmacol.* 2010, 15 (2):158-166.

Dyer, L. A., and C. Patterson. "Development of the endothelium: an emphasis on heterogeneity." *Semin Thromb Hemost* 36 (3): 227–35.
Dysken, M. W., M. Sano, S. Asthana, J. E. Ventrees, M. Pallaki, M. Llorente, S. Love, G. d. Schellenberg, J. R. McCarten, J. Malphurs, S. Prieto, P. Chen, D. J. Loreck, G. Trapp, R. S. Bakshi, J. E. Mintzer, J. L Heidebrink, A. Vidal-Cardona, L. M. Arroyo, A. R. Cruz, S. Zachariah, N. Kowell, M. P. Chopra, S. Craft, S. Thielke, C. L. Turvey, C. Woodman, K. A. Monnell, K. Gordan, J. Tomaska, Y. Segal, P. N. Peduzzi, and P. D. Guarina, "Effect of vitamin E and memantine on functional decline in Alzheimer disease the TEAM-AD cooperative randomized trial," *JAMA*. 2014, 311 (1): 33-44.

Eiselein, L., D. W. Wilson, M. W. Lame, and J. C. Rutledge. "Lipolysis products from triglyceride rich lipoproteins increase endothelial permeability, perturb zonula occludens 1 and F actin, and induce apoptosis." *Am J Physiol—Heart and Circ Physiol* 292 (6): H2745–53.

Eleftheriadis, T., G. Antoniadi, G. Pissas, V. Liakopoulos, and I. Stefanidis. "The renal endothelium in diabetic nephropathy." *J Ren Fail* 35 (4): 592–99.

Enzmann, G., C. Mysiorek, R. Gorina, Y. J. Cheng, S. Ghavampour, M. J. Hannocks, V. Prinz, U. Dirnagl, M. Endres, M. Prinz, R. Beschorner, P. N. Harter, M. Mittelbronn, B. Engelhardt, and L. Sorokin. "The neurovascular unit as a selective barrier to polymorphonuclear (PMN) infiltration into the brain after ischemic injury." *Acta Neuropathol* 125 (3): 395–412.

Ertek, S., E. Akgul, A. F. Cicero, U. Kutuk, S. Demirtas, S. Cehreli, and G. Erdogan. "1,25-dihydroxyvitamin D levels and endothelial vasodilator function in normotensive women." *Arch Med Sci* 8 (2012) (1): 47–52.

Ewaschuk, J. B.,H. Diaz, L. Meddings, B. Diederichs, A. Dmytrash, J. Backer, M. Looijer-van Langen, and K. L. Madsen, "Secreted bioactive factors from *Bifidobacterium infantis* enhance epithelial cell barrier function," *American Journal of Physiology-Gastrointestinal and Liver Physiology*, 2008, 295(5): G1025-G1034.

Fahadi, I. E., V. Gaddam, L. Garza, F. Romeo, and J. L. Mehta. "Inflammation, infection and atherosclerosis." *Brain Behav Immun* 17 (4): 238–44.

Foster, W., D. Carruthers, G. Y. Lip, and A. D. Blann. "Relationships between endothelial, inflammatory and angiogenesis markers in rheumatoid arthritis: implications for cardiovascular pathophysiology." *Thromb Res* 124 (4): 659–64.

Fouty, B. "Diabetes and the pulmonary circulation." *Am J Physiol Lung Cell Mol Physiol* 295 (5): 1725–26.

Frances, J. W., N. C. Drosu, W. J. Gibson, V. C. Chitalia, and E. R. Edelman. "Dysfunctional endothelial cells directly stimulate cancer inflammation and metastasis." *Int J Cancer* 133 (6): 1334–44.

Francis, A. A., and G. N. Pierce. "An integrated approach for the mechanisms responsible for atherosclerotic plaque regression." *Exp Clin Cardiol* 16 (3): 77–86.

Fraser, P. A. "The role of free radical generation in increasing cerebrovascular permeability." *Free Radic Biol Med* 51 (5): 967–77. Frick, M., A. Suessenbacher, H. F. Alber, and O. Pachinger. "Endothelial dysfunction and peripheral arterial disease." *Eur Heart* 28 (15): 1910; author reply, 1910–11.

Frigerio, S., M. Gelati, G. Boncoraglio, E. Ciusani, D. Croci, M. de Curtis, E. Parati, and A. Salmaggi. "Pravastatin in vivo reduces mononuclear cell migration through endothelial monolayers." *Neurol Sci* 27 (4): 261–65.

Fu, P., and K. G. Birukov. "Oxidized phospholipids in control of inflammation and endothelial barrier." *Transl Res* 153 (4): 166–76. Fuentes, J. C., A. A. Salmon, and M. A. Silver. "Acute and chronic oral magnesium supplementation: effects on endothelial function, exercise capacity, and quality of life in patients with symptomatic heart failure." *Congest Heart Fail* 12 (1): 9–13.

Futrakul, N., T. Panichakul, S. Siririnha, P. Futrakul, and P. Siriviryakul. "Glomerular endothelial dysfunction in chronic kidney disease." *Ren Fail* 26 (3): 259–64.

Gage, M. C., N. Y. Yulasheva, H. Viswambharan, P. Sukumar, R. M. Cubbon, S. Galloway, H. Imrie, A. Skromna, J. Smith, C. L. Jackson, M. T. Kearney, and S. B. Wheatcroft. "Endothelium specific insulin resistance leads to accelerated atherosclerosis in areas with disturbed flow patterns: a role for reactive oxygen species." *Atherosclerosis* 230 (1): 131–39.

Galgauskas, S., D. Krasauskaite, M. M. Pajaujis, G. Juodaite, and R. S. Asoklis. "Central corneal thickness and corneal endothelial characteristics in healthy, cataract, and glaucoma patients." *J. Clin Ophthalmol* 6 (2012): 1195–99.

Galgauskas, S., D. Norvydaite, D. Krasauskaite, S. Stech, and R. S. Asoklis. "Age-related changes in corneal thickness and endothelial characteristics." *Clin Interv Aging* 8 (2013): 1445–50. Galle, J., T. Quaschning, S. Seibold, and C. Wanner. "Endothelial dysfunction and inflammation: What is the link?" *Kidney Int* 63 (2003): S45–49.

Gans, R. O. "The metabolic syndrome, depression, and cardiovascular disease: interrelated conditions that share pathophysiological mechanisms." *Med Clin North Am* 90 (4): 573–91.

Gloddek, B., K. Lamm, and W. Arnold. "Pharmacological influence on inner-ear endothelial cells in relation to the pathogenesis of sensorineural hearing loss." *Adv Otorhinolaryngol* 59 (2002): 75–83.

Golbidi, S., M. Badran, N. Ayas, and I. Laher. "Cardiovascular consequences of sleep apnea." *Lung* 190 (2): 113–32.

Goldin, A., J. A. Beckman, A. M. Schmidt, and M. A. Creager. "Advanced glycation end products: sparking the development of diabetic vascular injury." *Circulation* 114 (2006): 597–605.

Goligorsky, M. S. "Endothelial-cell dysfunction and nitric oxide synthetase." *Kidney Int* 58 (3): 1360–76.

Goni de Cerio, F., A. Alvarez, F. J. Alvarez, M. C. Rey-Santano, D. Alonso-Alcondo, V. E. Mielgo, E. Gastiasoro, and E. Hilario. "MgSO4 treatment preserves the ischemia-induced reduction in S 100 protein without modification of the expression of endothelial tight junction molecules." *Histol Histopathol* 24 (9): 1129–38.

Greaves, C.J., and L. Farbus, "Effects of creative and social activity on the health and well-being of socially isolated older people: outcomes from a multi-method observational study," *Perspectives in Public Health* May 2006, vol. 126 (3): 134-142.

Greene, A. K., S. Wiener, M. Puder, A. Yoshida, B. Shi, A. R. Perez-Atayde, J. A. Efstathiou, L. Holmgren, A. P. Adamis, M. Rupnick, J. Folkman, and M. S. O'Reilly. "Endothelial directed hepatic regeneration after partial hepatectomy." *Ann Surg* 237 (4): 530–35. Greenstein, A. S., A. Price, K. Sonoyama, A. Paisley, K. Khavandi, S. Withers, L. Shaw, O. Paniagua, R. A. Malik, and A. M. Heagerty. "Eutrophic remodeling of small arteries in type 1 diabetes mellitus is enabled by metabolic control: a ten-year follow-up study." *Hypertension* 54 (1): 134–41.

Grundy, S., "Prediabetes, metabolic syndrome and cardiovascular risk," *J. Am Coll Cardiol.* 2012; 59 (7): 635–643.

Haram, P. M., O. J. Kemi, and U. Wisloff. "Adaption of endothelium to exercise training: insights from experimental studies." *Front Biosci* 13 (2008): 336–46.

Hawkes, C. A., D. Michalski, R. Anders, S. Nissel, J. Grosche, I. Bechmann, R. O. Carare, and W. Hartig. "Stroke induced opposite and age dependent changes of vessel associated markers in comorbid transgenic mice with Alzheimer's-like alterations." *Exp Neurol* 250 (2013): 270–81.

Hayashi, T., Nihon, Rohen, Igakki, Zasshi. "Senescence and endothelial dysfunction/atherosclerosis." *Japanese J Geriatrics* 48 (2): 142–45.

Heal, D. J., S. L. Smith, and R. L. Jones, "Central Regulation of food intake and energy expenditure," *Neuropharmacology* 2012, 63 (1): 1–168.

Heermeiet, K., R. Schneider, A. Heinloth, C. Wanner, S. Dimmeler, and J. Galle. "Oxidative stress mediates apoptosis induced by oxidized low density lipoprotein and oxidized lipoprotein (a)." *J Kidney Int* 56 (4): 1310–12.

Hernandez-Guerra, M., J. C. Garcia-Pagan, J. Turnes, P. Bellot, R. Deulofey, J. G. Abraldes, and J. Bosch. "Ascorbic acid improves the intrahepatic endothelial dysfunction of patients with cirrhosis and portal hypertension." *J Hepatology* 43 (3): 485–91.

Hoenig, M. R., C. Bianchi, A. Rosenzweig, and F. W. Selke. "Decreased vascular repair and neovascularization with aging: mechanisms and clinical relevance with an emphasis on hypoxia inducible factor 1." *Curr Mol Med* 8 (8): 754–67.

Hoffman, R. P., A. S. Dye, and J. A. Bauer. "Ascorbic acid blocks hyperglycemic impairment of endothelial function in adolescents with type 1 diabetes." *Pediatr Diabetes* 13 (8): 607–10. Holman, D. W., R. S. Klein, and R. M. Ransohoff. "The blood-brain barrier, chemokines and multiple sclerosis." *Biochem, Biophys Acta* 181 (2): 220–30.

Hornstra, G. "The influence of dietary fats on experimental arterial thrombosis in vivo in rats." *Acta Univ Carol Med Monogr* 53 (1972): 421–26.

Huang, X. L., Y. L. Ling, T. N. Zhu, Zhongguo, Ying, Yong, Sheng, Li, Xue, Zhi. "The role of N-acetylcysteine against the injury of pulmonary artery induced by LPS." *Chinese J Appl Physiol* 18 (4): 370–73.

Hudlicka, O. "Microcirculation in skeletal muscle." *Muscles, Ligaments and Tendons J* 1 (1): 3–11.

Hwa, C., and A. Sebastian. "Endothelial biomedicine: its status as an interdisciplinary field, its progress as a basic science, and its translational bench to bedside gap." *Aird WC Endothelium* 12 (3): 139–51.

Ignarro, L. J. "Physiology and pathophysiology of nitric oxide." *Kidney Int* 49 (suppl. 55): S2–5.

Inagami, T., M. Naruse, and R. Hoover. "Endothelium as an endocrine organ." *Ann Rev Physiol* 57 (1995): 171–89.

Iwakiri, Y., and R. J. Groszman. "Vascular endothelial dysfunction in cirrhosis." *J Hepatology* 46 (5): 927–33.

Jaimes, E. A., P. Hua, R. X. Tian, and L. Raij. "Human glomerular endothelium: interplay among glucose, free fatty acids, angiotensin II and oxidative stress." *Am J Physiol Renal Physiol* 298 (1): f125–32.

Jane-Wit, D., and H. J. Chun. "Mechanisms of dysfunction in senescent pulmonary endothelium." *J Gerontol A Biol Sci Med Sci* 67 (3): 236–41.

Jang, Y., O. Y. Kim, H. J. Ryu, J. Y. Kim, S. H. Song, J. M. Ordovas, and J. H. Lee. "Visceral fat accumulation determines postprandial lipemic response, lipid peroxidation, DNA damage, and endothelial dysfunction in nonobese Korean men." *J Lipd Res* 44 (12): 2356–64.

Jelic, S., D. J. Lederer, T. Adams, M. Padeletti, P. C. Colombo, P. Factor, and T. H. LeJemtel. "Endothelial repair capacity and apoptosis are inversely related in obstructive sleep apnea." *Vasc Health Risk Manag* 5 (2009): 909–20.

Ji, H-F., and L. Shem. "Berberine: A potential multipotent natural product to combat Alzheimer's disease," *Molecules* 2011, 16 (8): 6732–40.

Jochum, T., M. Weissenfels, A. Seeck, S. Schulz, M. K. Boettger, and K. J. Bar. "Endothelial dysfunction during acute alcohol withdrawal syndrome." *Drug Alcohol Depend* 119 (1–2): 113–22.

Kalanuria, A. A., P. Nyquist, and G. Ling. "The prevention and regression of atherosclerotic plaques: emerging treatments." *Vasc Health Risk Manag* 8 (2012): 549–61.

Kals, J., P. Kampus, M. Kals, A. Pulges, R. Teesalu, K. Zilmer, T. Kulisaar, T. Salum, J. Eha, and M. Zilmer. "Inflammation and oxidative stress are associated differently with endothelial function and arterial stiffness in healthy subjects and in patients with atherosclerosis." *Scand J Clin Lab Invest* 68 (7): 594–601.

Kapachi, P., and J. Vijg. "Aging—lost in translation?" *N Engl J Med* 361 (2009): 2669–70.

Karatzi, K., C. Papamichael, E. Karatzis, T. G. Papaioannou, P. T. Voidonikola, G. D. Vamvakou, J. Lekakis, and A. Zampelas. "Postprandial improvement of endothelial function by red wine and olive oil antioxidants: a synergistic effect of components of the Mediterranean diet." *J Am Coll Nutr* 27 (4): 448–53.

Karpenko, N., N. V. Bulkina, and E. V. Ponukalina. "Present views of the etiology and pathogenesis of rapidly progressive periodontitis." *Arkh Patol* 71 (1): 57–60.

Katusic, Z. S., and S. A. Austin. "Endothelial nitric oxide: protector of a healthy mind." *Eur Heart J* 35 (14) 888–94.

Kelleher, R. J., and R. L. Soiza. "Evidence of endothelial dysfunction in the development of Alzheimer's disease: is Alzheimer's a vascular disorder?" *Am J Cardiovasc Dis* 3 (4): 197–226.

Kellner, A., and D. C. Dju Chang. "Studies on the permeability of the endothelium to lipids in relation to atherosclerosis." *Am J Pathol* 27 (4): 683–84.

Kellog, N. J., and G. S. Savige. "Dietary advanced glycation end products restriction for the attenuation of insulin resistance, oxidative stress and endothelial dysfunction: a systemic review." *Eur J Clin Nutr* 67 (3): 239–48.

Kendall, M. J., and V. Toescu. "Nonlipid properties of statins." *J Clin Pharm Ther* 24 (1): 3–5.

Khattri, S., and G. Zandman-Goddard. "Statins and autoimmunity." *Immunol Res* 56 (2–3): 348–57.

Kim, S. Y., J. T. Park, J. K. Park, J. S. Lee, and J. C. Choi. "Aging impairs vasodilatory responses in rats." *Korean J Anesthesiol* 61 (6): 506–10.

Kimura, Y., M. Matsumoto, Y. B. Deng, K. Iwai, J. Munehira, H. Hattori, T. Hoshino, K. Yamada, K. Kawanishi, and H. Tsuchiya. "Impaired endothelial function in hypertensive elderly patients evaluated by high resolution ultrasonography." J Cardiol 15 (5): 563–68.

Kimura, Y., M. Matsumoto, E. Miyauchi, Y. B. Deng, K. Iwai, and H. Hattori. "Noninvasive detection of endothelial dysfunction in elderly with NIDDM by ultrasonography." *Echocardiography* 18 (7): 559–64.

Kliche, S., and J. Waltenberger. "VEGF receptor signaling and endothelial function." *IUBMB Life* 52 (1–2): 61–66.

Koenig, W. "Inflammation and coronary artery disease: an overview." *Cardiol Rev* 9 (1): 31–35.

Koh, K. K., S. H. Han, P. C. Oh, E. K. Shin, and M. J. Quon. "Combination therapy for treatment or prevention of atherosclerosis: focus on the lipid R AAS interaction." *Atherosclerosis* 209 (2): 307–13.

Kotimaa, A. A., A. M. Zainana, E. Pulkkinen, L. Huusko, S. E. Heinonen, I. Kholova, H. Stedt, H. P. Lesch, and S. J. Vla-Herttuala. "Endothelium specific overexpression of human vascular endothelial growth factor D in mice leads to increased tumor frequency and a reduced lifespan." *Gene Med* 14 (3): 182–90.

Kris-Etherton, P. M., W. S. Harris, and L. J. Appel (for the AHA Nutrition Committee), "Omega-3 Fatty Acids and Cardiovascular Disease," *Arteriosclerosis, Thrombosis, and Vascular Biology* 2003 (23): 151–52.

Kronenberg F, and A. Fugh-Berman. "Complementary and alternative medicine for menopausal symptoms: a review of randomized, controlled trials," *Ann Intern Med* 2002, 137 (10): 805–13

Kuo, L., N. Thengchaisri, and T. W. Hein. "Regulation of coronary vasomotor function by reactive oxygen species." *Mol Med Ther* 1 (1): 100–101.

Kvandal, P., A. Stefanovska, M. Veber, H. D. Kvernma, and K. A. Kirkeboen. "Regulation of human cutaneous circulation evaluated by laser Doppler flowmetry ionophoresis and spectral analysis: importance of nitric oxide and prostaglandins." *Microvasc Res* 65 (3): 160–71.

Lahera, V., M. Goicoechea, S. G. De Vinuesa, M. Miana, N. de las Heras, V. Cachofeiro, and J. Luno. "Endothelial dysfunction, oxidative stress and inflammation in atherosclerosis: beneficial effects of statins." *Curr Med Chem* 14 (2): 243–48.

Lahteenmaki, T. A., L. Seppo, J. Laakso, R. Korpela, H. Vanhanen, M. J. Tikkanen, and H. Vapaatalo. "Oxidized LDL from subjects with different dietary habits modifies atherogenic processes in endothelial and smooth muscle cells." *Life Sci* 66 (5): 455–65.

Langer, H. F., and T. Chavakis. "Leukocyte-endothelial interactions in inflammation." *J Cell Mol Med* 13 (7): 1211–20.

Lee, S. A., H. J. Kim, K. C. Chang, J. C. Baek, J. K. Park, J. K. Shin, W. J. Choi, J. H. Lee, and W. Y. Paik. "DHA and EPA down-regulate COX 2 expression through suppression of NF kappa B activity in LPS treated human umbilical vein endothelial cells." *Korean J Physiol Pharmacol* 13 (4): 301–07.

Leech, S., J. Kirk, J. Plumb, and S. McQuaid. "Persistent endothelial abnormalities and blood-brain barrier leak in primary and secondary multiple sclerosis." *Neuropathol Appl Neurobiol* 33 (1): 86–98.

Lele, R. D. "Causation, prevention and reversal of vascular endothelial dysfunction." *J Assoc Physicians India* 55 (2007): 643–51.

Lerman, A., and A. M. Zeiher. "Contemporary Reviews in Cardiovascular Medicine: Endothelial function: cardiac events." *Circulation* 111 (2005): 363–68.

Li, Q., K. Park, C. Li, C. Rask-Madsen, A. Mima, W. Qi, K.

Mizutani, P. Huang, and G. L. King. "Induction of vascular insulin resistance and endothelin-1 expression and acceleration of atherosclerosis by the overexpression of protein kinase beta isoform in the endothelium." *Circ Res* 113 (4): 418–27.

Lippi, G., M. Montagnana, E. J. Favaloro, E. J., and M. Franchini. "Mental depression and cardiovascular disease: a multifaceted bidirectional association." *Semin Thromb Hemost* 35 (3): 325–36. Littarru, G. P., L. Tiano, R. Belardinelli, and G. F. Watts. "Coenzyme Q_{10}, endothelial function, and cardiovascular disease." *Biofactors* 37 (5): 366–73.

Liu, M., J. Woo, S. H. Wu, and S. C. Ho. "The role of vitamin D in blood pressure, endothelial and renal function in postmenopausal women." *Nutrients* 5 (7): 2590–2610.

Liu, Z., S. H. Ko, W. Chai, and W. Cao. "Regulation of muscle microcirculation in health and diabetes." *Diabetes Metab J* 36 (2): 83–89.

Lopez-Lopez, J. G., J. Moral-Sanz, G. Frazziano, M. J. Gomez-Villalobos, J. Flores-Hernandez, E. Monjaraz, A. Cogolludo, and F. Perez-Vizcaino. "Diabetes induces pulmonary artery endothelial dysfunction by NADPH oxidase induction." *Am J Physiol Lung Cell Mol Physiol* 295 (5): 1727–32.

Low, Dog T. "Menopause: a review of botanical dietary supplements." *Am J Med* 2005; 118 (12 Suppl 2): 98–108.

Luiking, Y. C., M. P. Engelen, and N. E. Deutz. "Regulation of nitric oxide production in health and disease." *Curr Opin Clin Nutr Metab Care* 13 (1): 97–104.

Lum, H., and K. A. Roebuck. "Oxidative stress and endothelial-cell dysfunction." *Am J Physiol-Cell Physiol* 280 (4): C719–41.

Maclay, J. D., D. A. McAllister, N. L. Mills, F. P. Paterson, C. A. Ludlam, E. M. Drost, D. E. Newby, and W. Macnee. "Vascular dysfunction in chronic obstructive pulmonary disease." *Am J Respir Crit Care Med* 180 (6): 513–20.

Manrique, C., G. Lastra, M. Gardner, and J. R. Sowers. "The renin angiotensin aldosterone system in hypertension: roles of insulin resistance and oxidative stress." *Med Clin North Am* 93 (3): 569–82.

Marin E., and W. C. Sessa. "Role of endothelial-derived nitric oxide in hypertension and renal disease." *Curr Opin Nephrol Hypertens* 16 (2): 105–10.

McCarty, M. F. "Gamma tocopherol may promote effective NO synthetase function in protecting tetrahydrobiopterin from peroxynitrite." *Med Hypothesis* 69 (6): 1367–70.

Mehrotra, D., J. Wu, I. Papangeli, and H. J. Chun. "Endothelium as a gatekeeper of fatty acid transport." *Trends Endocrinol Metab* 25 (2): 99–106.

Mendes-Ribeiro, A.C., G. E. Mann, L. R. De Meirelles, M. B. Moss, C. Matsuura, and T. M. Brunini. "The role of exercise on L-arginine oxide pathway in chronic heart failure." *Open Biochem J* 3 (2009): 55–65.

Meuwese, M. C., H. L. Mooij, M. Nieuwdorp, B. van Lith, R. March, H. Vink, J. J. Kastelein, and E. S. Stroes. "Partial recovery of the endothelial glycocalyx upon rosuvastatin therapy in patients with heterozygous familial hypercholesterolemia." *J Lipid Res* 50 (1): 148–53.

Michaels, C. J. "Endothelial-cell functions." *Cell Physiol* 196 (2003): 430–43.

Middleton, L.E., and K. Yaffe," Promising strategies for the prevention of dementia," *Arch Neuro 2009* 66 (10): 1210–15. Miettinen, T. A., and H. Gylling. "Vascular effects of diets, especially plant sterol ester consumption." *J Am Coll Cardiol* 51 (16): 1562–63.

Miller, D. W., A. M. Joussen, and F. G. Holz. "The molecular mechanisms of neovascular age-related macular degeneration." *Der Ophthalmologe* 100 (2): 92–96.

Mori, T. A. "Omega-3 fatty acids and blood pressure." *Cell Mol Biol (noisy le grand)* 56 (1): 83–92.

Moyna, N. M. "The effect of physical activity on endothelial function in man." *Acta Physiol Scand* 180 (2): 113–23.

Murphy, B. P., T. Stanton, and F. G. Dunn. "Hypertension and myocardial ischemia." *Med Clin North Am* 93 (3): 681–95.

Musa, M. G., C. Torrens, and G. F. Clough. "The microvasculature: a target for nutritional programming and later risk of cardiometabolic disease." *Acta Physiol (Oxf)* 210 (1): 31–45.

Myers, Jonathon. "Exercise and cardiovascular health," *Circulation 2003,* 107: e2–e5.

Nag, S., A. Kapadia, and D. J. Stewart. "Review: molecular pathogenesis of blood-brain barrier breakdown in acute brain injury." *Neuropathol Appl Neurobiol* 37 (1): 3–23.

Nathanson, D., and T. Nystrom. "Hypoglycemic pharmacological treatment of type 2 diabetes: targeting the endothelium." *Mol Cell Endocrinol* 297 (1–2): 112–26.

Neri, S., S. Calvagno, B. Mauceri, M. Misseri, A. Tsami, C. Vecchio, G. Mastrosimone, A. Di Pino, D. Maiorca, A. Judica, G. Romano, and A. Rizzotto. "Effects of antioxidants on postprandial oxidative stress and endothelial dysfunction in subjects with impaired glucose tolerance and type 2 diabetes." *Eur J Nutr* 49 (7): 409–16.

Nishikawa, S. I., M. Hirashima, S. Nishikawa, and M. Ogawa. "Cell biology of vascular endothelial cells." *Ann N Y Acad Sci* 947: 35–40; discussion, 41.

Oh, S. J., W. C. Ha, J. I. Lee, T. S. Sohn, J. H. Kim, J. M. Lee, S. A.

Chang, O. K. Hong, and H. S. Son. "Angiotensin II inhibits insulin binding to endothelial cells." *Diabetes Metab J* 35 (3): 243–47.

Okaji, Y., N. H. Tsuno, J. Kitayama, S. Saito, T. Takahashi, K. Kawai, K. Yazawa, M. Asakage, N. Hori, T. Watanabe, Y. Shibata, K. Takahashi, and H. Nagawa. "Vaccination with autologous endothelium inhibits angiogenesis and metastasis of colon cancer through autoimmunity." *Cancer Sci* 95 (1): 85–90.

O'Keefe, J. H., K. A. Bybee, and C. J. Lavie. "Alcohol and cardiovascular health, the razor-sharp double-edged sword," *J Am Coll Cardiol* 2007, 50 (11): 1009–14.

Olgac, U., J. Knight, D. Poilikakos, S. C. Saur, H. Alkadhi, L. M. Desbiolles, P. C. Cattin, and V. Kurtcuoglu. "Computed high concentrations of low density lipoprotein correlate with plaque locations in human coronary arteries." *J Biomech* 44 (13): 2466–71.

Onetti, Y., M. Jimenez, F. Altayo, M. Heras, E. Vila, and A. P. Dantas. "Western type diet induces senescense, modifies vascular function in nonsenescent mice and triggers adaptive mechanisms in senescent ones." *Exp Gerontol* 48 (12): 1410–19.

Otani, H. "Oxidative stress as pathogenesis of cardiovascular risk associated with metabolic syndrome." *Antioxid Redox Signal* 15 (7): 1911–26.

Ouchi, N., S. Kihara, T. Funahashi, Y. Matsuzawa, and K. Walsh. "Obesity, adinonectin and vascular inflammatory disease." *Curr Opin Lipidol* 14 (6): 561–66.

Oyama, N., Y. Yagita, T. Sasaki, E. Omura-Matsuoka, Y. Terasaki, Y. Sugiyama, S. Sakoda, and K. J. Kitagawa. "An angiotensin II type 1 blocker can preserve endothelial function and attenuate brain ischemic damage in spontaneously hypertensive rats." *Neurosci Res* 88 (13): 2889–98.

Ozkul, A., M. Ayhan, C. Yenisey, A. Akyol, E. Guney, and F. A. Ergin. "The role of oxidative stress and endothelial injury in diabetic neuropathy and neuropathic pain." *Neuro Endocrinol Lett* 31 (2): 261–64.

Padade, F., I. D. Alexa, D. Azoicai, L. Panaghiu, and G. Ungureanu. "Oxidative stress in atherosclerosis." *Rev Med Chir Soc Med Nat Iasi* 107 (3): 502–11.

Palomo, I., R. Morre-Carrasco, M. Alarcon, A. Rojas, F. Espana, V. Andres, and H. Gonzalez-Navarro. "Pathophysiology of the proantherothrombotic state in the metabolic syndrome." *Front Biosci* (school ed.) (2010) 1; 2: 194–208.

Patti, G., R. Melfi, and G. Di Sciascio. "The role of endothelial dysfunction in the pathogenesis and in the clinical practice of atherosclerosis, current evidences." *Recenti Prog Med* 96 (10): 499–507.

Pedata, P., N. Bergamasco, A. D'Anna, P. Minutolo, L. Servillo, N.

Sannolo, and M. L. Balestrieri. "Apoptotic and proinflammatory effect of combustion generated organic nanoparticles in endothelial cells." *Toxicol Lett* 219 (3): 307–14.

Pericleous, C., I. Giles, and A. Rahman. "Are endothelial microparticles potential markers of vascular dysfunction in the antiphospholipid syndrome?" *Lupus* 18 (8): 671–75.

Petersson, H., L. Lind, J. Hulthe, A. Elmgren, T. Cederholm, and U. Riserus. "Relationships between serum fatty acid composition and multiple markers of inflammation and endothelial function in an elderly population." *Atherosclerosis* 201 (1): 298–303.

Pezzini, A., E. Del Zotto, I. Volonghu, A. Giossi, P. Costa, and A. Padovani. "New insights into pleiotrophic effects of statins for stroke prevention." *Mini Rev Med Chem* 9 (7): 794–804.

Pham, D., K. Hayakawa, J. H. Seo, M. N. Nguyen, A. T. Som, B. J. Lee, S. Guo, K. W. Kim, E. H. Lo, and K. Arai. "Crosstalk between oligodendrocytes and cerebral endothelium contributes to vascular remodeling after white matter injury." *Glia* 60 (6): 875–81.

Physicians Committee for Responsible Medicine, "A natural approach to Menopause." Washington D.C.

Pober, J. S. "Endothelial activation: intracellular signaling pathways." *Arthritis Res* 4 (suppl. 3): s109–16.

Poitras, V. J., D. J. Slattery, B. M. Levac, S. Fergus, B. J. Gurd, and K. E. Pyke. "The combined influence of fat consumption and repeated mental stress on brachial artery flow mediated dilation: a preliminary study." *Exp Physiol* 99 (4): 715–28.

Prisby, R. D., M. W. Ramsey, B. J. Behnke, J. M. Dominquez, II, A. J. Donato, M. R. Allen, and M. D. Delp. "Aging reduces skeletal blood flow, endothelial dependent vasodilation and NO bioavailability in rats." *J Bone Miner Res* 22 (8): 1280–88.

Rajendran, P., T. Rengarajan, J. Thangavel, Y. Nishigaki, D. Sakthisekaran, G. Sethi, and I. Nishigaki. "The vascular endothelium and human disease." *Int J Biol Sci* 9 (10): 1057–69.

Rangel-Huerta, O. D., C. M. Aguillera, M. D. Mesa, and A. Gil. "Omega-3 long chain polyunsaturated fatty acids supplementation on inflammatory biomarkers: a systematic review of randomized clinical trials." *Br J Nutr* 107 (suppl. 2): s159–70.

Repo. H., and J. M. Harlan. "Mechanisms and consequences of phagocyte adhesion to endothelium." *Ann Med* 31 (3): 156–65.

Rizza, S., M. Tesauro, C. Cardillo, A. Gali, M. Lantorno, F. Gigli, P. Sbraccia, M. Rederici, M. J. Quon, and D. Lauro. "Fish oil supplementation improves endothelial function in normoglycemic offspring of patients with type 2 diabetes." *Atherosclerosis* 206 (2): 569–74.

Robert, C., R. C. Fuhlbrigge, J. D. Kieffer, S. Ayehunie, R. O. Hynes, G. Cheng, S. Grabbe, U. H. Von Andrian, and T. S. Kupper. "Interaction of dendritic cells with skin endothelium: A new perspective on immunosurveillance." *J Exp Med* 189 (4): 627–36.

Rosei, E. A., and D. Rizzoni. "Small artery remodeling in diabetes." *J Cell Mol Med* 14 (5): 1030–36.

Ross, R. "Mechanisms of Disease. Atherosclerosis: an inflammatory disease." *N Engl J Med* 340 (1999): 115–26.

Rozen, T. D., M. L. Oshinsky, C. A. Gebeline, K. C. Bradley, W. B. Young, A.L. Shechter, and S. D. Silberstein, "Open label trial of coenzyme Q10 as a migraine preventative," *Cephalgia, An International Journal of Headache* 2002, 22 (2): 137–141.

Ruszczak, Z. "Human skin microvascular endothelial cells." In *Endothelial Cell Culture.* 1st ed., 77–90. Roy Bickell, ed. Cambridge: Cambridge University Press: 1996.

Sahebkar, A. "Effect of niacin on endothelial function: a systematic review and meta-analysis of randomized controlled trials." *Vasc Med* 19 (1): 54–56.

Sandoo, A., J. J. Van Zanten, G. S. Metsios, D. Carroll, and G. D. Kitas. "The endothelium and its role in regulating vascular tone." *Open Cardiovasc Med J* (2010) 4: 302–12.

Santillan, R. M. "Effect of L-arginine, vitamins C and E, and omega-3 acids (DHA, EPA) on oxidative stress and endothelial dysfunction in the mouse model of renal insufficiency." *An R Acad Nac Med (Madr)* 124 (3): 623–34.

Sawada, N., and J. K. Liao, "Targeting eNOS and beyond: emerging heterogeneity of the role of endothelial Rho proteins in stroke prevention." *Expert Rev Neurother* 9 (8): 1171–86.

Schweitzer, K. S., H. Hatoum, M. B. Brown, M. Gupta, M. J. Justice, B. Beteck, B., M. Van Demark, Y. Gu, R. G. Presson, W. C. Hubbard, and I. Petrache. "Mechanisms of lung endothelial barrier disruption induced by cigarette smoke: role of oxidative stress and ceramides." *Am J Physiol Lung Cell Mol Physiol* 301 (6): 1836–46.

Scott, D. W., and R. P. Patel. "Endothelial heterogeneity and adhesion molecules N-glycosylation: implications in leukocyte trafficking inflammation." *Glycobiology* 23 (6): 622–33.

Sena, C. M., A.M. Pereira, and R. Seica. "Endothelial dysfunction—a major mediator of diabetic vascular disease." *Biochem, Biophys Acta* 1832 (12): 2216–31.

Siddiqi, F., and A. Advani. "Endothelial podocyte crosstalk: the missing link between endothelial dysfunction and albuminuria in diabetes." *Diabetes* 62 (11): 3647–55.

Simka, M. "Blood-brain barrier compromise with endothelial inflammation may lead to autoimmune loss of myelin during multiple sclerosis." *Curr Neurovasc Res* 6 (2): 132–39.

Slater, S. J., J. L. Seiz, A. C. Cook, B. A. Stagliano, and C. J. Buzas. "Inhibition of protein kinase by resveratrol." *Biochem, Biophys Acta* 1637 (1): 59–69.

Smoliga, J. M., J. A. Baur, and H. A. Hausenblas, "Reseveratrol and health- A comprehensive review of human clinical trials," *Molecular Nutrition & Food Research* 2011, 55 (8): 1129–1141.

Soares, M. P., Y. Lin, K. Sato, K. M. Stuhlmeier, and F. H. Bach. "Accommodation." *Immunol Today* 20 (10): 434–37.

Song, J. W., and L. L. Munn. "Fluid forces control endothelial sprouting." *Proc Natl Acad Sci USA* 108 (37): 15342–47.

Spence, J.D., and J.C. Peterson, "Vitamins and progression of atherosclerosis in hyper-homocysteinemia," *The Lancet* 1998, 351 (9098): 263.

Stanhope, K. L., A. A. Bremer, V. Medici, K Nakajima, Y. Ito, T. Nakano, G. Chen, T. Hou Fong, V. Lee, R. Menorca, N. L. Keim, and P. J Havel. "Consumption of fructose and high frustose corn syrup increase postprandial triglycerides, LDL- cholesterol, apolipoprotein-B in young men and women," *The J of Clin End & Met* 2011, 96 (10): 1596-1605.

Stefanec, T. "How the endothelium and its bone marrow derived progenitors influence development of disease." *Med Hypotheses* 62 (2): 247–51.

Stockklauser-Farber, K., T. Ballhausen, A. Laufer, and P. Rosen. "Influence of diabetes on cardiac nitric oxide synthetase expression and activity." *Biochem, Biophys Acta* 1535 (1): 10–20.

Sugden, J. A., J. I. Davies, M. D. Witham, A. D. Morris, and A.D. Struthers. "Vitamin D improves endothelial function in patients with type 2 diabetes mellitus and low vitamin D levels." *Diabet Med* 25 (3): 320–25.

Sun J., Y. Xu, S. Sun, Y. Sun, and X. Wang. "Intermittent high glucose enhances cell proliferation and VEGF expression in retinal endothelial cells: the role of mitochondrial reactive oxygen species." *Mol Cell Biochem* 343 (1–2): 27–35.

Sun, Y., K. Xun, Y. Wang, and X. Chen, "A systemic review of the anticancer properties of berberine, a natural product from Chinese herbs," *Anti-Cancer Drugs* 2009, 20(9): 757–69.

Tamler, R. "Diabetes, obesity and erectile dysfunction." *Gender Med* 6 (suppl. 1): 4–16.

Tanabe, T., S. Maeda, T. Miyauchi, M. Lemitsu, M. Takanashi, Y. Irukayama-Tomobe, T. Yokota, H. Ohmori, and M. Matsuda. "Exercise training improves ageing induced decrease in ENOS expression in the aorta." *Acta Physiol Scand* 178 (1): 3–10.

Taslipinar, A., H. Yaman, M. I. Yilmaz, S. Demirbas, M. Saglam, M. Y. Taslipinar, M. Agilli, Y. G. Kurt, A. Sonmez, O. Azal, E. Bolu, M. Yenicesu, and M. Kutlu. "The relationship between inflammation, endothelial dysfunction and proteinuria in patients with diabetic nephropathy." *Scand J Clin Lab Invest* 71 (7): 606–12.

Taylor, S. Y., H. M. Dixon, S. Yogonayagam, N. Price, and D. Lang. "Folic acid modulates eNOS activity via effects on posttranslational modification and protein interaction." *Eur J Pharmacol* 714 (1–3): 193–201.

Theones, M., A. Ogucki, S. Nagamia, C. S. Vaccari, R. Hammoud, G. E. Umpierrez, and B. V. Khan. "The effects of extended release niacin on carotid intimal media thickness, endothelial function and inflammatory markers in patients with the metabolic syndrome." *Int J Clin Pract* 61 (11): 1942–48.

Thorin-Trescases, N., G. Voghel, N. Farhat, A. Drouin, M. E. Gendron, and E. Throin. "Age dependent oxidative stress: toward an irreversible failure in endothelial maintenance." *Med Sci (Paris)* 26 (10): 875–80.

Tousoulis, D., A. Plastiras, G. Siasos, E. Oikonomou, A. Vereniotis, E. Kokkou, K. Maniatis, N. Gouliopoulos, A. Miliou, and T. Stefanadis Paraskevopoulos. "Omega-3 PUFAs improved endothelial function and arterial stiffness with a parallel anti-inflammatory effect in adults with metabolic syndrome." *Atherosclerosis* 232 (1): 6–10.

Tsao, C. W., S. Seshadri, A. S. Beiser, A. J. Westwood, C. Decarli, R. Au, J. L. Himali, N. M. Hamburg, J. A. Vita, D. Levy, M. G. Larson, E. J. Benjamin, P. A. Wolf, R. S. Vasan, and G. F. Mitchell. "Relations of arterial stiffness and endothelial function to brain aging in the community." *Neurology* 81 (11): 984–91.

Tsuda, K. "Statins and nitric oxide production against ischemic stroke." *Stroke* 39 (11): e170; author reply, e171.

Turner, R., N. Etienne, M. G. Alonso, S. de Pascual-Teresa, A. M. Minehane, P. D. Weinber, and G. Rimbach. "Antioxidant and antiatherogenic activities of olive oil phenolics." *Int J Vitam Nutr Res* 75 (1): 61–70.

Uchino, B.N., "Social support and health: a review of physiological processes potentially underlying links to disease outcomes," *J of Behavioral Medicine* 2006, 29(4): 377–87.

Ukena, S. N., A. Singh, U. Dringenberg, R. Engelhardt, U. Seidler, W. Hansen, A. Bleich, D. Bruder, A. Franzke, G. Rogler, S. Suerbaum, J. Buer, F. Gunzer, and A. M. Westendorf, "Probiotic Escherichia coli Nissle 1917 inhibits leaky gut by enhancing mucosal integrity." *PloS one, 2007,* 12 (2): e1308.

Ullrich, V., and M. Bachschmid. "Superoxide as a messenger of endothelial function." *Biochem Biophys Res Commun* 278 (1): 1–8. Ungvari, Z., W. E. Sonntag, and A. Csiszar. "Mitochondria and aging in the vascular system." *J Mol Med (Berl)* 88 (10): 1021–27.

Van Brussel, B. C., S. S. Soedamah-Muthu, R. M. Henry, C. G. Schalkwijk, I. Ferreira, N. Chaturvedi, M. Toeller, J. H. Fuller, and C. D. Stehouwer. "Unhealthy dietary patterns associated with inflammation and endothelial dysfunction in type 1 diabetes: The EURODIAB study." *EURODAB Prospective Complications Study Group Nutr Metab Cardiovasc Dis* 23 (8): 758–64.

Ventura, H. O., and M. Reddy. "The eye as an indicator of heart failure in diabetic patients." *J Am Coll Cardiol* 51 (16): 1579–80.

Vestweber, D. "Adhesion and signaling molecules controlling the transmigration of leukocytes through endothelium." *Immunol Rev* 218 (2007 Aug): 178–96.

Victor, M., N. Apostolova, R. Herance, A. Hernandez-Mijares, and M. Rocha. "Oxidative stress and mitochondrial dysfunction in atherosclerosis: mitochondria targeted antioxidants as potential therapy." *Curr Med Chem* 16 (35): 4654–67.

Vingtdeux, V., L. Giliberto, H. Zhao. P. Chandakkar, Q. Wu, J. E. Simon, E. M. Janle, J. Lobo, M. G. Ferruzzi, P. Davies, and P. Marambaud. "AMP-activated protein kinase signaling activation by reseveratrol modulates amyloid beta peptide metabolism," *The Journal of Biological Chemistry,* 2010, (285): 9100–13.

Virdis, A., A. Bacca, R. Colucci, E. Duranti, M. Fornai, G. Materazzi, C. Ippolito, N. Bernardini, C. Blandizzi, G. Bernini, and S. Taddei. "Endothelial dysfunction in small arteries of essential hypertensive patients: role of cyclooxygenase 2 in oxidative stress generation." *Hypertension* 62 (2): 337–44.

Voelkel, N., and S. Rounds. "The Pulmonary Endothelium: Function In Health And Disease", *In Murray and Nadel's Textbook of Respiratory Medicine,* 337–54. Hoboken, NJ: John Wiley and Sons, 2009.

Voidonikola, P. T., K. S. Stametelopoulos, M. Alevizaki, G. E. Kollias, N. A. Zakopoulos, J. P. Lekakis, E. Anastasiou, M. J. Theodorakis, A. G. Pittas, and C. M. Papamichael. "The association between glycemia and endothelial function in nondiabetic individuals: the importance of body weight." *Obesity (Silver Spring)* 16 (12): 2658–62.

Volk, T., and W. J. Kox. "Endothelium function in sepsis." *Inflamm Res* 49 (5): 185–98.

Vrentzos, G. E., Paraskevas, K. I., and D. P. Mikhailidis. "Dyslipidemia as a risk factor for erectile dysfunction." *Current Med Chem* 14 (16): 1765–70.

Wang, Y., Q. Liu, and H. Thorlacius. "Docosahexaenoic acid inhibits cytokine induced expression of P selectin and neutrophil adhesion to endothelial cells." *Eur J Pharmacol* 459 (2–3): 269–73. Wanner, A., and E. S. Mendes. "Airway endothelial dysfunction in asthma and chronic obstructive pulmonary disease: a challenge for future research." *Am J Respir Crit Care Med* 182 (11): 1344–51. Wassmann, S., and G. Nickenig. "Interrelationship of free oxygen radicals and endothelial dysfunction-modulation by statins." *Endothelium* 10 (1): 23–33.

Weingartner, O., D. Lutjohann, S. Ji, N. Weisshoff, F. List, T. Sudhop, K. Von Bergmann, K. Gerts, J. Konig, H. J. Schafers, M. Endres, M. Bohm, and U. Laufs. "Vascular effects of diet supplementation with plant sterols." *J Am Coll Cardiol* 51 (16): 1553–61.

Wexler, D. J., F. B. Hu, J. E. Manson, N. Rifai, and J. B. Meigs. "Mediating effects of inflammatory biomarkers on insulin resistance associated with obesity." *Obes Res* 13 (10): 1772–83.

Willemsen, J. M., J. W. Westerink, G. M. Dallinga-Thie, A. J. Van Zonneveld, C. A. Gaillard, T. J. Rabelink, and E. J. de Koning. "Angiotensin II type 1 receptor blockade improves hyperglycemia induced endothelial dysfunction and reduces proinflammatory cytokine release from leukocytes." *J Cardiovasc Pharmacol* 49 (1): 6–12.

Witham, M. D., F. J. Dove, J. A. Sugden, A. S. Doney, and A. D. Struthers. "The effect of vitamin D replacement on markers of vascular health in stroke patients." *Nutr Metab Cardiovasc Dis* 22 (10): 864–70.

Wolf, F. I., V. Trapani, M. Simonacci, S. Ferre, and J. A. Maier. "Magnesium deficiency and endothelial dysfunction: is oxidative stress involved?" *Magnes Res* 21 (1): 58–64.

Wolk, R., A. S. Gami, A. Garcia-Touchard, and V. K. Somers. "Sleep and cardiovascular disease." *Curr Probl Cardiol* 30 (12): 625–62.

Wustmann, K., M. Klaey, A. Burow, S. G. Shaw, O. M. Hess, and Y. Alleman. "Additive effect of homocysteine and cholesterol lowering therapy on endothelium dependent vasodilation in patients with cardiovascular disease." *Cardiovasc Ther* 30 (5): 277–86.

Xiao, L., Y. Liu, and N. Wang. "New paradigms in inflammatory signaling in vascular endothelial cells." *Am J Physiol Heart Circ Physiol* 306 (3): h317–25.

Yanishlieva, N. V., E. Marinova, and J. Pokorny, "Natural antioxidants from herbs and spices (review article)," *European Journal of Lipid Science and Technology*, 2006, 108 (9): 776–793.

Yao, Y., M. Jumabay, A. Ly, M. Radparvar, M. R. Cubberly, and K. I. Bostrom. "A role for the endothelium in vascular calcification." *Circ Res* 113 (5): 495–504.

Yun, C. H., K. H. Jung, K. Chu, S. H. Kim, K. H. Ji, H. K. Park, H. C.

Kim, S. T. Lee, S. K. Lee, and J. K. Roh. "Increased circulating endothelial microparticles and carotid atherosclerosis in obstructive sleep apnea." *J Clin Neurol* 6 (2): 89–98.

Zhan-Zhou, H., P. Zou, and Y. You. "Endothelial cells: a novel key player in immunoregulation in acute graft versus host disease?" *Med Hypotheses* 72 (5): 567–69.

Zhang, G., F. Yue, H. Jin, H. Shen, M. M. Ori, and Z. Wang. "Effect of CoQ (10) on apoptosis and proliferation of cultured mouse microvascular endothelial cells and its mechanisms." *Chinese J Pathophysiol* 20 (1): 17–21.

Zhang, L., P. Papadopoulos, and E. Hamel. "Endothelial TRV4 channels mediate dilation of cerebral arteries: impairment and recovery in cerebrovascular pathologies related to Alzheimer's disease." *Br J Pharmacol* 170 (3): 661–70.

Zhang-Jianping, G., U. Liqun, H. Xiufeng, Z. Bohua, and Z. Zhiyong. "Protective effects of riboflavin on vascular endothelial dysfunction induced by hyperlipidemia." *Acta Academiae Medicinae Wannan* 22 (3): 163–65.

Zieman, S., and D. Kass. "Advanced glycation end product cross-linking: pathophysiologic role and therapeutic target in cardiovascular disease." *Congest Heart Fail* 10 (3): 144–51.

Zlokovic, B. V. "Neurovascular pathways to neurodegeneration in Alzheimer's disease and other disorders." *Nat Rev Neurosci* 12 (12): 723–38.

Appendix

Graph 1
Endothelial-Cell Inflammation/Dysfunction, Aging Acceleration and Reversal

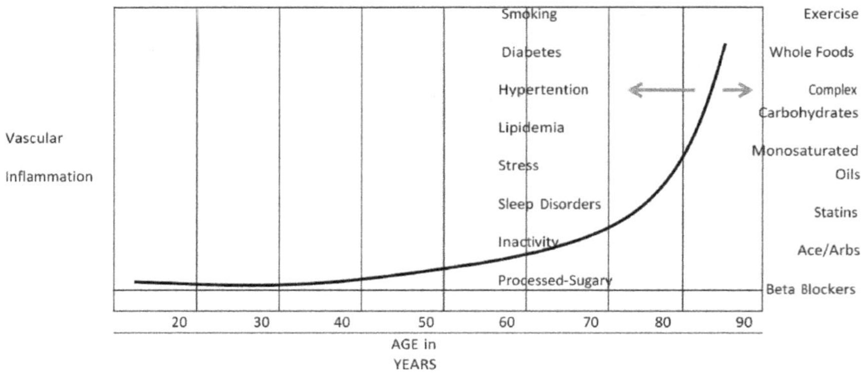

Graph 1 shows selected risk factors that produce an accumulative increase in vascular inflammation, resulting in arterial-tree dysfunction by adversely affecting capillary cells' coordination of end-organ function. As inflammation continues and endothelial-cell dysfunction advances, end-organ function declines and aging increases. The process tends to accelerate with age. At a critical point, the inflammatory process becomes irreversible, and death to the end organ (in human organisms) occurs. Depending on genetic vulnerabilities and environmental influences (smoking, alcoholism, drugs, air pollution), life span can be cut in half from what would be expected. On the right side of the graph are selected interventions, behavioral and medicinal, that have the opposite effect. These interventions decrease vascular inflammation, stabilize capillary-cell function, and then improve end-organ function. These interventions, when practiced in aggregate, can reverse aging and add decades of relevant quality of life.

Graph 2
Age-Accumulative Endothelial-Cell Inflammation and Changes in Endothelial Cell Markers of Function

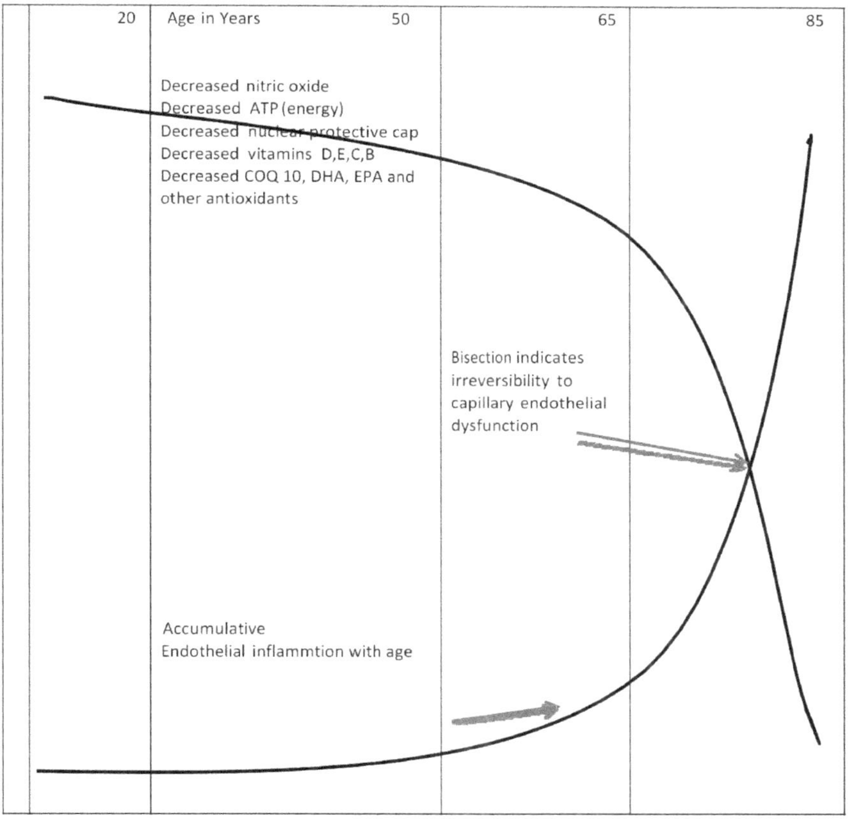

This graph demonstrates increasing endothelial inflammation with age and associated reductions in antioxidants, energy and smooth muscle relaxing molecules in the endothelial cell. With aging important changes occur inside the capillary endothelial cell that contribute to dysfunction. As antioxidant and other biomarkers in the capillary endothelial cell fall, dysfunction increases and reduced signaling/ coordination efforts from the blood and end organ are lost.

Graph 3
Endothelial-Cell Inflammation and Extra-/ Intracellular Markers of Inflammation, with Age

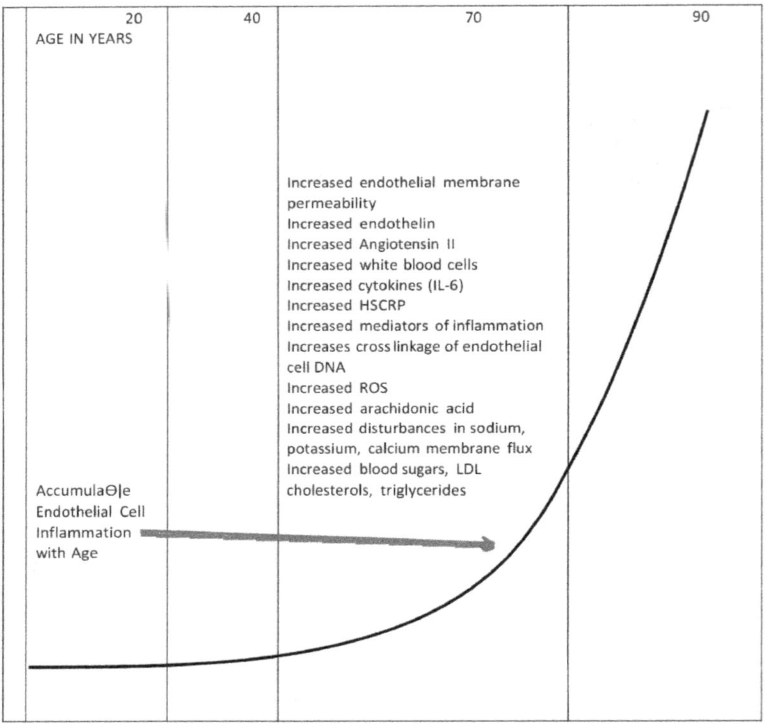

This graph represents changes in intracellular and extracellular capillary-endothelial-cell inflammatory markers with age. As antioxidants, nitric oxide and ATP energy levels fall, inflammation increases making permeability of the capillary endothelial-cell membrane vulnerable to toxins from the blood. This has the net effect of exposing the internal workings of the endothelial cell as well as the end organs they serve to molecules that disrupt function creating cascades of adverse effects involving signaling, coordination, clotting, immune function, smooth-muscle relaxation, as well as passive and active transport. These adverse changes accumulate until the endothelial cell can no longer function.

Graph 4
Endothelial-Cell Inflammation And Increased Clinical Expression of Disease with Age

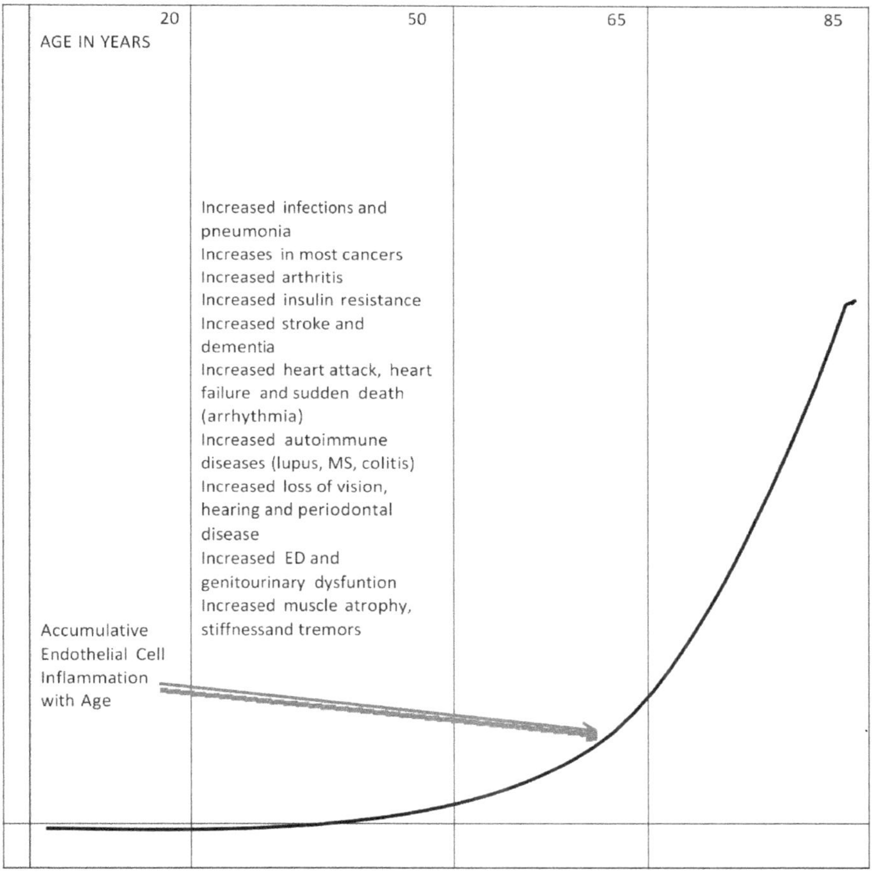

This graph shows the relationship of accumulative capillary-endothelial-cell inflammation and the associated increase in multiple end-organ diseases including infections, cancers, metabolism derangement, vascular and autoimmune diseases. This dysfunction creates deficiencies in managing immune function, clotting, smooth-muscle relaxation as well as passive and active diffusion.

Graph 5
Effect of Endothelial-Cell Inflammation and Stacking of Clinical Inflammatory Risk Factors on Mortality, with Age

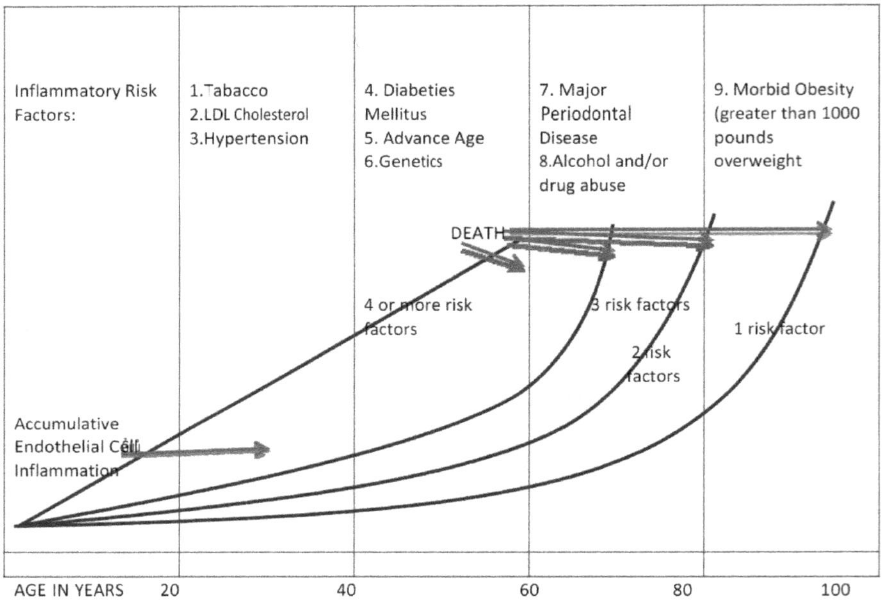

This graph demonstrates the stacking of clinical vascular endothelial risk factors for inflammation and rates of all causes of mortality. As the numbers of risk factors increase, the acceleration of vascular endothelial-cell inflammation increases as does all - cause mortality. The difference between one and four or more risk factors can be as much as thirty or more years of life span. Most with four or more risk factors will not live beyond 60 years of age.

Figure 1
Cross Section of Capillary Endothelial Cells

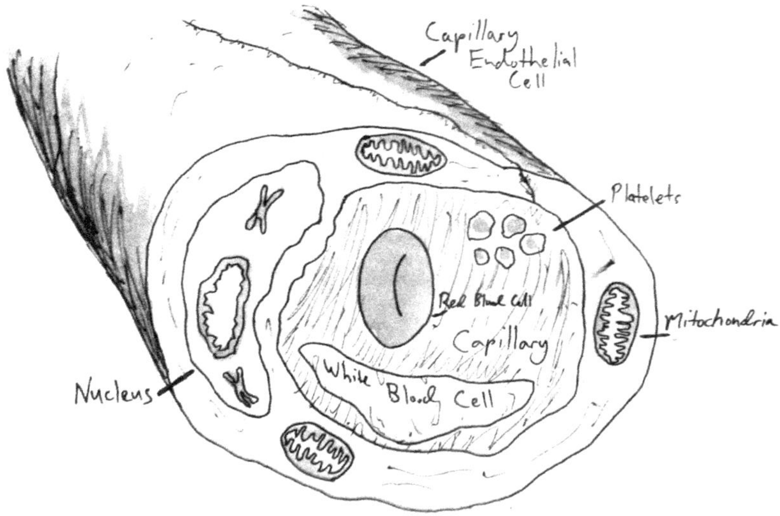

Figure 1 depicts a cross section of a capillary endothelial cell, with its nucleus, cytoplasm, and gap junctions between each cell. In contrast to larger-bored arteries, capillary cells have no smooth muscle to regulate the diameter of their lumens. These cells, and the ways in which they function, provide the cornerstone of effective end-organ homeostasis and ultimately determine the course of aging acceleration or reversal.

Figure 2
Medium- or Large-Bored Endothelium, Smooth Muscle, and Nitric Oxide

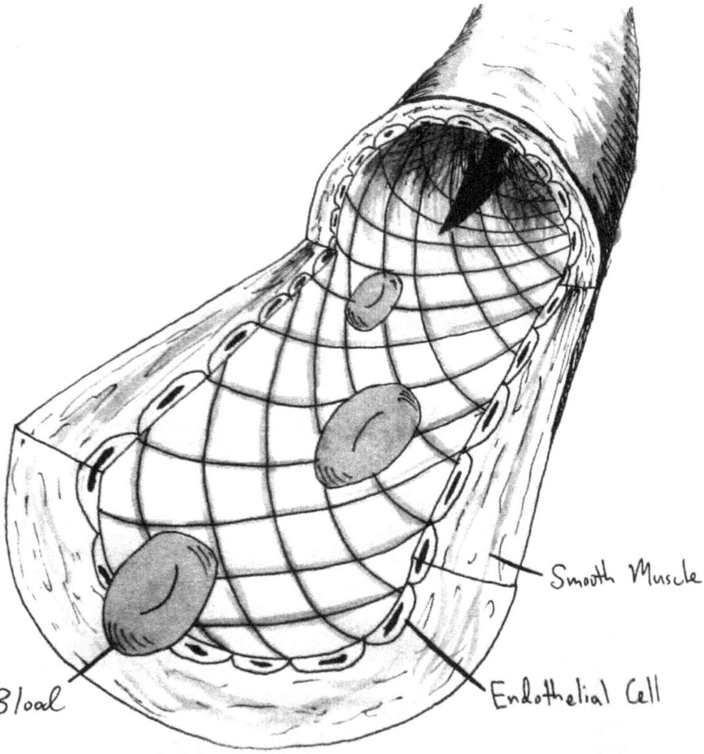

Figure 2 is a rendering of a longitudinal section of a large arterial blood vessel that has been transected. As can be seen, large-vessel endothelial cells line the innermost part of the vessel, have a thick layer of smooth-muscle cells on their basement membrane side, and function primarily as tubes carrying blood to capillaries and end organs. The smooth muscle around the endothelial cells responds to nitric oxide and angiotensin II, in order to relax or constrict, thereby affecting blood flow upstream to the cells. These larger vessels, when bifurcated, are prone to membrane thickening and plaque development on their basement membrane side.

Figure 13
Capillary Endothelium and Kidney Glomerulus

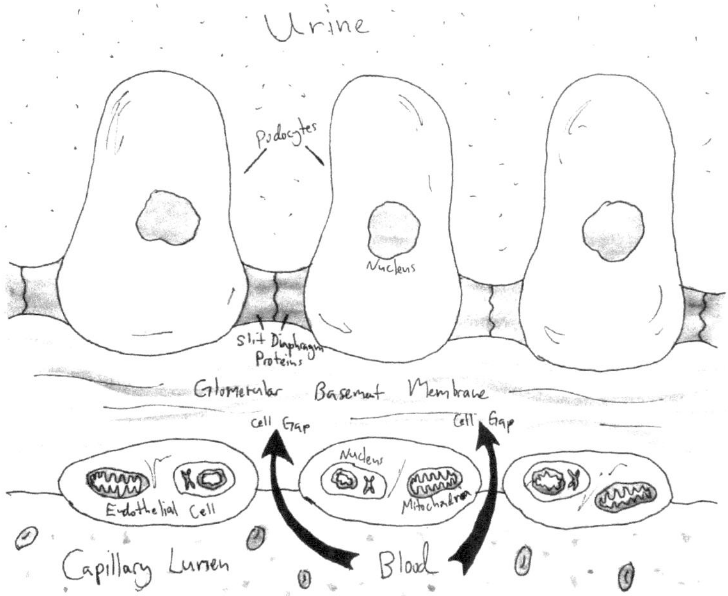

Figure 3 demonstrates the kidney glomerulus, which is critical in making urine. At the bottom of the figure in cross section are the porous capillary cells with wide gap junctions. On the other side of the capillary cells (basement membrane side) are the specialized epithelial cells of the glomerulus, known as podocytes. They take the filtrate that has been presented to them and ultrafilter it to make urine. The filtering process in not passive, and so it requires energy and nutritional support from the capillary endothelial cells. What is equally important is what the capillary cells present to the podocyte in the filtrate. Exposure to proteins, bacteria, or inflammatory molecules reduces podocyte function.

Figure 4
Capillary Endothelial-Cell Membrane White Blood Cell Adhesion

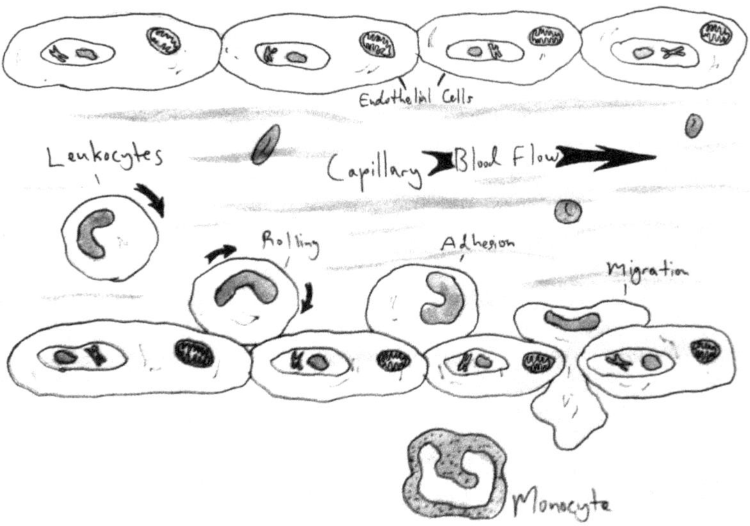

Figure 4 demonstrates how the capillary endothelial cell facilitates inflammatory cells (white blood cells) to be captured from the blood, to eventually traverse the gap junction and make their way to the end organ. Once there, they are part of the immune surveillance team that assists in fighting infection and removing cancer cells, particulates, or foreign molecules. The healthy processing of immune surveillance by capillary cells defines their health.

Figure 5
Capillary Endothelial Cell Migration through the Gap Junction

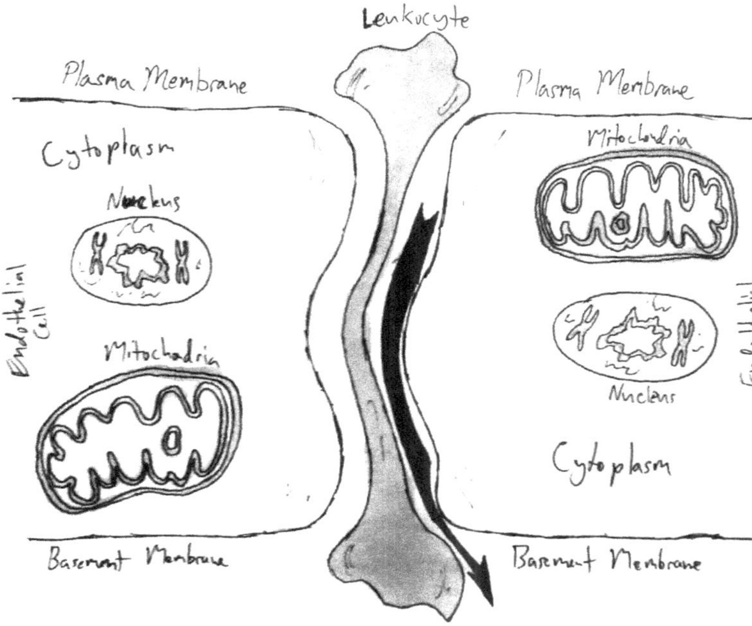

Figure 5 demonstrates how the gap junction between capillary endothelial cells facilitates immune surveillance by facilitating transport of white blood cells from blood to the end organ and back again. In this figure, the leukocyte (white blood cell), also known as an inflammatory cell, is in the final stages of making its way through the capillary-cell gap junction to the end organ.

Figure 6
Capillary Endothelium, Gas Exchange, and Lung Alveolus

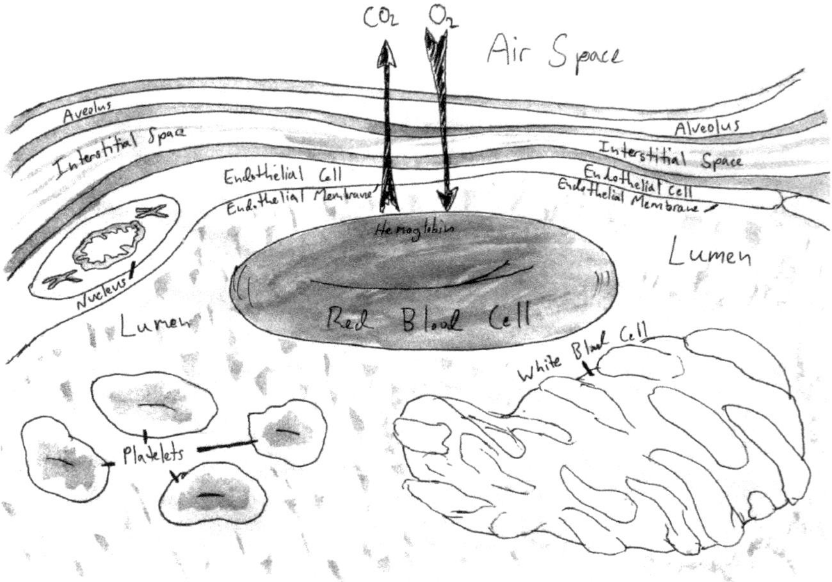

Figure 6 represents a longitudinal cross section of a capillary endothelial cell and epithelial alveolar lung cell. In the lung, the capillary endothelial cell coordinates gas exchange of oxygen and carbon dioxide with the alveolar epithelial cell and the red blood cell found in the blood circulation. In addition to coordinating gas exchange, the capillary endothelial cells of the lung facilitate immune surveillance in order to protect alveoli from infection, cancer cells, and foreign particulates. They also a regulate blood flow to the alveolus through nitric oxide production, based upon increasing or decreasing oxygen requirements from heart and skeletal muscle.

Figure 7
Endothelial-Cell Dysfunction and Progression of Arteriosclerosis

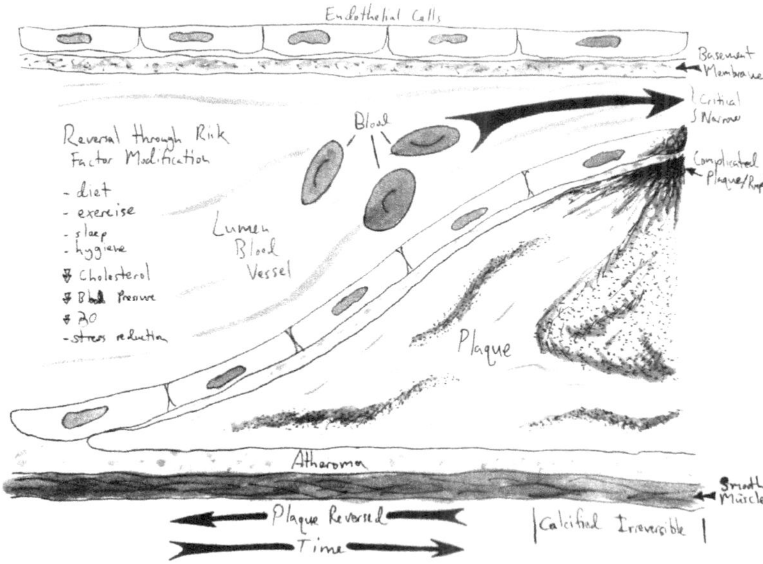

Figure 7 demonstrates the progression of plaque development in a medium to large lumen artery. As the plaque forms and grows, there is a progressive diminution of lumen diameter. This reduction decreases blood flow upstream and disrupts capillary-cell function to the end organ. Once the plaque obstructs the lumen by 70 percent or more, symptoms from the end organ become evident. As the lumen diameter closes, the risk for complete occlusion and loss of blood flow increases. This blood-supply cutoff will cause death to capillary and end-organ cells upstream. The degree to which the end organ dies will depend on how large the affected vessel is and whether there is any collateral circulation to the affected tissue. As large-vessel plaque progresses, the capacity of the endothelial cell to function is compromised not only at the level of the plaque but also upstream. Processes like this tend to be occurring throughout the arterial tree, with predilection to bifurcating arteries where one large artery divides into two and shear stress increases.

Figure 8
Capillary Endothelium of the Blood-Brain Barrier

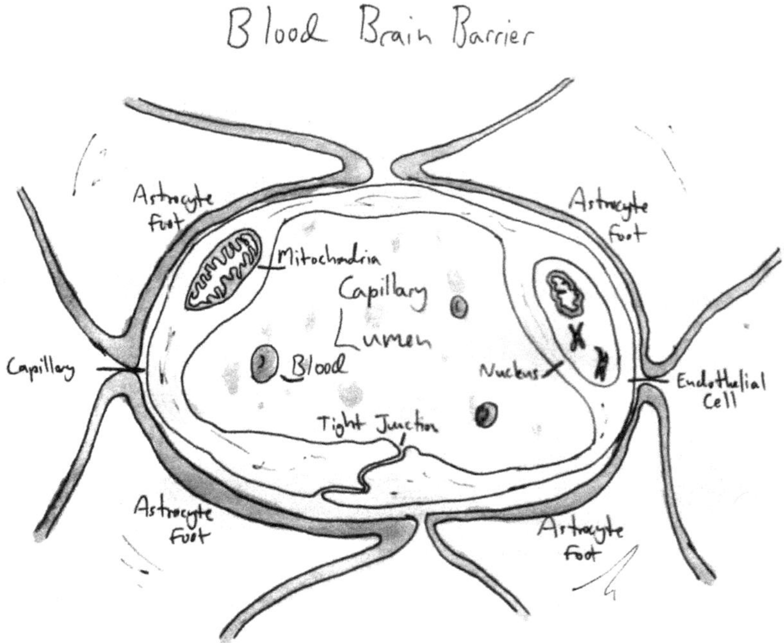

Figure 8 depicts a schematic of the blood-brain barrier and how the capillary endothelial cell has adapted to control the influx of molecules from the blood into the bath known as the cerebrospinal fluid. The capillary endothelial cell in the blood-brain barrier has a tight gap junction that limits blood-plasma access. Paracellular and vesicle transport of the blood-brain barrier is tightly maintained, and the basement membrane to the capillary endothelium is sealed and without pores. Maintaining the blood-brain barrier requires more energy, as compared to energy requirements of other end organs. Further protection of the blood-brain barrier unit comes from pericytes and brain glial cells called astrocytes, which are depicted in the figure. The capillary endothelial cells of the blood-brain barrier coordinate oxygen and energy delivery to the brain, as well as managing immune surveillance and clotting functions. They also coordinate with astrocytes in maintaining proper electrolyte balance in the cerebrospinal fluid. Other capillary cells, known as the choroid plexus, are specialized cells found in the brain ventricles that secrete cerebrospinal fluid. Capillary cells then either make the fluid or use the fluid for purposes of feeding the brain what it needs to function. Brain-cell integrity is only as good as the vascular endothelium that supplies what it needs from the blood.

Figure 9
Capillary Endothelium and Liver Hepatocytes Forming a Liver Sinusoid

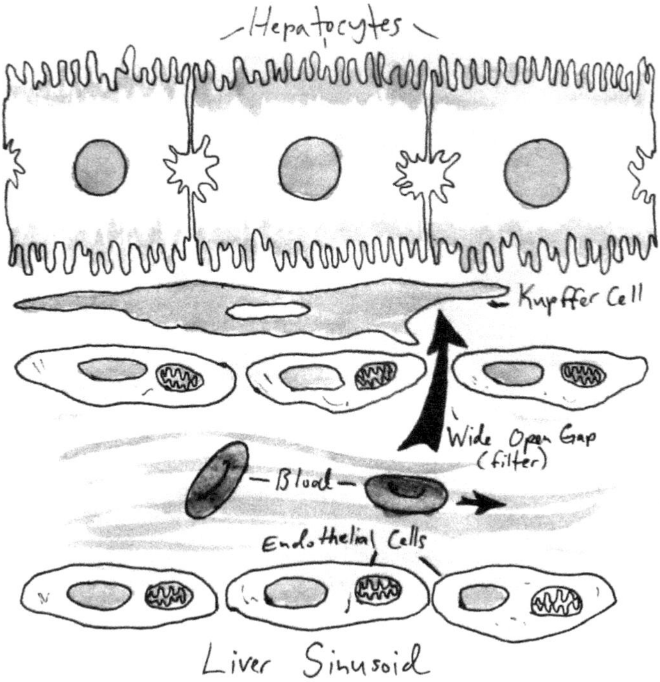

Figure 9 shows a capillary endothelial cell in relation to a liver hepatocyte. Together, these cells compose a liver sinusoid. Similar to the endothelial cells that compose the kidney glomerulus, liver capillary cell basement membranes are fenestrated with loosely appended gap junctions. This facilitates a more rapid transport of nutrients to the hepatocyte (liver cell). The downside to porous capillary membranes is increased exposure of the end organ to viruses and chemical toxicity. Because of this vulnerability, the Kupffer cell has partnered with the capillary cell to assist in patrolling the liver epithelial cells for infection and other foreign particulates. Since liver cells manufacture proteins, manage clotting factors, and package fatty acids, capillary cells coordinate the distribution of these products to the rest of the body.

Figure 10
Capillary Endothelium and Methods of Active Transport

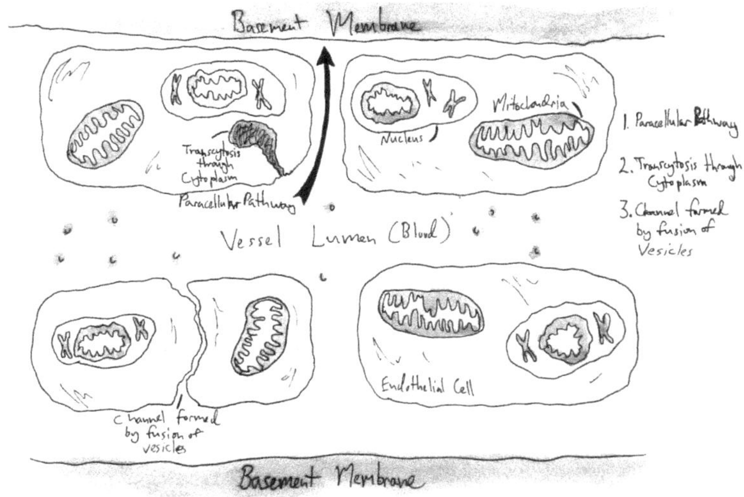

Figure 10 summarizes the different ways that the capillary endothelial cell can facilitate transport of molecules to and from the blood and end organ. The paracellular pathway is through the gap junction and requires coordination of membranes between both endothelial cells. Vesicles may fuse to form a channel for transport, or an individual vesicle can also facilitate transport across the capillary membrane or gap junction. In addition to active transport mechanisms that require energy for transporting molecules, the capillary endothelial-cell membrane facilitates transport of molecules, such as oxygen and carbon dioxide gases, by passive diffusion. Depending on the end organ, active transport processes can be more or less restrictive to molecule movement. For example, the blood-brain barrier is more restrictive, while the liver sinusoid is much less so. More-restrictive management of capillary-cell membranes is more energy dependent. Changes in the capacity of the capillary cell to manage membrane integrity directly affects end-organ function.

Figure 11
Sampling of Endothelial-Cell Inflammatory Mediators

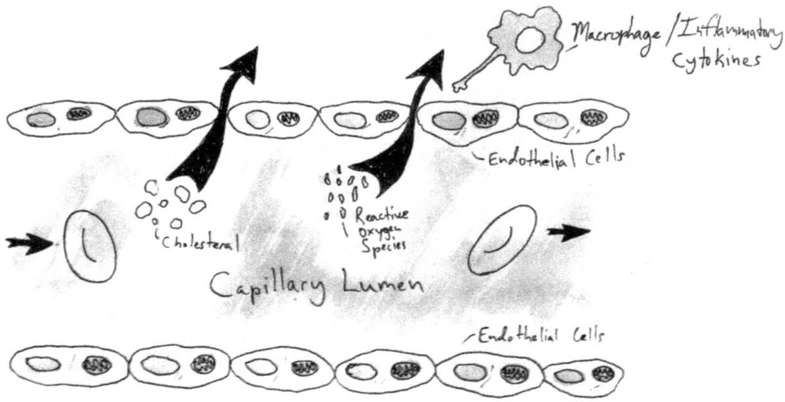

This figure reflects a longitudinal cross section of capillary endothelial cells. The gray represents blood plasma, and as can be seen, demonstrates a variety of blood constituents that the endothelial cell reacts to. These include, but are not limited to, platelets, clotting factors, inflammatory cells, inflammatory blood proteins, foreign molecules, infectious agents, cancer cells, cholesterol particles, other small particles from endothelial cells, reactive oxygen species (ROS), and inflammatory granules. On the other side of the endothelial cell (where the end-organ epithelial cell resides), in addition to nutrient support to the end organ (not shown), immune surveillance occurs. Various mediators may create inflammatory responses, including cytokines, oxidized LDL cholesterol (Ox-LDL), white blood cells, and reactive oxygen species (ROS). All of these processes are orchestrated by the capillary endothelial cell.

Vascular Dysfunction

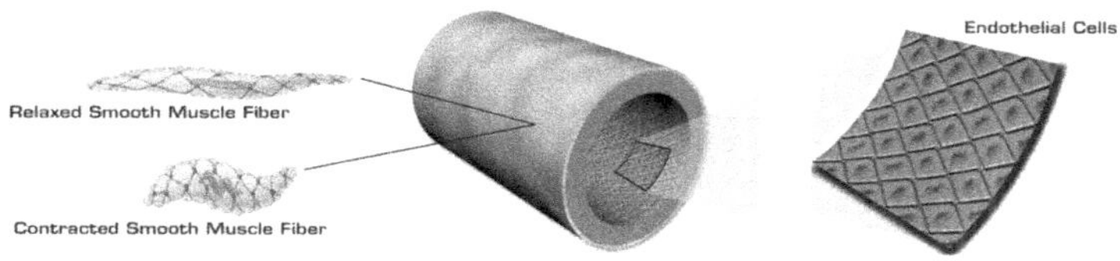

is Present in or a Precursor of:

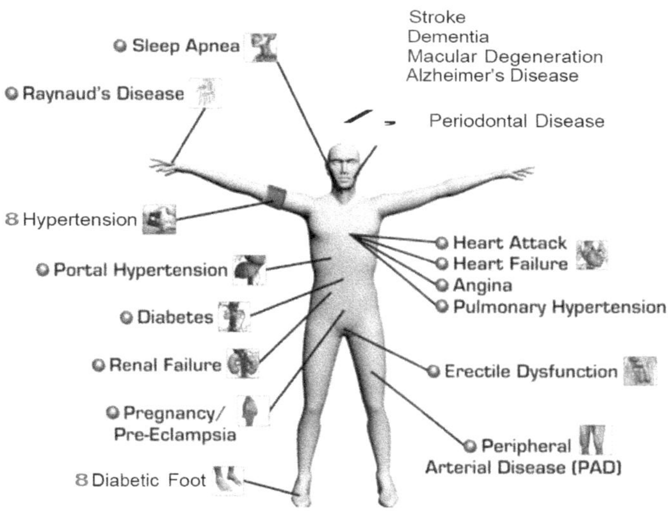

and the Result of:

Smoking, High Cholesterol, High Blood Pressure, Overweight or Obesity, Diabetes, Poor Diet, Stress, Genetics, and Other Factors

About the Author

Robert L. Buckingham, MD, FACP, has been a practicing physician in Ojai, California, for thirty-six years. During this time, Dr. Buckingham has had the privilege of taking care of a broad swath of patients, both in the office and in the intensive care unit of the local community hospital. During this time, he has seen recurrent patterns of disease emerge associated with serious illnesses and concomitant vascular risk factors. At the same time, patient interventions, noninvasive testing, and associated clinical outcomes, coupled with newer research, have resulted in insights into the depths of disease origin that have created a new paradigm of understanding cause and effect. The relationships of vascular inflammation, endothelial function, and disease progression is the theme that has played out over and over again as Dr. Buckingham manages the complex array of multiple end-organ-system failure that occurs with aging. It is in this context that Dr. Buckingham has spent hundreds of hours in his "off time" to put together this timely book that has the potential to be a game changer in terms of people's lives, as well as creating a paradigm shift in medical practices from disease diagnosis to prevention.

Dr. Buckingham received his medical degree from the University of Illinois College of Medicine, where he graduated as a James Scholar with an MD and a master's degree in pharmacology. After publishing a series of papers on the neuropharmacology of sleep, he went on to residency training at Northwestern University in Chicago. After completion of training in 1979, to the chagrin of the program director,

Dr. Buckingham eschewed academics for a career as a practicing internist in Ojai, California. It has been during this time that Dr. Buckingham has had the unique opportunity to be involved firsthand with multiple complex patterns of disease in outpatient as well as critical-care settings. This unique perspective has provided a frame of reference in understanding the origins of illness and the merging factors that mitigate it.

Dr. Buckingham hopes that this book will provide insight to those with all levels of medical knowledge. Because of that goal, writing this book became a challenge, as he had to keep it interesting to beginners as well as experts in the field of endothelial function. In the process of writing this book, it became evident that progress in endothelial-cell research requires a fundamental knowledge of mitochondrial and nuclear function within the cell. Future books will set out to explore how these organelles of the endothelial-cell work and integrate the complex energy and signaling functions that are critical to endothelial-cell function.

If this book provides insight into changing behaviors, improving the quality of life, and even saving lives, then it has been a success. If it provides insight into basic science research and stimulated thought about how health-care providers think about disease prevention, then all the goals of this book have been met. So sit back and enjoy the read. There should be useful information for just about everyone who chooses to be informed about health, longevity, and antiaging.

Index

B

C

D

G

H

L

M

N

O

R

S

T

U

V

W

T

U

V

W

Y

Z

CPSIA information can be obtained
at www.ICGtesting.com
Printed in the USA
LVHW041041210323
742132LV00009B/450

9 781948 779104